Tony **Martin**

A RIGHT TO KILL?

First published in Great Britain in 2004
by Artnik Foundation
341b Queenstown Road
London SW8 4LH UK

Published by Artnik Foundation
Reg. 210025734

© Artnik Foundation 2004

ISBN 1-903906-36-9

Printed and bound in Spain by Cayfosa-Quebecor

A RIGHT TO KILL?

Tony Martin's story

as told to **John McVicar** (editor)
and **Douglas Wallace** (assist. ed.)

ARTNIK • LONDON

The profits from this book will be shared between
the POW Trust and the Artnik Foundation

Acknowledgements

The publisher wishes to thank all those who contributed to this
book, in particular Mr and Mrs Malcolm Starr and Mr M. Coleman
for their hospitality in Norfolk.
The publisher further wishes to compliment Mr Tony Martin for
being most gracious to her, and for his unique sense of humour
which brightened up her trips to Norfolk considerably.

CONTENTS

INTRODUCTION

In June 2003 Peter Sainsbury of the POW Trust, the charity which was critical in obtaining Tony Martin's early release, offered Artnik the publishing rights to the Martin story. But at a price: profits were to go to the POW Trust. Artnik agreed on the condition that Martin was handed to them on a plate, with a ghostwriter to boot. The deal was struck – Artnik would have its production costs and the prestige, POW the rest.

At the end of July 2003, Martin was released, collected by the *Daily Mirror* and then whisked off to Somerset where he took a cool £150,000 for his story. Meanwhile, the ghost-writer supplied by POW was working on the book…well, sort of.

A chop-whiskered man as thick as his portfolio of unpublished works, he had no access to Martin who was too busy cashing in on his "horrendous experience", as he always called it, to co-operate. With both POW and Artnik on his back for a manuscript but with no means of delivering it, the poor ghostwriter buckled and was taken away by the men in white coats.

Artnik were left with no ghostwriter, no access to Martin, no manuscript, just a massive commitment to the publishing trade to produce a book that it could neither profit from nor, it seemed, get anything from other than egg on its face.

Peter Sainsbury acted. He began recruiting alternative ghostwriters. His contribution is epitomised by one interview that he conducted with a young female writer who, a few days before, had broken up with her boyfriend. When Sainsbury discovered this, he enthused, "Splendid, splendid. No distractions. Give you more time to devote to the book." She left in tears.

The book's so-called editor, John McVicar, was taken off his whisky drip in the geriatric ward, wheeled into a crisis meeting and asked what should be done. He repeated a word three times in a phrase that to this day makes Sainsbury shudder, "Money, money, money." With promises of percentages, serialisation deals and film rights, Sainsbury managed to persuade Martin to come to London to meet McVicar.

They met September 4th 2003 in the Cubana restaurant at Waterloo. Martin did not like the food, the noise, the company... Over dinner, ex-Treasury Minister Phillip Oppenheim, who owns Cubana, told the Norfolk farmer that he had managed to persuade William Hague to do the foreword to his book.

Martin replied, "Hague used to be okay, but he's no good now." McVicar was not amused. Martin decided that he would never speak to McVicar again. Indeed, in early January 2004, when through an intermediary, McVicar asked to speak to Martin to put to him the allegations in *A Right to Kill*, the farmer said that he would only talk to him in the presence of the police.

An increasingly desperate Sainsbury now appealed to Artnik's founder, Valentina Artsrunik, to save the project from the scrapheap. She charmed the smelly old farmer's socks off and eventually he allowed the Artnik team to listen to him talking about his case, his past and his philosophy of life. It is an experience that has scarred us all for life. If Artnik was a respectable organisation that carried proper insurance for compensating its staff from exposure to natural disasters like Tony Martin, we would probably all be set up for life.

Meantime, while we were scurrying back and forth to Norfolk and generally dogsbodying for McVicar, he began reading the trial transcripts. He latched onto one reply that Martin gave in the witness box, which turned the whole focus of the book.

Martin was asked a question about his use of the term *pikies* for Gypsies. On oath, Martin replied, "I have never used that word in my life." In fact, Martin uses it all the time.

McVicar pointed out that a defendant on trial for murder, who casually lies about something that has no bearing on the verdict and over which he could easily have been exposed as a liar, is not only cavalier with the truth but also cavalier about lying.

The one thing we trust any reader of *A Right to Kill?* will take from this book is that we are not cavalier with the truth.

Douglas Wallace
Ellie Mathieson
Robert Huntington

CHAPTER 1

TURNING OVER THE "OLD NUTTER"

On 20th August 1999, Fred Barras was exactly 16 years, eight months, three weeks and five days old. He was a stringy, runty lad with a cherubic face who, while virtually illiterate, could calculate the permutations on a *super-yankee* quicker than your normal punter could fill out his betting slip. His schooling had been rudimentary – he had been "excluded" (school-speak for being expelled) a number of times. Two years earlier he had decided to leave school and go to work with his maternal uncle, Tony Joynes, a Newark market trader, but Fred's real job was thieving, a trade he'd been plying for three years, during which time he had racked up twenty nine convictions for fraud and assault, as well as another seven for theft.

He was a feckless, arrest-prone criminal, but to his mother he was "a loveable rogue" and to his five older sisters he was just a scamp who undeservedly had his own bedroom because he was the only man of the house. Whatever they said, his sisters fussed over and mollycoddled him every bit as much as his mum.

Around six that evening, Ellen Barras, 44, ordered her son a takeaway meal of chicken and chips. A gaunt-looking woman who lived off state benefits and whatever her six children managed to put into the house, Ellen was a loving, indulgent mother. She had left Fred's father – also named Fred – when Fred junior was a baby and moved back to her mother's home in Devon Road on the Hawkville Estate, Newark. She had met Fred senior in 1970 when they were both fifteen but, after she left him, they lost contact and he never saw his son again.

Originally 'the Ville', as the estate was known among the locals, had been a redbrick haven from the high-rise apartment blocks of the bigger cities, but many of the itinerants who used to flood into the fens during harvest time had settled there as their traditional seasonal work dried up. Some still kept horses and traps, and hunted with dogs, so the estate had a gypsy-like air to it. Yet some parts of the estate retained the outward appearance of the respectable working class with their manicured hedges bordering postage-stamp gardens, lace curtains and Sunday-best front rooms. Devon Road with its abandoned burnt-out cars, rusting prams and dumped sofas was definitely in the underclass sector.

As Fred's mother busied herself in the kitchen, he sat in front of the TV hammering lightly at the plaster cast on his right leg to soften it up before he hacked it off with a carving knife. Three months before he had fallen from a tree while out scrumping and had broken his tibia. This had handicapped his thieving but, nonetheless, a week previously he had managed to get himself arrested for nicking some garden furniture. He had been given bail despite the police asking for him to be remanded in custody. His release form was still in his pocket.

Ellen came in with his meal and saw what he was doing. "Fred!", she objected, "yunno you should let the hospital do that. That's not gunna heal…you'll be a cripple."

Fred ignored her. He was used to people telling him what to do and then doing the opposite. "Here you goo boy," said Ellen as she put the plate on the table in between the sofa and the TV. "I'll get you some ketchup." By the time she returned Fred had all but finished his last supper.

Fred ripped through the plaster cast, then, ignoring the debris at his feet, he bolted down the last remains of his meal. He was hungry but had other things on his mind, too. He had been waiting for this night for a long time. His idol, Brendon Fearon, had invited him some months ago to join a night-time raid on a farmhouse. Without a father to model himself on, Fred had taken to identifying with the older local *tealeaves* (thieves). He especially looked up to Brendon, who was 29 and had numerous convictions for theft, assault, GBH, obtaining property by deception...

Wiry and fit, with a shock of black hair and an earring in his right lobe, Brendon took his role with Fred seriously. Later he was to say that he had invited Fred on the job "to keep him out of trouble". He meant this genuinely: thieving was work, and it kept idle hands from mischief. In fact, Fred had been badgering him for some time to let him come along and, while the boy had been serving time at Glen Parva Young Offenders Institution, Brendon had told him that he had some work for him when he came out that would set him up.

This was Fred's first *big 'un*. He was determined to show that he was up for it. As soon as he finished his meal, he dashed out to the backyard. As he left, his sister Sara-Jane, 19, shouted, "Get that mess cleared, before you go down town to see your mates – we're not yer skivvies, y' know." Fred ignored her. He rummaged around in their outhouse for some rubber gloves, a chisel and a screwdriver that he had hidden under an old orange crate. Tucking them in his jacket pocket, he returned to the kitchen and kissed his mum goodbye. It was the last time they would ever see each other.

Meanwhile, Darren Bark also left his mother's and got into a clapped-out white Ford Granada. At 33, Darren had racked up 52 convictions for similar offences to Brendon and Fred, including car theft. The Granada was his but the wheels, the radio, and the battery had all been nicked from other cars.

He drove the few hundred metres to Brendon Fearon's who came out carrying three *holders* (holdalls), which he put in the boot. Inside one of them was a torch and a load of black binbags. As he got in the passenger's seat Darren said, "Y'right ba?"

Brendon replied, "Yeh. Y'right? You got gloves?"

Darren patted his pocket, "Got'em."

"We gonna get Fred," Brendon said.

Darren had set up the raid but Brendon had only agreed to come if they took Fred along. Brendon had met Darren's reservations about "working" with a mere lad by saying, "He may be a lad, but he's game and he don't grass." They drove off and parked at the end of Devon Road where they waited for Fred who, incongruously wearing trainers, limped into sight a few minutes later and jumped in the back.

They were off to work...

The tip for the job had come from another burglar, Christopher Webster, whom Bark and Fearon knew. Webster had been involved in raiding Tony Martin's farmhouse some three months previously. The thieves had stolen china, silverware, a bureau and some other furniture worth in the region of £6,000. Webster had told Bark that Bleak House's owner was "a fucking old nutter" who had taken a pot-shot at a mate of theirs, Newark gypsy Mark Aldin, five years before.

Webster told them that the farmer was rarely there and, as a bonus, Aldin had bragged to him that Martin had lost his gun licence over the incident. Webster's gang hadn't had time to clear the place out and there was still a load of valuable *smalls* (burglar-speak for baggable trinkets and antiques) lying about waiting to be nicked. Tonight Brendon, Darren and Fred planned to finish off what Webster had begun. The latter was sentenced in November 2000 to

2 years imprisonment for handling the property stolen from Bleak House in May 1999.

Although Martin lived in squalor, he was relatively wealthy – in 1999 his farm was worth roughly £750,000 – yet his main income came not from farming but from contracting-out part of the 350 acres and from "set-aside" subsidies worth over £20,000 a year. He was what the locals called a "roadside" farmer, one who was more interested in playing at farming rather than actually being one. He also wheeled and dealed in antiques, which resulted in his farmhouse acquiring a reputation among the Newark burgling community for being a bit of an Aladdin's cave.

The May raid, which had been set up by Webster, embittered an already vengeful man – Martin came home to find his bureau dumped on his drive but the thieves had made off with a table, two chests of drawers and a grandfather clock. When he rang the Norwich police to report the theft, he told the female constable who fielded the call, "If they come back on my land again, I'll blow their heads off." She was later to give evidence at his trial, and she was not alone.

Martin was already seeing the police as part of the "enemy" that colluded in the licence that thieves enjoyed in the Norwich area. He felt utter contempt for the way they did nothing about the "light-fingered *pikies*" (gypsies). However, what made him vow to take the law into his own hands occurred a few days later when his neighbour Paul Leet rang him.

Paul, 55, an easy-going farmer who rarely gets het up about anything, had been working on his property and found some old letters, model ships and some cassette tapes. He put one of the tapes in the player in his tractor and he knew instantly whom he was hearing. He told Artnik "I knew straight away who that voice was. It was Tony. It was Tony talking about when he worked on a pig farm in Australia. It turned out that instead of sending letters he'd make a tape and send it to his family."

"Well, I rang Tony to tell him. When I told him what was there in the conifers – the burglars obviously chucked it there when they took the antiques – it was the worst I seen him. This was stuff from his childhood: little ships he'd built as a boy... And I gave him them back and that's when he got irated, really irated with 'em. And that's when he said that if anyone else came on his land he'd shoot the thieving pikies. He meant it.

"And he kept to his word, kept to his word, 'cos he did shoot 'em," Paul added with a chuckle.

Tony said later, "The shock of seeing the property, which is part of my history, missing from my home really affected me. From that time I became very security conscious. I felt almost as if I had let down the people who passed it on to me."

Certainly the three crooks driving to Wisbech reckoned on earning at least a grand apiece for their planned evening's work. Fred's mood was upbeat. He had bought a four-pack of Stella from the local off-licence and he began to drink one in the back of the car.

At ten past eight, when they were on the Wisbech road near Balderton, a patrol began tailing them. Darren told the others, "Watch it, there's a piglet on our *bottle*." The patrol car swiftly pulled alongside and flagged Darren over. PC Knight was on his own and had no reason to stop them, except that the Granada didn't look right. Then he recognised Bark and Fearon as known thieves and this decided the matter.

All three were suddenly jumpy. Given their previous form for burglary and housebreaking, what they carried was enough for the police to charge them with conspiracy: they all had gloves on them – even though it was a warm August evening – plus the three holdalls in the boot, inside which were their tools for breaking in.

To Brendon's relief, Darren swiftly produced his insurance and without further ado improvised the perfect bit-part for their predicament: "We're just out for a drink at the King's Head officer." Then he added with a grin, "You shoulda waited until I was on me way back." PC Knight, disarmed by Bark's cheek, gave him a Produce Form for his licence, but did not search them or look in the boot.

They continued on their way. Relieved at their near miss, all of them felt it was a good omen for the raid. "We're on a roll tonight boys," Fearon said before producing a joint. "I was saving this for on the way back but I think we just earned it." They all had a puff as it was passed round.

Fred began boasting to Bark about his criminal past. Bark wasn't impressed, telling him to "Put a sock in it boy, you're doin' me head in".

Fearon wasn't in the mood for having his protegé *dissed*. "*Darren*," Fearon warned firmly. He knew that his mucker would not take offence – they had been mates since they met in the nick in 1994. But this was the first time they'd done a *screwer* (burglary) together.

It was nearly half-past nine when they approached Bleak House. Dusk was beginning to turn into night but it was still light enough to drive with just sidelights. They drove slowly alongside the apple orchard that bordered the Outwell Road, which runs alongside Martin's farm. Darren parked on the gravel drive that led down to the gate, which opened up onto the farmyard. They couldn't see the house from there nor could they see any lights through the trees. They had been told that Martin often did not come back to Bleak House at night or, if he did, not until the pubs shut. It looked deserted. Fearon and Bark had cased the place in the daylight four days previously and they knew the house was about forty yards down the track leading from the gate, inside the gate there was a barn and cottage, then the old nutter's ramshackle house.

Their main worry was Martin's Rottweilers, which might be loose in the grounds. Webster had told Fearon that, although the dogs looked fierce, they were "pussycats". Fearon was also confident in his ability to handle them, but Darren had ruled himself out as a candidate for going near the house as he didn't like any kind of dog, never mind a pack of Rottweilers. Fred wasn't too keen on big dogs either but he put his trust in Brendon.

Darren said to them, "You ready, mush?" Brendon nodded. "Let's hope the old nutter is away." He drove down the drive and stopped the car with the bonnet pointing at the gate. He put the headlights on full beam and flicked them in the direction of the house. They all waited tensely for any signs of life.

"It looks dead," Darren said. Fred and Brendon put on their gloves and took the holdalls out of the boot. Brendon came to the driver's window and Darren said, "I'll pull out onto the main and watch in case anything comes down here. If it does, I'll buzz you. You'll have to leg it and I'll pick you up later. But if it's OK, I'll wait for you to give me the shout to come back for the load-up." He grinned wolfishly. Brendon nodded in anticipation.

Then, while Darren reversed the car to drive back up to the main road, Brendon and Fred went round the side of the gate and began walking into the farmyard. They didn't talk but they were not that careful about making a noise either. Fred was virtually clinging to Brendon's shoulder, worried about the dogs but happy that he was with his mentor whom he knew would stick with him come what may. Fearon stopped suddenly. "Fucking 'ell," he cursed. He'd left his mobile in the glove compartment. In the flap of getting the holders out of the boot, putting his gloves on and stringing a Petzl torch-lamp on a lanyard round his neck... "Wait here, I need to talk to Darren," he muttered to the mystified Fred.

He sprinted back, round the gate and up the drive. He could see the Granada's lights but then it pulled out onto the highway...he gave up. The plan was that as soon as they had packed the smalls in the holders he was going to ring Darren to pick them up. "This is turning into a real boo-boo," he thought. He shrugged, "Darren will tumble I've left it and drive back after a while. It'll be *cushty*."

When he joined up with Fred, he didn't tell him that he'd forgotten his mobile. "What's the point? Just worry him." Suddenly a thick, black shape came towards them...it was Bruno, one of Tony Martin's three Rottweilers. "He was shaking its mouth," Fearon later told the police. The other two dogs, Otto and Daniel, were locked up in a run-down brick shed next to the house, which looked like an abandoned pig-sty because of Martin's habitual DIY disasters.

Fearon dropped onto one knee and began chanting softly, "Good boy, there's a good boy..." Bruno stopped and gazed inquisitively at the two intruders. Fearon pulled out a Mars Bar from his pocket and crackled the wrapper. Bruno looked expectantly at the snack. Fearon ripped open the treat and tore the sticky bar in half, offering the dog a piece on his upturned palm. Bruno swallowed it in one gulp, then sat up, wagging his stubby tail as he waited for more.

Fearon patted him, stood up, bit off a piece for himself, then threw the rest into the undergrowth for Bruno to scamper after. "Come on Fred", he said coolly, "he's me mate for life."

The two burglars continued down the drive with Bruno following, before the dog lost interest in getting any more treats. From the recce he'd done, after Webster had briefed him and Bark about the job, Fearon knew their best entry. It was an unbarred ground floor window on the side of the house. The house looked completely deserted. No lights, nothing. When they came to the window, Fearon ripped away some ivy that had grown over it. It was double-glazed! Fred, eager to impress, began trying to open it up with his chisel. It was stuck. "Just smash it," Brendon told him. He began breaking the glass with the hammer end of the tool.

Tony Martin had left his mother's house just after nine o'clock that evening after having tea and cake. The light faded as he drove back along the twisting road from the hamlet of Elm. The earlier rainy and overcast skyline that loomed over the brooding fens was beginning to lift and it looked like a bright moonlight night was in the offing. This augured well for the morning. He had wanted to do some ploughing back at the farm for days now…well, after he'd fixed the tractor. He had been prevented from doing that by the un-seasonable, Fen-ish weather.

He soon arrived back at the farm and, given the way the weather was turning, resolved to rise at dawn the next morning to begin work. However, it was rare for him to begin work early. He rarely slept at Bleak House, so by the time he got back and got himself organised it would be midday. But he often worked on the land in the dark, much to the bemusement of his neighbours.

As Martin drove in and parked his Nissan Bluebird outside the farmhouse next to his front door, Bruno went ballistic and jumped up at him. He roughed the dog playfully, then took one of the torches that he had in the car and went to see his other two "bowsie wowsies". His Rottweilers looked fierce enough but even he admitted that as guard dogs they were useless. He walked over to the cottage to see Otto and Daniel. He didn't let them out, just made sure they had feed.

He went in the side door of the house… he couldn't use the front door next to where he parked his car as, after his burglary in May, he'd rendered that unopenable.

Later he described how he did it, "I just put steel bars because the house is not nicely furnished inside. I just went up the blacksmith's shop, got these steel straps, drilled holes in them, got coach bolts, put them against the door, got a spanner, drilled it in like that, put them as best I could on the door and because the door's the weak link on the house, or it turned out to be some time ago, a few months ago, I got an RSJ which I laid down between that and the wall and a brick, just to make up for lack of distance. So I thought, well, I can't really do... do any more, that's as good as rock or anything else."

It had taken him over a week to put all this together, working compulsively like some religious fanatic at his devotions.

He turned on his one downstairs light, a 15-watt bulb in the hallway. He'd had trouble with his grid feed two years ago and, as temporary measure, he'd taken a low voltage feed from his barn, which was enough to power the landing bulb, his fax machine and another 15-watt bulb in his bedroom.

He checked for faxes. Nothing.

He heard a car pull up out on the drive. This wasn't right. He didn't have visitors, except uninvited ones. He walked back to the door and saw the light from the car's headlights flooding the yard. The driver was flicking them on and off. They were back – they were checking to see if he was around. He heard car doors open and shut...He went back into the house, turning off his torch. His "Magnum", as he called it, was propped up next to the door. He picked it up. The judge at his trial was to describe his pump-action shotgun as "a fearful weapon". It was..."and it put the fear of God into those pikies, I tell you" he was to tell Artnik later. Then he walked over to the light switch and turned off the landing bulb. He heard the car drive off.

He always knew they would return. The pikies saw him as easy pickings. They often drove past slowly and even drove down his driveway as if they were lost.

Well, this time he was ready for them. He scooped up some cartridges from a box on the floor, and put them in his pocket.

Should he confront them in the grounds? They were already trespassing. He decided against it, mainly on the memory of how the previous incident with Aldin had turned against him. As he'd taken a potshot at Aldin's car, he'd become the villain! If they were burglars caught in the act rather than just trespassers, poachers, he would have had a better case. But one thing he knew was that if they broke into his house, they were going to pay for it.

He thought about ringing the police... "Useless, useless. By the time they took particulars over the phone, the pikies would have taken what they wanted and gone." He had the right to defend himself. Absolutely. He knew that. *An Englishman's home is his castle.*

As he didn't know if they were going to break in or, if they did, where they would make their entry, he stationed himself in the hallway near the bottom of the stairs as it gave him the best vantage point for defending his property.

The staircase had two gaping holes, one at the top and one at the bottom, where he had removed steps in several botched attempts to repair and change the layout of the hallway. For no particular reason that he could remember, he had dismantled the dog-leg at the top of the staircase. He had wanted it to turn the other way, but once he'd removed two treads he had realised that it was impossible. The prosecution at his trial turned this botching into a deliberate boobytrap to catch burglars.

One of his neighbours, Mike Coleman, had roared with laughter when he saw the mess he'd made, "You've bastard'd your own staircase."

And he had.

"Bastard'd"…the word had struck home. The farm and house were littered with the remains of every bodged, botched and unfinished job imaginable. Tractors, threshers, roofs, doors, cars, taps…everything he turned his hand to got bastard'd. He sighed and shrugged. So what? – it was his staircase, his farm, his life…

He turned off his torch and waited, then after about ten minutes, which seemed like ten hours, he heard footsteps outside. It was them. He was right. The same burglars had come back to finish off the job. "What do they have against me…hadn't they done enough last time, stealing my possessions, dumping all my letters and photographs over the drive… And the car's right outside, so they don't care that I'm here." This spooked him…so these pikies were prepared to use violence to subdue him.

Like Aldin, for example. The police had told him that he had a long record for "violence and intimidation". As these thoughts whirled around in his head, he wondered if they had actually watched him drive up before making their move! This was why he sometimes drove in from the back entrance. They must have…they'd certainly been watching him. So they were going to take him. Well, they could try.

Although Martin couldn't have known it, in the darkness Barras and Fearon hadn't noticed his Nissan Bluebird, which was parked near the front door, unlocked with its keys in the ignition.

Tony heard the window break… it was from a small room that led into the hallway… the easiest way of forcing an entry into the house. He had left this unbarred when he'd tried after the May burglary to make the place impregnable because from the outside it was virtually hidden by ivy. They knew the layout of the place! This confirmed to him that it was the same thieves who had burgled him in May.

The image of Robby Augur came to mind, another farmer who'd

been burgled; he was bound and gagged in his own home in exactly the same circumstances. It haunted Martin. He also thought of his uncle Arthur who had been tied up and left to rot by intruders. His heart began to flutter and he found it hard to breathe.

They had climbed through the broken window and were in the house. There were two of them at least – he could hear them talking...they were pikies, he recognised their lingo. One of them had a torch as he could see a beam of orange light flickering around. He backed away from the foot of the stairs as they were coming into the hallway. He heard the chink of a bottle brushed aside by feet, feet that were getting nearer... Maybe if they took him, they would violate him... He tightened his grip on the pump-action. It helped break the clamp of fear that was enveloping him.

He used the gun regularly on vermin and "two-legged rats" – pigeons and gypsies. It was another of his jokes, which not everyone found funny. But he could handle this gun. It was the best maintained piece of machinery in the farm. Reassured, he embraced the heavy firearm tightly, but there was a problem. He didn't have a cartridge in the breech as it shortened the life of the spring mechanism. His left hand cradled the foregrip but as he habitually went to rack a cartridge into the breech he stalled the impulse. The noise would echo round the house and it was a sound that anyone with even a passing acquaintance with firearms would recognise. This might frighten them off – but equally so it might trip them into rushing him... He would have to wait until the last moment to prime the gun, but he could and did click back the safety catch.

He had given them every chance. He had not ambushed them on his grounds but waited until they broke in. Whatever they got they deserved...every last pellet of it.

But his breathing was becoming more laboured. Nightmarish thoughts flashed before his mind's eye. His thrombosis. Both he and his brother Robin had it. A clot had dislodged itself and was blocking the blood flow to his heart, his brain...

"Christ!" he scolded himself.

"Not much frightens me, but what about my heart? It's thumping away..." The image of a jack rabbit pounding the ground with its hind feet came into his head. "How much can your body take of this? Heart attack. That's how I'll go... No. They are not going to get me." He reassured himself, "They are not going to get the upper hand. If it's the last thing I do, I'll get them first."

It was like a horror movie, he thought, as his head span with confusion and panic, but to reassure himself he thought, "At least I am directing the shoot, and they are the rats... Rats in a trap."

They came out into the hallway and crossed over into the breakfast room. One of them had a torch clipped to his chest like miners have in their hats. He watched them, wondering when he should move on his unsuspecting quarry. There were two of them...no, three of them. There must be one driving the car. He edged towards the breakfast room...

Fred picked his way through the strewn rubble, discarded newspapers and empty cans of dog food towards the hallway that led to the stairs. He moved fearlessly into the darkness – adrenaline was pumping him on. Ancient Christmas cards and old yellowing magazines lay on the floor pinned down by broken bricks. Fearon, the more experienced of the two, lingered in the first room they'd entered, looking for any smalls missed by his young apprentice.

After a few minutes Fearon moved on. He had his Petzl torch-lamp strung round his neck on a piece of string but sometimes he used his hand to focus it. He flicked it over newspaper clippings Sellotape'd along the dusty walls here and there. A long forgotten Christmas tree decked with cobwebbed pine cones lay diagonally across the floor. Years of dust coated an old boiler that sat incongruously in the middle of the room, and a jar of Coleman's mustard balanced on top of a pile of paper. Fearon craned his neck forward in amazement as he spotted a copy of the *Eastern Daily Press* from 1987!

"Jesus", scoffed Fearon as he looked around for Barras, "what a fuckin' nutter." Then he saw a dresser. He opened it up and found two silver jugs. He checked the hallmark and turned to look for Barras who was carrying the holders. He said, "Mush, bin this." He shone the torch on the jugs. Fred squatted on his haunches as he carefully put one in the first bag and the other in the second to stop them chinking. He was still trying not to make any unnecessary noise.

Fearon heard a creak in the hallway – someone was there. He flicked the torch towards the sound and caught the white, fearful face of the aging farmer. The old nutter was very close...only five yards or so. He had something cradled in his right arm, which Fearon thought was the sort of long torch that poachers sometimes used for hunting rabbits at night.

Martin was blinded by the light and panicked. The burning orange light dazzled him...he couldn't see anything else. He went on automatic pilot: aiming the gun beneath the light and pulling the trigger...nothing happened.

There was no cartridge in the breech! He rammed back the foregrip and heard the shell slam home. He pulled the trigger again.

The noise of a 12-bore at night in this enclosed space was deafening. The muzzleflash lit up the room and he saw two figures clear as day, then everything went black again. He thought he heard a scream but he couldn't be sure and now his ears were ringing from the noise of the shot. Nonetheless, even in the dark, he fancied he'd got at least one of them – any seasoned shooter knows from the feedback of his senses whether or not he's hit the target. But he told himself he wasn't sure...he did not want to be sure because he knew the damage a 12-bore does at such close range.

Fearon saw the barrel flash before he heard the noise. He heard Fred say, "He got me... I'm sorry. Mum. Please don't. Mush."

Fearon's mind went blank but not enough to stop him bolting like a rat from a sinking ship. Martin could hear their panicked movements and there was some light from the torch even though the person with it had his back to him. He reloaded as he walked towards them and squeezed the trigger for the second shot. Again firing down.

Fearon took the blast in his right thigh, throwing him around like a rag doll. The pain ripped through his leg; he could hear Fred whimpering forlornly for his mother.

Martin could hear nothing as the momentum of his action carried him on...he reloaded. The ejected cartridge shell ricocheted to his right. In the face of death, Fearon found escape. He frantically scrabbled away from the sound of the gun, dragging his bleeding leg behind. He came against a wall, which he clawed at desperately, blindly. By pure chance, Fearon's gloved fingers and his arm went clean through a windowpane. He clenched his fingers around the bars that covered the opening. With a monumental effort he ripped the entire unit out of the wall. In fact the frame was merely laid in. He saw light and what it meant – escape from that deadly, thundering gun.

Fred instinctively followed the noise of Fearon, clinging to his only hope of staying alive. Suddenly the third shot rang out and both of them took pellets in the legs. Fearon dived through the opening, tumbling clumsily onto the grass...but he was free. He didn't know whether Fred had followed him because he was already staggering off across the yard.

It was every man for himself and even a boy could understand that.

Martin saw them hauling themselves through the patch of moonlight coming in through the ripped out window. The jitters that he had felt earlier had lifted – he was in charge and in the right. The scum deserved everything he'd given them.

He deliberately let off another shot. He stood panting in the darkness, the acrid smell of cordite in his nostrils. Shaking with relief, he turned and made his way back to the staircase. He reloaded the shotgun but out of habit he put only four into the magazine, leaving the spent cartridge in the chamber.

He fancied he'd bagged a couple of two-legged rats, but he had no means of knowing how badly. He'd fired down below the waist but as they'd taken off like March hares they obviously weren't badly hurt.

Fred was fatally wounded. And while he had made it to the window, it was only the force of the shot that had proppeled him over the sill. He dropped like a sack of potatoes onto the dank earth next to the house, the pain in his gaping back shooting up his spine as he took a deep breath of the warm night air. He shouted to Fearon, "Mush, mush..." But Brendon was away. Alone, Fred slid off like a dying animal towards the sanctuary of the undergrowth, which was only a few metres away.

Once he reached a thicket he curled up. Breathing was painful as he rocked weakly from side to side. The pain would not abate. He tried rolling onto his back, but it only aggravated the agony. He rolled onto his front. His only relief from the pain was unconsciousness that he was aware was gradually sucking him into a darkness from which he would never emerge. He must have known he was dying but surely held onto the hope that his mush,

Brendon, would come back for him.

Darren Bark was waiting in the Grenada a little way along the main road, watching the drive leading down to Martin's house. He heard two muffled shots in quick succession, then Bruno's ferocious barks, which were soon bolstered by a cacophony of baying and snarling from Otto and Daniel who started tearing at the rotten shed door, desperate to break loose. Their barks masked the next two shots but there was enough poacher in Darren Bark to know that the first two came from a 12-bore.

Darren was terrified of dogs. When he heard of the old nutter's trio of Rottweilers he'd told Fearon to "blot me out, I don't wanna know". But Fearon had sweet-talked him back on the job. Now it was dogs and gunfire. Brendon and Fred didn't have a gun... And no car had come off the main road and down the drive to the farmhouse. The farmer must have turned the tables on them. Webster's story about the old nutter losing his shotgun licence over taking a potshot at Aldin had been a lie. Their so-called roll was over.

Darren was racked with fear and uncertainty. The smoke from his Lambert and Butler snaked up to draw tears from his eyeballs, jolting him back to the present. Was the farmer ringing Old Bill? What should he do? He drove back to the top of the drive with the nose of the car pointing down. He put his headlights on full beam...nothing. He turned his lights off, then turned off his engine. He rang Brendon's mobile. He heard it ringing...It was in the glove compartment! The stupid, idiot gypo...

He didn't know what to do but someone must have rung the police...they always do. "Move off the plot, just in case," he decided.

He waited a little while before turning the ignition key of the Granada. This time the clapped-out engine didn't catch. The carb had flooded? The starter motor whirled. "Please, please you bastard…" Suddenly the engine caught and roared into life. As he took off, he thought how he hadn't wanted to do the job anyway. Fearon and the kid would look after themselves.

He drove off along the road but, to placate his conscience, he parked in a lay-by a mile or so from the farmer's house. Maybe Brendon or Fred would come this way…at least when anyone blamed him for driving off he'd be able to say that he'd kept close by.

Fred Barras died in the grounds of Bleak House next to a weather-beaten garden chair on a bed of leaves. He lingered on for half an hour or more, drifting in and out of consciousness before, as the autopsy showed, he suffocated to death. His had been a short but eventful, even exciting, life. At least he had been much loved and this must have softened his end.

His two accomplices had both left the scene of the crime and would later deny that Fred had accompanied them on the raid. Fearon did this within the window that could have given Barras a chance of survival. By the time he made it to a nearby cottage Barras's life might still have been saved.

Contrary to media reports that Barras died within five minutes or less, an autopsy by Mr. Alastair Wilson, lead clinician at the Royal London Hospital, proves that he lived for at least thirty minutes and maybe longer. There was no life-threatening damage to any vital organs (only one of his lungs was shot up), nor any damage to major blood vessels. Despite the gunshot wound he was not losing life-threatening quantities of blood. Air was escaping through an entry wound on Fred's back.

Perversely, this hole kept him alive as it helped him gasp for air more easily. Untreated, though, this opening became clogged with bloodied clothing and pressure built up in Fred's chest. This made his breathing laboured and shallow, until he suffocated to death. Had paramedics been called, a relatively simple emergency procedure would have saved his life.

A RIGHT TO KILL?

CHAPTER 2

"A LAW UNTO HIMSELF"

Brendon Fearon fought his way through the dense briar of sequoia, pine and walnut trees that surrounded Bleak House and tripped over a wooden pallet that lay by the side of an irrigation ditch at the back of the property. The white-hot agony that he had felt immediately after being hit in the thighs by Martin's 12-bore had developed into an intense, deep, searing pain from his knees right up to his groin.

He lay on his back in the damp grass with his legs outstretched before him. With some considerable effort he raised his upper body and slumped forward to inspect his wounds. His hands throbbed from wrenching the window frame clear out of the wall moments earlier. He briefly wondered where that superhuman strength had come from, before inching off his black, blood-sodden gloves one at a time. He hadn't realised that he'd been holding his wounds. He took the torch, which was still on, from around his neck and threw it. He knew he had to go to hospital and without even knowing it he started getting rid of anything that tagged him as a burglar.

Looking down at his legs made him retch – they were heavily peppered with shot and seeping rivulets of blood. His tracksuit bottoms were torn apart and he could see where his skin was missing. His right leg was badly ripped by the blast and was pulsing blood, but his left leg was worse: it had been lacerated above the knee. A thick flap of his thigh muscle, larger then his own hand, draped itself lazily over his kneecap and the lurid yellow of the exposed sub-cutaneous fat turned his stomach. But there was little blood coming from what was by far the worst wound.

He knew that, even if he lived, he would be crippled for life. He also knew that he would have to get to hospital for treatment, which meant the police and arrest. "The bastard, the stinking scumbag doing this to me…" Almost automatically his mind went to how he would explain his presence in the house to the police: they had run out of petrol…they had gone down some driveway to seek help…the dogs had scared them…they had been backed up against a seemingly deserted outhouse…

But he had to get to hospital. And Fred? How was the boy? What would he say to Fred's mum? And where was Darren? If he could find Darren… If only he hadn't forgotten his mobile… But most of all: "Don't let me become a cripple, please…"

He had to get to hospital. Fearon twisted his head away from Bleak House and the pain – to his right and beyond the irrigation ditch was an expansive wheat field. On the other side of the field he could quite clearly make out the lights of an adjoining farmhouse. If only he'd not forgotten his mobile. How had he done that? Crazy, mush, crazy.

He weighed up his options: trek back along the gravel path to where Darren had been parked or go across the field towards the farm. Trying to find Darren would be chancy. He'd have heard the shots, the dogs, and known it was only a matter of time before the police arrived. It was odds on Darren had pulled off the plot and was already half-way to Newark. Brendon faced Hobson's choice – it was either the next farmhouse or death.

Martin stood before the ripped out window, through which the two

burglars had made their escape. Call the police? He knew that'd be
trouble – his shotgun licence had been revoked in 1994 when he'd
fired at the car of the pikey whom he'd caught on his land. When
challenged Mark Aldin, the gypo had replied cockily that he was just
scrumping; Martin ordered him off his land and he refused to leave.
In response, Martin set his three Rottweilers on him; Aldin backed
off but came back in his car and drove at the dogs, injuring Otto.

An incandescent Martin retrieved his double-barrelled 12-bore
and blasted the rear wing of Aldin's car, who took off like he was the
getaway driver on a bank robbery. With righteous indignation,
Martin called the police and demanded that they take action…they
did, they revoked his gun licence.

There was another problem with his 'Magnum' as he called – for
licencing purposes a pump-action shotgun was classed as a firearm,
not a shotgun, and he'd never even held such a licence. He grimaced.
This was serious. "Talk a lot and say nothing," he told himself. It was
a technique that he'd developed over the years; his habit of going on
verbal walkabouts had the added advantage that it aggravated his
listeners.

"Anyway, the police are bloody useless," he mused. "They are
more concerned about nicking drivers for speeding than catching
burglars, especially gypos. 'Itinerants are a discriminated
minority'…" he intoned sarcastically in his mind. He snorted in
derision. No, he decided, there was no point in calling the police.

He retrieved his torch that he had left by the staircase, then went
back into the breakfast room. With the pulled-out window frame
lying on the floor, it looked even more shambolic than before. The
old Christmas tree still lay diagonally across the floor, the collapsible
ladder was there, a rusty boiler sitting next to it, a sardine can was
wedged under the split bag of cement. He looked for blood, but
couldn't see any. Yet, he knew he'd hit at least one of them and

possibly heard a scream – but maybe it'd been in fright? They had certainly bolted.

Then he saw the three holdalls. He prodded the purple one with the end of his Winchester and heard a metallic clunk. He shone his torch into the bag and saw several of his aunt's antique silver jugs and an ornate pot.

"The bastards, the stinking, slimey, thieving, pikey bastards," he muttered to himself. All the rage flooded back...murderously. He'd shot down below the torchlight – he should have shot above it.

Craddling the shotgun in his right hand, Martin strode resolutely out of the side door. He shut it heavily, even though the gaping window provided easy access to the house. He let Otto and Daniel out of the shed to join Bruno... Then he heard the car at the bottom of the lane lazily turning over before catching and driving off. Even if they were uninjured, the other two could not have made it that far. It meant there were at least three of them.

He got into his Bluebird, started the engine and put the lights on full beam. The tyres span wildly in the deep gravel that covered the overgrown drive. Martin drove in large looping passes across the grounds to the front of the property, looking for any signs of them. He bumped and skidded over discarded plastic sheeting and broken wooden pallets. The shotgun – its safety catch off – jumped around on the passenger seat as Martin swung the car closer to the orchard. It wasn't dangerous. Out of habit he hadn't put one up the spout. Unable to see anyone, he took off in pursuit of the car he'd heard start up and drive away. Someone was going to pay a bit more for this.

Fearon heard the car wheeling backwards and forwards but he was already rising to his feet and edging his way across the ditch. There was some brackish rainwater in the bottom, which was punctuated by broken branches and clusters of stinging nettles. As he set foot on the dark soil on the other side of the ditch, his right leg gave way beneath him and he fainted. His baseball cap rolled into a furrow.

Darren Bark knew that if a police car came along the lane in answer to a 999 call, he was especially vulnerable. Without really thinking it out, he started the engine and barrelled back to Newark, thoughts of what had happened on the farm tormenting him as he sped home.

How had the "old nutter" sprung them? He'd obviously had a shotgun to hand. But had he shot them or just frightened them off? Maybe Fred or Brendon had copped it.

He'd deserted his mates. The getaway driver is honour-bound to stay on the plot until everyone is back in the car. "Fucking 'ell, it'd be funerals and gypos all steamed up and getting at me." Darren liked working with gypsies but if something happened to one of their own they would always lay the blame on a *gorjer* (non-gypsy) like him. Fred's sisters would be at his throat, too. Thoughts like this turned over in his mind as fast as the engine of the Granada.

Outside Newark, he pulled over into a lay-by and lit another cigarette. He'd been chain-smoking for much of the journey. He had to think. He looked at his watch – it was 11.40 – then he realised that he had returned to the same place on the road where they had been pulled over by the policeman earlier that evening… On a roll! Maybe it would have been better if they'd been nicked then!

Constantly nagging his mind was the question of whether or not he should go back to the area around the farm to look for Fred and Brendon. He took a long drag on his fag and flicked the ash out of the window, his fingers anxiously drumming the steering wheel. It was sixty miles from Bleak House to Newark. He didn't know what to do.

His reasoning – if grasping at straws can be called such – was that, if they were OK, Brendon and Fred would lay low until the morning, then thumb it back or get a bus. If taken in for questioning, of course, Fred would be charged with breaking bail – not that Darren cared. Brendon shouldn't have rowed him in, it was wrong to work with a kid.

Bark decided to ring his mum to see if there had been any messages from Brendon or Fred. It didn't make much sense – he had Brendon's mobile and Fred didn't have one nor did he have either his or his mother's number – but he was too panicky to work anything out logically. His mother said there had been no calls for him. Mulling it all over again…he decided to drive back, even though he knew finding the others would be a needle in a haystack job. He turned the car around and headed back to Emneth Hungate. Bark was aware that he was acting like a headless chicken, but he couldn't do anything about it.

Martin's search of his yard did not extend to where the teenager lay dying. Later he was to say, "I am glad I didn't find him because I don't like to think what I would have done." But this was when he had found a voice in deliberately upsetting the *Guardian* reader's sensibilities. In fact, Martin regards his dogs, even his teddy bears, as honourary human beings and he would certainly never leave a person – even a pikey – to die in agony. If he had spotted the teenager he would, however grudgingly, have called the emergency services... eventually.

In March, Tony Martin had gone to a meeting of "Farm Watch": an informal association of thirty farmers from Norfolk, which had the highest incidence of burglary in the counties. They weren't a bunch of vigilantes, but rather a network of eyes and ears. The group pooled information about raiders in the area in the hope of stemming the rising tide of rural crime. Tony's solution was rather more picaresque: "Herd them into a field and machine gun the lot." Unfortunately, when he was on trial for murder, evidence of this kind did not exactly endear him to the jury.

Martin gunned his Bluebird around Emneth looking for the car...any car that might look suspicious and anyone on foot who looked out of place. Gradually his anger dissipated, and he began to slow and calm down. As he turned back towards his farm, he saw the lights of his nearest neighbours, Paul and Jacqui Leet. They'd had their fair share of raiders but had no time for Farm Watch – "It don't do no good...just a bunch of farmers talking to each other," was Paul's comment. He drove into the driveway of "Foreman's Bungalow", the Leets' cottage.

Paul Leet was in the kitchen and from his window had seen Tony's car drive past like a bat out of hell. A few minutes later it returned at a much slower speed, swung into his driveway and parked outside his front door. Tony arrived at their door just before ten o'clock – oblivious to the fact that one of the wounded burglars was dragging himself there, too.

Paul Leet stepped outside to meet Tony. Although their respective houses were only 400 metres apart, Paul and Jacqui had never invited him inside their bungalow. A thick-set man of about 52 with dark, heavy Mediterranean features, Paul would see Tony a lot while they were working, but he never regarded him as a friend. Paul told Artnik "Friends go out together; we never did that. You'd see Tony twice a day. He'd come and see what you were doing. And he'd do the same to his little bit of land. He is not really what you call a competent farmer."

His wife Jacqui, a bubbly, chatty lady butted in as is her want, "But in his mind he is." She laughed.

Paul chuckled in agreement, "He buys these machines all the time...he's just bought another fork lift. I don't know why he's bought it. Everything is stood out in the rain...you can just ride up there and see it all just rusting there in the open land. I don't know why he does it, just a waste….But to get back to me point, we never went out together for a drink like friends do. And he's never been in here…Jacqui would not have liked it." He looked wryly at his wife, who audibly sniffed. Paul added, "I used to think, 'Tony, you need a bath.' Living on his own and that, he forgot things."

Paul went back to his story of that evening: "I came out and said, 'Hello Tony.' He was just his normal self. He had his working clothes on, boots, jeans and a short-sleeved shirt. But he was right as normal as I have always seen him. Just normal. There was no nerves…

"This thing that Tony is a weak man is rubbish. Tony's not a weak man. Physically an' mentally, he's strong. This depression talk is silly. He's bright too, but a lot of people think he's not. But that's deliberate, too."

Jacqui chipped in again, "He hides behind his eccentricity… that's what I think. Instead of lying outright, he evades questions and waffles away. When he goes on his verbal walkabouts it is usually to cover something up."

Paul nodded, "Exactly. But when he arrived here, he was just as he always is. There were no nerves… If I'd done it, I tell you I'd be nervous…

"He said, 'I just come to warn you there are burglars about. I found three of them in my house when I came back from me Mum's. I took a shot at 'em but I don't know if I hit them.' He told me that he'd been looking for their car and came back 'cause he couldn't find it. He said it was a blue car…how he knew that he didn't say.

"I said, 'You'd better tell the police, Tony.' He didn't say nothing. He just got in his car, backed out and went.

"At the time I asked meself: had he shot them? I didn't know what to believe, but after the last burglary he has always said that if anyone else goes on his land he is going to shoot them. He told everyone that.

"I thought have you done it, Tony, or haven't you? I didn't know whether to believe him or not. I never heard the shots, so...." Paul shrugged.

Jacqui took up the story, "You came in and told me, because I said, 'What the bloody hell does he want?' You said, 'He reckons he came back from his Mum's and found some burglars in his place and he took a shot at them.' And I said to you I think we ought to phone the police, didn't I?"

"That's right," Paul replied. "And I said Tony's just gone home to do it. I didn't want to do it..."

On Tony's mind as he drove off was Paul's advice – "ring the police". For all his misgivings, Martin knew that if he had hit one of them the police would have to investigate and, when they found out he'd used an unlicenced firearm, he'd be in the dock. He decided against making the call. "That'd be letting the fox into the henhouse." The burglars had got away; if they were wounded, they probably would get patched up by some pikey witch doctor...like him they would not want the authorities involved.

He decided to drive back to his mother's to think out what he was going to do. Increasingly, though, the knowledge of what he had done was forcing itself into the forefront of his mind. Just as that gun would shred a rabbit, so it would a leg. They'd have to go to hospital, have to. He knew that even though he was still hiding from it.

Meanwhile, Fearon had regained consciousness and was scrambling his way across the wheat field to the lights of the Leets' house. He was badly disorientated by the pain, which his exertions aggravated. Even though he had the lodestar of the lights from the house, Fearon still found himself meandering off course. Then, unexpectedly, he came upon a narrow unlit road that crossed the field between the two farms. And virtually straight away he saw a pair of headlights coming from the direction of the Leets'. Fearon stood on the verge and, as best he could, frantically flagged down the car.

The driver, John Spalter, was a professional eel catcher and was returning home after checking his nets in the River Ouse. He saw a down-and-out looming up on the roadside waving his hands like a drunken madman, and decided that as he didn't know him he was not stopping, even though he looked "more than a bit sorry for himself".

Fearon sobbed as he cursed the passing driver in Romany. "*Prastlo ming gorjer...*" He despaired at ever reaching hospital, but he kept to the road rather than going back into the field. Thankfully, the road actually led straight to the Leets' cottage. It was almost eleven o'clock when he finally scrambled onto the same doorstep that Martin had vacated some 45 minutes earlier.

Jacqui Leet was in the kitchen putting "the crocks in the disher" before she and Paul went to bed. "I heard this moaning, deep moaning and groaning. I looked out the window and saw this head above the hedge walking towards the entrance of our gateway. As he saw me, he came into the yard. He was dragging his leg. I could see he was hurt as it was all shot away. We have a dusk-to-dawn yard light and it showed up his injuries pretty well. I ran into the bathroom to tell Paul. Part of me wanted to believe it was someone who had had an accident, you know...you don't think about people being shot around here. But I think I did know this must be who Tony had said he'd shot because I ran to the bathroom and told Paul that I thought it could be something to do with Tony. Paul said, "You better ring the police."

Jacqui dialled 999. It was 10.55pm.

"Hello? Police."

"Look, there's someone outside and they're screaming they've been shot. We daren't go out," said Mrs Leet.

The operator responded, "Right."

"I think that he's been shot, you need to come quickly."

"What makes you think he's been shot?" he asked.

Jacqui replied, "Because he said so." She told Artnik that she didn't want to get Tony into trouble ..."but then in the end I said to them that Tony had been round earlier and said that he'd shot at three burglars and they'd run across the field."

The operator took down the address and warned her, "Don't go outside until we arrive. We have an ambulance on the way."

Jacqui returned to Paul by the window.

"What'd they say, love?" he asked.

"Not to go out 'til they get here." she replied. "Don't forget we don't know where the other two are and they could be armed."

Paul told her, "He keeps saying that he's leg been blown away and needs water. I'm going out there." He described Fearon to Artnik: he was wearing a dark leather jacket and black tracksuit bottoms, and the right leg was blown away and his thigh was hanging down to his ankle."

He explained, "I thought 'I've got to go out', as he was hurt. I asked how he'd been hurt. At first I wasn't sure he'd been shot. But when I heard the groaning and moaning...

"I thought, 'Tony, you got him.'" Paul nodded emphatically.

"Truthfully deep down I believe Tony did know he'd shot 'em... I used to use a gun when I was on the farm and you always know if you've hit something. If you're shooting pheasant and you hit one, it's a different sound...thwump. You know.

"I let matey have a drink out of my standpipe. The funny thing was he knew where it was and you can't see that standpipe unless you know where it is. There'd been an attempted burglary on our place a little before this, so maybe...

"Then matey collapsed on the lawn. He said he was cold, so I went and got a blanket out of the garage and put it over him. I thought he didn't have long... If we hadn't reported it and the ambulance hadn't arrived quickly, I'd have been putting the blanket over his head.

"It would not have been loss of blood. The police told me afterwards that the pellets sealed the blood vessels, so he didn't bleed much. The blanket that I wrapped him in only had a couple of spots of blood on it. It was shock that he'd have died from, shock. But he didn't go into shock until near the ambulance arrived. Up to then he was quite coherent. I asked him if anyone else was hurt and he just said, 'No.' It was when I heard the sound of the ambulance, that's when he lapsed into unconsciousness. Shock...it can kill you."

Around 11.20 the wailing ambulance drove into the driveway rapidly disgorging a paramedic, Derek Sand, and a technician, Michael Kiff. Sand began injecting Fearon with adrenaline and diamorphine, as Kiff examined and dressed his wounds. Fearon came out of his faint. Sands asked him his name and immediately began calling him by his first name. "Brendon, were you on your own or was there anyone else with you?"

"I was on my own."

Sands had been briefed that more than one person had been shot, so he kept asking Rearon whether anyone else had been with him. Each time, Fearon said that he was on his own.

Sands also said, "Don't worry. We'll keep you warm and look after you." Fearon knew he was going to live now.

After Sands and Kiff had finished dressing the wounds, they strapped Fearon onto a stretcher and wheeled him into the ambulance. Just as they did a police car arrived.

Jacqui related what happened, "One officer got into the ambulance and asked Fearon was anyone else shot and he said 'No' again. Three times he was asked by people, three times he said no there wasn't anyone else hurt. Reminds me of someone else...

"The Judas. He knew that boy was there, shot. He could have saved that boy's life, I say that more than anyone he was to blame. Fearon could have saved that boy's life and he didn't." Jacqui looked indignant.

"With Tony it's pikey this, pikey that... He just did na' like gypsies." She pronounced the word in a way that emphasised she didn't use derogatory terms for gypsies. "He would come straight out and tell you he didn't like them. I'm not saying anything bad about gypsies because we've got very good friends who are gypsies. And there is good and bad in all walks of life. I'm not being down on them because they were gypsies and did the burglaries. I am down on burglars.

"When all's said and done, they shouldn't have been there. And who's to say what they would have done to Tony if he hadn't had a gun.

"Tony's no saint but when all said and done, what right had they to be there? It's not robbing lorries, cargoes or what have you, but it's someone's house. It's your property and no one should have the right to be on your property. The law should favour the householder – you can't be *reasonable* when someone is on your property trying to steal from you because anger takes over."

The ambulance took off with its sirens wailing, heading for King's Lynn General Hospital some 23 miles away. Fearon was stable and would live. He would not be crippled for life, although in public he was still staggering around on a walking stick three years after the event. Yet, one prisoner described Fearon as "running round the gym like a ferret" only a year after the shooting.

After Martin left the Leets' cottage he drove to the neighbouring village of Elm, where his mother Hilary lived in Redmoor House. She was getting ready for bed with her sisters, Hilda and Rosemary. Rosemary had been married to the local neo-fascist Andrew Fountaine, who had founded the National Front. He started his career as a Tory squire much-loved by the rank and file.

His description of the then Labour Government at the 1948 Tory Party Conference was greeted with a rapturous standing ovation: "a group of conscientious objectors, national traitors, semi-alien mongrels and hermaphrodite Communists." But his views became a little too extreme even for the Tory Party of the day and he was edged out. He involved himself in fascist politics, predictably becoming very concerned about the degeneration of Britain into "a mongrel race".

Fountaine's country home, Narford Hall, is 27 miles from Bleak House, but as a child Martin spent many weekends there during the school holidays when Fountaine organised Aryan summer camps for local boys. At these gatherings, Fountaine was famous for warning his own 'Hitler Youth' about the dangers to the bloodline of 'fenfolk' from interbreeding with gypsies: "Within a generation, the Norfolkman, his culture, purpose, and ethnic succession will be biologically extinguished."

Martin sat down with Hilary, while Hilda made coffee, as he told her what had happened. Tony complains about most things including his mother's coffee.

"...the torchlight hit me in the eyes and I fired at the floor, below the light...I don't know if I hit them." His voice betrayed that he thought he had.

"What did you shoot them with? Was it that old pistol you've got in the shed?" Hilary asked him, remembering that he hadn't had a gun licence for years.

"A Winchester shotgun, I haven't got a licence…" he replied, slightly shamefaced.

"Oh, Tony! What are you going to tell the police?" she cried, putting her hand on his knee.

"I'll have to tell them that a well-wisher gave it to me, one that heard I kept getting burgled. Maybe I can tell them that someone left it in my car…with a note or something."

He wasn't joking. It made sense to him. He could hardly say he'd bought in another farmer's firearm licence. As he checked out in his head whether or not this would stand up with the police, he switched off from interacting with his mother.

She knew the phenomenon well – a psychologist had diagnosed it as Asperger's Syndrome, which is a form of autism. Hilary had always known there was something wrong with her son – he was awkward when interacting with others, had developed a peculiar pedantry as a schoolchild and periodically developed obsessive hobbies. As Tony tested the lies about the illegal shotgun that he'd tell the police, his mother just looked on nonplussed.

They sat in silence. Martin spoke first, "I'm going to leave the gun here, Mum. It's for the best."

He walked his aged mother to the small toilet and showed her where he had propped the gun up behind the door on his way in. He'd already unloaded it in the car and thrown the cartridges onto the floor. "I'll collect it tomorrow," he said as she gave him a kiss on the cheek. "I'm going to Helen's." Helen Lilley was an old friend who lived nearby.

As she watched the Nissan roll back out on to the road, his mother said, almost as if in prayer, "Take care."

Martin had no intention of going back to Bleak House. The import of what he'd done was beginning to sink in. He still flirted with the hope that he'd only winged the gypsies and that they'd get patched up without going to hospital and the police becoming involved. On the way to Helen's he threw the last spent cartridge case out of the window. He couldn't think what difference it would make but it made some kind of sense to get rid of it.

Helen Lilley owns the Marmion House Hotel, which is really just a guest house for reps and lorry drivers, situated two miles away on the outskirts of Wisbech just off a busy roundabout. Martin often slept there – not in a room but on a sofa in the hotel lobby. A grotesquely overweight woman of 55, Helen has buck teeth and spectacles, and "as a friend" has known Martin for over twenty years. Helen is one of those women who says she is not going to talk but then can't stop herself. She often accompanied Martin to antiques auctions.

She tells the story about Tony being a very experienced bidder and sometimes, for a bit of fun, he'd bid a piece up. He was skilled enough to pull out before the final bid. He liked to go up afterwards to the new owner and say "you paid a lot of money for that!" Tony's got a perverse sense of humour.

Tony's keen to make it clear about Helen that she "was never a Sheila of mine... I only ever think of women as a dish and Helen...well, she is a lot of things but she is no dish."

Martin made no attempt to hide his car inside her car park. Having thought of a story to explain away the gun, his mind was completely absorbed with what he would tell the police. His mind was on overdrive cooking up an account that made him the prey and not the predator.

Helen was surprised to see him on her doorstep at 10.30,

generally he showed up after the pubs shut. Tony explained why tonight was different from other nights. His emotions were frazzled by now and the calm front that he'd maintained so far collapsed. Everything all poured out – except the truth.

"Something bad has happened at the house and the police will be here soon," he told her. He recounted his evolving version of what had happened with particular emphasis on how afraid he had been. "…I thought I was going to have a heart attack…my chest was pounding boom, boom as I pulled the trigger"

"…It was all just surreal, surreal…"

The two of them stood in the hotel kitchen as she made him tea to calm his nerves. Going through the story again – this was the third time that evening – stripped away the wishful thinking, which unwittingly he'd used to hide from the likely reality. The warning that he was given for using his shotgun in '94 was nagging.

In the face of reality, he decided to make some practical arrangements to protect his most important dependents – his dogs. "Helen", he asked, "if the worst comes to the worst will you look after the dogs for me?" He grew more despondent and insisted on repaying a small sum of money that he owed her before nestling down on the couch for the night.

Martin often roughed it during his three years in the Australian outback in the late '60s and he so liked the image of a sleep anywhere buckeroo it became an integral part of his lifestyle.

Meanwhile, the Norfolk police were becoming very busy. Firearms, Rottweilers and thieving gypsies were a heady mix for the local constabulary. They leased a helicopter which was soon circling overhead, its searchlights probing the grounds of Bleak House; five squad cars, two vans, a mobile Police Investigation Unit caravan and some dog handlers quickly assembled at the Leets'.

Paul Leet recalled, "They were worried about Tony's dogs being loose and they daren't go round in case Tony was holed up in the farm with his shotgun, so rather than storm his place they sort of used our place as a temporary base. Our yard was swarming with police...we were making cups of tea and that.

"The armed response officers arrived quite quickly as they had been dealing with an incident in King's Lynn. I told them to ring Tony before they entered his place as he might think they were the burglars returning. Even to my mind, they didn't seem to know what they were doing. But they were all on overtime and seemed happy enough.

"The first ones to arrive knew Tony over the gun incident in the past when he shot up a gypo's car. Their attitude, to my mind, was 'good on yer, Tony'. It wasn't until they found the body the next day that things changed. Until then they'd been on Tony's side."

Detective Chief Inspector Martin Wright of the Norfolk Constabulary was in charge of the operation. He quizzed the Leets about what they had seen and knew about the recent movements of their oddball neighbour. Armed officers were seconded to secure the grounds around Bleak House but not to move in to the place. As they did not know if Martin was there, a call was put out for his silver Nissan across the entire region.

Darren Bark arrived back in the area around the same time as the Chief Inspector. There was a lot of action with police cars going back and forth. Darren was in the dark as to the likely fate of his mates but to his mind, as the police were searching for them, they were alive and on the run. That was good news but, for him, the bad news was he would have to stay in the area. "If I cut out, they'll all say I'm a longtail…" Some Gypsies believe it is unlucky to use the term rat, so they use the euphemism *longtail.* Worry, tiredness, uncertainty and guilt all took their toll. He drove along the run leading to the Leets and saw all the police cars and vans. To disguise his car number he turned off his lights, which understandably attracted the attention of at least one police officer. DC Peters reported the sighting to his DCI Wright and there was some speculation as to whether or not this was the burglars' car. Paul Leet had told them that Tony had said they were in a blue car and the Granada was white. Nonetheless, a call was put out to arrest the driver.

DC Peters was in a squad car scouring the area when he spotted the Granada parked up on the verge at Hungate corner. Bark was sitting in the driver's seat, smoking, with the engine ticking over. Peters approached him and took one look at the unshaven, shell-suited, unkempt 32-year-old and thought immediately that this 'one's *sheet*'s (record) as long as me arm'. He said to Bark, "Can you turn off the ignition and step out of the vehicle so I can have a word, sir."

"Have a word" meant only one thing to Darren – in next to no time he'd be in handcuffs. He put the shift in drive and took off...to shouts of "Stop!" Unfortunately for him, for the first time in their history the Norfolk Constabulary had a helicopter up in the air and he was quickly spotted and tracked along the winding country lanes. Even after he'd turned off his lights, the chopper stayed with him. Bark ditched his battered Grenada and legged it. However, with Alsatian dogs on hand, the police swiftly picked up his scent and he was arrested only a few miles from Bleak House. Just like Fearon, Bark kept shtum when questioned about Fred Barras.

While this was all unfolding, Martin was sleeping like a log on Helen's sofa roughly eight miles away in Wisbech. But a patrol car spotted the Nissan outside Helen's and armed police raided the place at 6 am. By now Martin was already awake and greeted the officers affably, joking in typical chirpy style about their guns, "Good morning officers, I don't think you need those unless we are all going out to bag a few rabbits for the pot."

He was to be told that he was being arrested for the attempted murder of Brendon Fearon and for being in possession of an illegal firearm. The charge related only to Fearon, as the police still hadn't searched the grounds of Bleak House. The police had taken one look at Martin's three "bowsie wowsies" and decided they were "too aggressive" to tackle without back-up. Attempts were made to recruit an expert, who used drugged darts to subdue wild animals. While this was debated, the search was effectively stalled. The two obvious candidates for rounding up the dogs were, of course, Martin and Fearon. The Constabulary did not consider them appropriate candidates for the job.

Martin idolised his dogs and is, accordingly, very emotional about them. When the mother of Bruno, Otto and Daniel died, he wrapped her in a Persian rug and buried her in the spinney.

Paul Leet was emphatic on this point: "No one looks after his dogs better than Tony. They are well exercised and well fed. He liked nothing better than walking his land with them around him."

Jacqui nodded, "With his gun too. Tony's arrogant. He thinks he is above the law, above everything, a law unto himself. But the gypsies, they will get him in the end. They'll get him. It won't be now, won't be until all the kerfuffle has died down but they'll get him one of these nights. Definitely. I honestly think you'll find him dead in his car one day."

CHAPTER 3

"IN THIS COUNTRY WE DON'T GIVE BURGLARS CAPITAL PUNISHMENT"

Tony Martin was handcuffed to a policeman and the arresting officers walked him to the nearby Wisbech police station. He was his usual whacky self, "I know you chaps are only doing your job but I should be doing mine. It's harvest time and I should be getting the wheat in …And my dogs. What's happening to my dogs…they're loose." One officer reassured him that as far as he knew they hadn't been rounded up yet but, when they were, they would be looked after. At the station, the handcuffs were removed and he was driven to King's Lynn police station.

There the desk sergeant took him through the formalities: logging and bagging his personal property, making sure he understood why he had been arrested and so on. When the charge was read out by Desk Sergeant Dexter – "that you did unlawfully cause grievous bodily harm to Brendon Fearon with intent to do him grievous bodily harm" – he was formally cautioned and said nothing.

Before being led away to be photographed and fingerprinted, Dexter told him that he would be interviewed soon and that he had the right to have a solicitor of his choice present or, if he preferred, a free duty solicitor. Tony replied, "I've done nothing wrong, so why should I need a solicitor? I've had a horrendous experience."

As Martin wiped the last of the black ink off his hand he was told that he had the right to a phone call and was asked if there anyone he wanted to call. He declined, "Not yet, not yet, let's get this bloody interview out the way first." He was led with a mug of tea to the police cells. When the door was opened, he said, "Streuth, it certainly ain't the Ritz, is it?"

"We do our best Tony, we do our best," the cell officer replied. "Well, for some…we do our best, but not everyone gets that…" He winked.

Tony sat on the polystyrene mattress on the stone bunk, staring at his mug of tea and reflecting on his forthcoming interview. He felt confident about having the gun as he had his story for that…it had been put in his car, he had never used it until last night and he kept it as protection from the thieves who had been intimidating and robbing him for years. He kept it where he was at his most vulnerable…the bedroom. It would have to be under his bed, so at least if they came for him…it was at hand as his last line of defence, as a last resort.

But he'd shot them downstairs!

He had to come downstairs with the gun, then. He'd been in his bedroom…asleep. Yes, asleep. Then he heard noises and was terrified that they were going to come upstairs where all the real valuables were. He went downstairs because he was frightened of what they would do, truss him up, violate him. They shone the torch in his face…he did what anyone would do who just happened to have a gun under his bed at the time he was being burgled. He was defending his life and property, fighting back against years of intimidation and theft. The police never do their job and, under the circumstances, he had no choice but to do it for them. What he'd done was right and he had every right to have done it. And he was not going to back down…

DS Newton and DC Peters asked for Martin to be brought from the cells to the interview room at 10 am. They had prepared the tape recorder with dual cassettes – one for the Crown and one for the interviewee. And when Tony was brought in they again asked if he wanted a solicitor. "I've already told you, I've done nothing wrong. And if you've done nothing wrong you don't need a solicitor."

DC Peters said, "I take it, Mr Martin, that means you do not want a solicitor of your choice present or a duty solicitor supplied under legal aid? Is that correct?"

Tony looked at him as if he was a subnormal child, "I said I don't want a solicitor…how many times do I have to say it?" Newton reassured Tony that they there were various procedures that had to be followed, which were legal requirements to protect the suspect.

Tony immediately interjected, "That's the trouble with the law nowadays, it is all about protecting the criminal and not the law-abiding citizen. I've had previous break-ins. Perhaps the same people, the same man. And what do the police…"

"Mr Martin", Newton interrupted him, "can we wait until all the proper safeguards are in place before we begin to talk about what happened?" Tony nodded but his face conveyed his exasperation.

Peters started the tape recorder, established what time it was and who was present, then he cautioned Tony with the words that were to become all too familiar to him: "You do not have to say anything, but it may harm your defence if you do not mention when questioned something which you later rely on in court. Anything you do say may be given in evidence."

Peters began by explaining to Martin that he had been arrested in connection with the wounding by gunshot of a man named Brendon Fearon who had been on his property at roughly 9.15 the previous evening.

Tony shook his head, "That's not right. This man was *illegally* on my property, he broke into my farmhouse. I don't really understand how the law works but I know that, if someone breaks into your property and is prepared to use violence, you have a right to defend yourself. And that is all I did. I did nothing wrong. It was horrendous what happened to me. And as police officers you should be enforcing the law, not arresting a farmer who pays his taxes and just wants to farm his land and harvest his crops. You have arrested me and I've done nothing wrong...why don't you arrest this Fenion man or whatever his name is?"

Newton, who had some previous experience of Martin over the incident when he had taken a pot-shot at Aldin's car, intervened, "We know how you feel Mr Martin, but Fearon was badly wounded on your property and all we want to do is find out what happened. We have spoken to him and he says that he entered your property on his own after he got lost and was attacked by one of your dogs. He claims that while he held your dog, you shot him. Now at this stage we don't know if he is telling the truth or lying but we do know he was shot while he was on your premises and we want to know your side of things. Did you shoot Mr Fearon?"

Tony realised that the injured burglar had lied about being on his own. It meant that the other burglar – injured or not – had got away. He visibly perked up but neither detective knew why. Tony replied confidently, "Well, you must have asked him...what does he say?"

Peters answered, "The purpose of this interview Mr Martin is to find out your side of things. Will you, please, tell us what occurred at your home yesterday evening..." As an innner elated Tony continued to look stonily at him, he added, "Fearon says that a number of shots were fired at him in your home that resulted in him sustaining serious injuries... Did you shoot anyone in your house, Mr Martin?"

"That's correct, so would you if you'd been in my shoes. He should not have been in my house," Tony replied. "And my dogs have never attacked anyone. I have not reared my dogs up like that. They are big and they look fierce but they don't attack anyone. You're the police – have you ever had any complaints about my dogs? Have you?" Tony is a master at gabbling; it's a skill he has perfected over a lifetime.

Newton and Peters exchanged glances. Peters said, "I am not aware of your dogs having been the subject of a police enquiry, Mr Martin, but what we are here to establish is what happened at your home yesterday evening. But you didn't know that Fearon was a burglar...he could have been a trespasser, for example. People get lost and there are all sorts of abandoned machinery and scrap cars on your farm, he may just have thought…

"Trespasser? That's ridiculous." Martin changed tack, "I've had two previous break-ins this year in my house. I don't go out very often and I don't go very far this time of year, because I have a lot of work to do around the farm." Newton and Peters exchanged more glances.

Tony continued, "I have what I call my Magnum. Someone gave it to me...I don't know who. You might be able to find out. Perhaps you can, I don't know...I've had an horrendous experience. Horrendous."

Peters tried to pull the interview back to base, "Mr Martin, is your "Magnum", as you call it, the gun you shot Mr Fearon with, the man you found in your house?"

Tony never answers questions directly. He replied, "You're not interested in my side of things...I can tell. What is the point in me talking about what happened if you are not prepared to let me tell you? There is no point in me telling you...I wish I was in China, they'd put a bullet in my bloody head and I'd be finished and out of the way. What you prefer is the story of some thieving...some burglar who invaded my home. I'm not a criminal…"

Newton attempted to placate Martin by saying that Fearon, although still in hospital, was officially under arrest for burglary of his home, and that another man had been arrested in a car nearby who was also suspected of being involved. But when he returned to asking about the gun, Martin replied adamantly, "I have already said what happened to me was horrendous and I am not going to talk about it. Not now. Maybe some other time. I need time to get my thoughts in order."

The officers pressed Martin on the few points they had gleaned, but he continued to say that he'd had this horrendous experience and didn't want to talk about it. In fact, he repeated it 38 times.

Eventually the officers looked at each other in resignation...they knew they had to terminate the interview and did so. They told him they would like to finish the interview later, when he would be given bail. Martin went back to his cell, where the cell officer, on the instructions of Newton, gave him some sheets of paper and a ball point pen. The shirt-sleeved constable had a thick ring of keys harnessed to his belt. He said, "Tony, if you want anything, tea or a sandwich or you want to make a phone call, just press the bell here." He indicated the recessed buzzer next to the door.

"You're the butler here, are you? Does the general public know that these criminals get room service in our police cells?"

The officer grinned, "Tony, it's only our VIPs who get the five-star treatment." He winked conspiratorially at Tony.

Tony laughed, "Goodonyer!" He often uses Australian-isms. He says he does it to put at ease people who feel inferior when they realise that he is public-school educated. Inside the cell, he began to think about the import of how he was going to explain the gun. He was conscious during the interview how lame his explanation had sounded. He knew he was better than a politician at not answering questions but he also knew that the police were going to be like a dog with a bone over the Magnum. On the other hand, the good news was there was only one burglar injured...

Tony sat back on the bed and began doodling on the pad. He wrote down some scattered thoughts about the history of the way over the pikies…gypsies had put him and his property under siege. Then he remembered that he should organise the rounding up of his dogs. He pressed the buzzer and asked the cell officer if he could make a phone call to his friend Helen Lilley. This was arranged and he rang her from the telephone at the end of the cell unit, which can be, and usually is, monitored on a shared line by the desk sergeant. He rang her guest house and, when she answered, said, "Helen, it's Tony…" She was surprised at the call and thought for a moment that he had been released.

"No," he replied. "They are holding me on a trumped up charge of grievous bodily harm, whatever that means! It seems that once they conclude their inquiries they will give me bail to appear before the King's Lynn magistrates on Tuesday. But what I am ringing about is the dogs. They are still roaming around on the farm, according to the police. Could you get Roger (Roger Cotteril was her son-in-law and a tractor mechanic who often helped Tony out) to go over there and put them in the cottage. He can feed them and watch over them and the farm until I am back… Can you also go round to Hilary's – I put the Winchester in her toilet, it's standing up behind the door, unloaded – tell her not to worry and arrange to hand it into the police." Helen agreed. She has an extremely good relationship with the local police as they sometimes use her guest house to put up people who are remanded on bail but not allowed to live at home.

Roger Cotteril is married to Helen Lilley's daughter – he is Fenfolk born and bred. He is an ordinary looking bloke of around 38 but unlike some of the people around Tony he is polite and courteous… "the salt of the earth" is the way he is described. Unusually for a farming man, he has an air of humility about him, which probably comes from the devotion he gives his autistic son.

He told Artnik, "Helen rang me and I drove over to the farm

and spoke to the police surrounding the ground, explaining who I was and why I was there." The police at Bleak House convened a hasty conference about the propriety of this. One officer asking, "What if they turn on him? We'll really be in the shit then. We've got a duty of care…"

Sergeant Middlebrook, of sturdier country stock than his colleague, cut to the quick, "For Christ's sake, this man has known the dogs all his life. They're not polar bears." Roger was given the green light to round up the dogs Once they were under control the police decided that they would call off the search and bring in the detectives to examine the scene of the crime.

Roger recalled, "I found a bone and threw it into the cottage and Bruno and Daniel dived in after it. I just locked them in. But Otto went off into the orchard, so I followed him, then I saw this pair of trainers. That's what caught my eye and I thought 'what are they doing there?' I looked and it was a body, laying on its front. I could tell from the pallor of the face, the lad was dead. I told the police, who were virtually at the point of calling off the search, and suddenly everything started up again."

Fred Barras was still wearing his burglar's rubber gloves. It was 2.40 in the afternoon. The police were unable to contact his mother, Ellen, until much later that evening.

The police operation now went into murder overdrive. The body was cordoned off and the Police Investigation Unit summoned from the Leets'. Martin was informed by a detective of their find and told under caution that the investigation had now been upgraded to murder. He replied defiantly, "It wouldn't have happened if they hadn't burgled my place."

One detective, DCI Martin Wright, said to him in words that Martin remembers and repeats to this day, "In this country we don't give burglars capital punishment." But he was told that they planned to re-interview him on the Sunday partly to give him time to prepare his notes.

Back at the Ville, Ellen was dolling herself up for a night out in Skegness with some of her friends. The officer from the Norfolk Constabulary killed the evening's jollities when he told Ellen and her daughters of Fred's death.

Ellen was taken to the police forensic laboratory at King's Lynn where she formally identified Fred's body. Leaving the hospital, extremely distraught, she said to the waiting press:

"I don't think I will ever be happy again."

A RIGHT TO KILL?

CHAPTER 4

TONY'S BIG WHOPPER

Tony Martin went back to his cell. He was deflated by the discovery of the body but was not that surprised. He presumed the young pikey had died of loss of blood... He certainly did not feel any more responsibility than he had for winging Fearon. He had fired down, which had become his mantra and to his mind proved that he had not been guilty of murder or attempted murder. However, the change in his circumstances, his concern over his dogs, worry about the state of his farm began to get on top of him...

He started staring into space, just imagined how his life would now change... The cell officers became concerned about Martin's odd behaviour. He wouldn't talk or eat anything. In the end they contacted a local GP, Dr Dermott Gerard Tiernan.

Tiernan, who regularly examined offenders held in police custody, arrived at 11.38 am. Tony told him about the thrombosis in his leg and that he'd suffered from depression in the past. Tiernan asked the usual questions to test mental alertness such who was Prime Minister.

He found Tony withdrawn but not suffering from anything other than tiredness and concern at the predicament he faced. Tiernan saw Martin again that day and felt that a day respite from questioning was all that was needed. He pronounced Martin unfit to be interviewed on the Sunday but able to be questioned on the

Monday as long as an independent person was present in the interview room. The term for such a person is "appropriate adult" and this is someone, usually supplied by the local social services, who is supposed to protect the interests of the interviewee. This safeguard is mandatory for people such as juveniles, those with mental health problems or just those who are in bad health generally.

During the Sunday Martin drew up a long list of events that he wanted to talk about in the next interview. He also decided that it would be better if he did take advantage of his right to a solicitor but, rather than pay for one, he claimed the free one provided by the state. The duty solicitor for 23rd August was a Paul Croker of Kenneth Bush & Co. Before the interview Croker had a consultation with his client.

Tony explained what had happened at the first interview and how, after a while, he had refused to discuss events. Croker told Tony that he was surprised by this and he advised him to stick up for himself and tell his side of the story. Tony said that this time he wanted to consult his notes and he showed them to Croker. His notes were as voluminous as they were disorganised, but Croker advised him to stick with them and said that he would forewarn the officers of this. He encouraged Tony by saying that he was perfectly within his rights to consult them whenever he wished.

After Newton and Peters had installed the appropriate adult in the interview room, set up the tapes and Peters had delivered the caution, Croker rather pompously informed the officers: "In order to assist my client today in recounting these circumstances surrounding the offence which he is under arrest for, he has prepared some notes that he would wish to refer to during the course of this interview. Clearly I would be grateful if you, as officers, could show a degree of forbearance when he is going through those notes in trying to explain what happened during the material time…"

Tony told Artnik that he rather liked Croker's preamble but the body language of the two officers made it clear they didn't actually relish the idea of showing their *forbearance*… Both also looked uneasy as they clocked the madcap scrawl of writing on Martin's sheets of paper. After Croker had finished, Peters asked Tony to tell them what happened at his home on Friday evening.

Tony, peering at his notes, began talking: "Well, on this piece of paper that I have been writing things on while I was in custody last night, which I found is better, things are clearer. I've got down here that *lights appeared to be coming up the stairs* and then I've got down here *my car outside*… well, then I've got down here *were these the people I saw earlier in the year?* Is Taylor connected with any of these people? He drives by my property and has been on my property before. Ah, it is there, *my car being outside and me being broken into made me feel whoever is out there now.*"

John Taylor was another local gypsy whom Martin had suspected, not without cause, of stealing from and trespassing on his property. Martin had developed an obsessive interest in the local police taking action against Taylor and had made a number of complaints to that end.

As Martin went off on the Taylor tangent, Peters looked like he wanted to interrupt but didn't.

Tony went back to his notes, beginning to realise that he'd stumbled upon a wonderful prop for talking a lot and saying nothing. "Ah", he exclaimed as he spotted something supposedly relevant, "*my car being outside and me being broken into*…This is not quite in the order of how I've got it written down. Nothing is in order in this statement I'm making. I'm going from notes, from paper…And this particular night I went in probably, in the house, I didn't look at my watch, but maybe about 9 o'clock…"

Peter started to try to pin Martin down and interrupted his flow, "Can I just stop you for one second...can you just tell me where you parked your car, so that we know where we're talking about?"

Better men than Peters have given up at trying to elucidate what Tony is talking about when he decides to red herring the trail you want to go down.

After establishing that Peters knew the layout of Bleak House, Tony told him that he parked his car to the left of front door, behind the garage containing an abandoned Rover car. Peters was serenely ignorant that the Rover car was an elephant trap that Tony was setting up to spring on him.

Peters repeated that what he was trying to establish was where Tony parked his car.

Tony drew Peters in prior to springing the trap, "May I say that during the meeting we had the other day and you made a comment about scrap cars, I assume you were referring to the Rover car. Weren't you?"

"That's right," Peters replied innocently. "It's the only one we've seen. Can you describe the car again?"

Tony was enjoying this: "Well, may I say that I...You may not have meant it and you don't understand the situation, but I took offence to what you said about a scrap car." Tony paused before springing the trap, his voice already quivering. "It's a scrap car that belonged to my father."

It's obligatory, even for policemen, to show respect for the dead. Peters answered solemnly, "I see."

Martin began to blubber and said between sobs, "And my father...like everyone else's tried..."

After some more sobs and sniffs, Peters interjected, "Take your time." Which was rather redundant advice to give to Tony as if there is anything he does do is take his time and waste yours.

Tony continued, "My father has been dead for many years and I thought that when the car… I didn't really need it. I just had it for a period of time until I got another car because my garage has been broken into several times before, and has been locked and secured beyond reason. I decided to park that car against one of the doors and I never use one of those doors and it has sat there ever since. Yes, it does look like scrap, but in that car is everything that is my father…" just as Peters went to intervene, Tony stalled him with some more sobs…" with his keys, with his land owner's badge, country land owner's badge, a knife in there with a bone handle – really it is for cutting up beef – but he used to eat asparagus with it and to me that is just a little time warp here."

Peters knew he was trapped and stopped struggling, "Right." He nodded in resignation. Newton just sat dumbfounded by the sight of a 54-year-old man accused of murder crying over the car of his long-dead father. Walter Martin died of lung cancer in 1979.

Tony continued, "And his little flask bottle for whisky in his tin. But it's funny, I've been having a little clear out of it just lately, for one reason or another…and I redone the drive and I had a look in there and I'm afraid as the years have gone by it does get damp in there, things are beginning to rust and maybe it's time for the car to be moved. But that is beside the point. I just wanted to let you know."

Newton and Peters eyes were glazed over. They had not come into the police force for this nor had their training, such as it was, seasoned them to listen to Tony Martin on full-throttle verbal walkabout.

This was ten minutes into the interview; the sobs had subsided and Peters was out of the trap, but the person making the running was Martin. Yet, what Martin rarely appreciates is that for all his success at taking people on his digressions, his tangents, his obfuscations, their gut reaction is that he is obscuring the truth for his own ends. The wily, contrary Norfolk Farmer may run rings round people with his bizarre style of social intercourse, but often it's not to his own advantage.

Peters doggedly ploughed on, but Tony was in full flight, "I'll try to get back to the point. I might be going over what I've said and my car being outside and me being broken into, I mean, I didn't know this... but my brain... I told you earlier on. Can I explain something? I've had experience of this...that...when you see something different or you tend to think not the worst but it might be something else... And I don't know whether we control our brain or whether our brain controls us but, basically, your brain, when you think, instantly, if that is the correct answer, you know, if you think you're being broken into but then you're not...or somebody's left or there's a door there that you know you closed and you see it open, you think, well, maybe I did leave it open. But your brain has already told you that you didn't leave that door open – it's closed...And there's something wrong, but the door has got nothing to do with what I'm talking...it's just an example..."

Tony ranted on as Peters and Newton listened and interjected the odd comment, but it was established who was setting the agenda. The interview was punctuated by long silences as Tony struggled with deciphering his notes – "I find it difficult to read my own writing". In default the detectives just let him waffle on. And he did.

"A man also came onto my property several years ago, which I felt the seriousness of the threat. I'm not going into details, unless you want to know about it, I don't suppose you do, of the threat that I ended up fetching my gun for protection – not use – but for protection and a witness was there when it all happened. The threat was carried out...well, it wasn't actually carried out but it was attempted. I felt I had no choice but to fire a warning shot and this was not at the man, this was at the vehicle, at a tyre...this was the incident I reported to the police and I ended up being the loser and, if you want to know any more about that, you can do...all you need to know."

Of course, all Peters wanted to know about, as he had already made abundantly clear, was what happened when Fearon and Barras were shot and, as Tony gabbled on and the Aldin incident ran its course, he attempted to get back to that: "Well, if we go into what...if we go into that at a later stage... because what we really want to get to do is Friday night."

Tony wanted to keep away from Friday night for as long as possible. He replied, "Right. Okay... I was the loser because it wasn't something I wanted to do. I decided you can't wait for police cars and all sorts of things, you're in a situation" – he turned to his solicitor and asked if he was doing okay. Croker assured him that he was. Martin continued, "This is a situation where, you know, it's not a rehearsal. Things are happening and we're talking about... this was the lives of my dogs actually. I reported this to the police and there was... I was very worried because when I found out I didn't know where the man was, he went away and then he came back. It was premeditated actually. And then he came back and then, when he went, I went on my searches and I wrote, first time, not necessarily...but it happened that way..."

Tony chatted on like this for another two minutes without interruption, before Peters established that this all took place in 1994. When the year was confirmed, Tony reflected, "My goodness me. My dogs are seven years old. I thought they were four."

Gradually he was inched towards the events of Friday evening.

"I hardly get...I work hard all the time, just when, you know, I hardly go out in the evening now, only when it's light and not late, It seems I can't get it right any more. I go out and get burgled, I stay at home I end up like this. This house or area seems to have a history of violence. The incredible voices in the house that night. I still can't understand or explain the voices from people, as it's turned out, it's not audible. What a nightmare.

"The gun I've had for some time. I only decided to use as I was… The gun I've only had for some time. I only decided to use it as I was sure people were coming up the stairs. Maybe some of the banging, the noises – I still don't understand – might have been from opening drawers. I say this because when I got down the house eventually I had the courage to go downstairs and go and get a torch I noticed one of the drawers had been opened and a cupboard. But whether when they arrived the drawers in the house were already open I don't know. That's all I saw."

Martin grass-hopped around the sequence of events, talking one minute about his electrics and the next his stairs but, in between these topics, he talked about coming out onto the landing and seeing the torchlight of the burglars. "And I went out there and I saw these lights, like car lights. Now these – when I say car lights, not from the outside, this was from inside and there seemed to be a lot of lights and…err – Tony took time out by consulting his notes – at that stage I'm afraid…*started to become very frightened, fearful, terrified… I couldn't stand it any longer.* What I did…I didn't want to go downstairs – I couldn't face whatever was going to happen. *I couldn't stand it any longer, so I took the gun out and loaded it.*"

Peters asked, "With how many shots, please?"

Tony answered, "Can't remember, just till it was loaded."

Peters pushed, "What does it normally take?"

"Don't know."

"Okay, fine."

Tony suddenly introduced the big whopper, "Never used it before."

All Peters wanted at that stage was the story of what happened, he was not yet looking to catch Martin out and so responded to this claim with a simple, "Okay."

Tony added, "Err…'the uncertainty…loaded the gun.' The uncertainty I couldn't bear any longer, yeah."

There was a break to insert a new tape and Tony asked, "Have I already said the gun I've had for some time?"

"Yes" Peters replied crisply.

"I only decided to use it as I'm sure people were coming up the stairs."

Peters asked, "Yes. You haven't told us where you got the gun from, though?"

Tony replied, "I'll tell you later. Maybe some of the banging or knocking opening drawers, I did that bit, didn't I?"

Peters answered deadpan, "Yeah."

The interviewing technique lapsed into letting Martin ramble on in the hope that he would eventually entangle himself in his web of implausible and evasive answers.

But Tony can talk Martinese until the cows come home: "This is in hindsight, not at the time… *I thought something was coming up the stairs.* In fact, I really thought somebody was on the landing. In fact, I didn't really know where the noise was coming from. I mean, I've never had anybody in that house all the years that I've lived there, so I wouldn't know about noises. I mean, I know when a cat comes in or a dog comes in, which they can't get in anymore. I was going to stay in the bedroom after going out of it once, but *I couldn't stand it any longer and loaded the gun.* The uncertainty I couldn't bear.

"Anyway, as I say, I've done that and then I've done the one about the ill omen I've found. (No one has ever ascertained what this 'omen' was.) Had I not taken the bottom of the stairs out or made it look unused at the end, this could have been a different story maybe. *So many different noises. A nightmare.* My home has just been a place of sleep and a place to store some things, which are not safe anywhere else. Now nothing is safe. Now, I've got down here downstairs, up the stairs, out of the house. Basically, when I'd been the first time out of my bedroom on the landing I felt, well, I didn't know what was going on, but I felt maybe somebody was coming up the stairs and this was very frightening. And I went back into the bedroom to try to hide or do something. And then it sounded like somebody really coming up. There was this *knock, knock, knock, knock*. And I can't say it sounded like that, it's indescribable…but it certainly…my staircase hasn't got carpet on it and that definitely sounded like the banging of wood. But where I don't know. And it was very, very consistent and the stage we're talking, maybe in trillionths of seconds I have to make decisions and I'm not prepared at that stage to wait for the unknown and I had no choice. I got the gun out, loaded it, waited and it seemed like forever.

"Nothing was coming, but there was this *knock, knock, knock* and there were other noises, which I didn't understand, like a kind of scrape. Like I don't know whether snakes make a noise when they move in the sand or whatever they do, but it was something like something slivering around. And then there was this crashing and there was noise like my central heating, which is not central heating, it's just a solid fuel boiler, which I did use last week and once it goes on it's finished and there was this kind of gurgling and banging and this whole confusion. I mean, I knew someone was down there because there's lights. I'd seen the light…"

Newton grinned wryly.

"…and there was this banging and this gurgling and *knock, knock, knock* and there's like air kind of get out of something and there was this consistent *tap, tap, tap, tap, tap* and I just, I don't know how long, whether it was seconds, half a minute or whatever it was. And in the end I couldn't stand it. I just thought I can't wait

for somebody to walk into the bedroom. I walked out of the bedroom along the landing, down the stairs, halfway down the stairs,
and that was difficult because I've got this problem getting from the
top on to it and then down there. I see some reflection of feet and
it looked like a lot of feet to me and I'd also heard this murmuring,
not audible speech, murmuring. Then this light shined in my face
and how. I mean all these things were all in a flash. And I just
couldn't stand it any longer and then I just let the gun off. Anyway
after that I couldn't see anything. I never even heard anything.
Never heard anything."

Peters nodded, "Right. Do you remember how many times you
fired the gun?"

"Can't remember."

"Until it was empty?" Peters suggested.

"Until it was empty…Well I don't… I've never used the gun
before. In fact, I don't know whether I…Where are we going? I could
tell you now, but I could tell you later, whatever way you wanted."

Peters, like Newton, looked surprised, "Tell us what?"

"Well, the gun that I had."

Both Peters and Newton nodded, "Mmm."

Tony dangled the bait, as he often did, and pulled it away as the
officers went to bite, "I have since I owned it. I've never used it
because I'm not a man who shoots game. I didn't get any pleasure
out of it. I did get a gun licence many years ago to buy a gun because
I was having trouble with pigeons. But I don't grow rape any more.
I got fed up shooting at pigeons and it doesn't make any difference.
I'm not really interested in shooting rabbits around the house or
anything else and I've never used the gun and I didn't actually know
whether it worked and that was a terrifying experience in itself."

"Can you tell us where you got the gun, Tony?" Peters asked.

"I'll tell you that at the end."

They got back to Tony's account of the shooting. Tony used his notes as prompts but, as he only thinks in sentences not paragraphs, whatever coherence there was in them did not translate into speech. Each point tended to turn into a cue for a digression. He explained that after he discharged the gun he ran up the stairs. After going into his bedroom he came back out and went downstairs, went out to his car to retrieve a torch, then came back into the breakfast room and saw the burglar's bags with "stuff" in them. He also noticed a cupboard that had its drawer open. In his account, he only noticed the window that Fearon tore out to make his escape after he'd been outside. "Well, this window, suddenly I've noticed the window's missing and it's laying on the ground and I don't know any more than that. But that's where the window laid. And I went outside again."

People with Asperger's Syndrome characteristically see things with blinkers on, they often focus on the detail without seeing the wider picture within which the details are intertwined. Tony's account was rendered incoherent by this trait and didn't even get close to meeting the facts. For example, as Tony Martin returned to the breakfast room, after the shooting, he could not have missed the window through which Fearon and Barras made their escape as it was a bright moonlit night and light would be have been flooding in through it. In a pitch black room, it would immediately catch your eye long before you saw the bag or the cupboard. Tony also claimed in the context of another burglary, "I can see quite well in the dark, whether through use or habit or the way I live or whether other people are the same." This kind of lack of attention to detail was later to damn him at trial.

The detectives went on to clarify that Tony shot towards the torch but below it. He also explained how he drove round the grounds of his house searching "for where these people had gone" but he admitted that he was "hoping that I might see a car with lights on there." Peters did not press him on how he knew the burglars had a car. Tony then described how he went out onto the highway looking for their car and described seeing a man driving a pale blue car, which he chased for a while but gave up as "I can't just keep chasing after ghosts".

Peters suddenly asked, "Did you have the gun with you when you went for your drive around?"

"I could hardly leave it in the house, could I? There might have been somebody still in the house. I mean, I'll now go back in time…" And he did for five minutes as he evaded the question by telling them in minute detail of an incident that had occurred twenty years earlier. But the detectives let him go there as by now they could see he would hang himself.

As his diversion ran down, Tony asked Peters, "Is that alright?"

"Yeah, I think you're back," Peters commented sardonically. He had Tony's measure and pulled him back from twenty years ago to Friday evening. Tony kept to his version of events, describing how he had given up chasing the burglar's car and dropped in on the Leets, before driving to his mother's.

At the first mention of Tony visiting Hilary, Peters interrupted with another question that threw Tony, "Did you leave the gun with your Mum?"

Tony wobbled, "Well, I didn't know what to do, what I would do with this gun, I'm going to have to give myself up and I…I wanted a little bit of time left for a little bit of freedom to get me into a state of rationality and everything. And I hid it in the toilet."
Peters saw the opening and countered flush on Tony's chin, "You say that you had to give yourself up. For what? What did you think you had done other than discharge your gun."

Peters had given Tony all the rope that he needed to pull the trapdoor on himself.

"Well…" On the story that Tony had told, there was no plausible answer.

Peters struck home his point, "Did you know you had hit someone?"

"No, I didn't know I'd hit anybody, but I just felt that obviously there was somebody in the house. I couldn't see what was in the room, not very much, even with a torch really. When you're in the room there like that you don't really…I mean, I don't know. There's lots of things on your mind and you…Where are these people? Can I catch them? And all that sort of thing. Anyway…"

Again Peters cut in, "You hid the gun in the toilet at your mum's. Was that…

"Pardon?"

"You hid the gun in the toilet." Peters stated flatly.

"I didn't *hide* it. I just put it there. I just put it there and I left. It wasn't going to be any good to me. *Getting sick and tired of…no more use for it.* Then, I thought 'shall I go home?'. No. I didn't want to go home. What was there to go home to? The dogs were there. So then I went up the hotel and I just thought, well, if anything happened or if anything comes to light… I thought, well, everyone knows where Tony is. And the police turned up in the morning at Helen Lilley's. Then they called my mother. And, then, it was only what, two or three years ago I had break-ins…well, they weren't break-ins." Tony wittered on for a few minutes until he mentioned his thrombosis, which he didn't want his mother to know about… "I don't want this…any of this to get back to my mother, who will not be here for much longer." This became another cue for a sobbing breakdown. When he recovered from this he stated emphatically, "The gun I used on Friday I've never used before, never, not even on game. I was also terrified as I didn't know if it worked or actually how to operate it, and which was the safety switch."

Very soon after this the police gave Tony a two hour break to compose himself before beginning another interview. In the interval he spoke to his solicitor. When the interview resumed, he said, "Well, I feel reading back earlier, I haven't made it clear to you my horrendous experience – this break-in with my gun on the staircase. I want to make it clear that when I fired my gun I genuinely thought my life was in danger..."

Soon afterwards Newton asked where he got the gun from. This time Tony decided that he had to grasp the nettle and he launched into his account, "This gun relates back to Robbie Augur. This gun was a surprise and I found it in my car with a small note. It's apparently somebody who'd admired my uncle Arthur or was a friend of many, many years ago and there was just a brief letter. I can't remember exactly what the words were, but they know of my predicament...what was happening down at Hungate and the problems I'd been having and they just mentioned that they knew my problem and that they, basically, didn't need the gun and they thought I might need it."

Peters attempted to establish how long ago this happened and Tony replied, "I don't know. I mean it's like you're saying I don't..." The detective tried to get Tony to date it by what car he had.

Current car? "No, no, no."

What car then? "I've had stacks of cars."

What car? "I don't know. I can't remember. Well, I mean, I had about three cars a year."

In Martinese, a "well" at the beginning of a sentence is usually a trailer for a red herring. Actually, Martin recruited an elderly neighbour, Aubrey Millard, who held a firearm certificate, and drove with him to Spalding in Lincolnshire where they bought the Winchester. The police hold a statement to this effect, and a *Telegraph* journalist retains a taped interview in which Aubrey talks abou the purchase. Millard has since passed away.

Peters asked Martin if he was given the pump-action shotgun before or after his own shotgun certificates had been revoked.

"After."

Peters said, "After. Right. So we know it's after '94."

"Well, I don't know when that was."

Peters confirmed, "Yes, we think it's '94."

"'94. As long as that?"

An exasperated Peters said, "Do you realise that you should have handed the gun in?" Tony pretended that he didn't know what gun they were talking about. Peters then showed him the Winchester that was wrapped in cellophane to protect it for fingerprinting.

As his story was that he only ever used the gun once, Tony decided that it would be best if he was unsure whether it was the same gun, "It looks like it, yes."

"That is the gun that was recovered."

"It looks like it, yes. I don't really remember much about it." Tony had come back from the dead but this time Peters was determined to nail home his coffin, "But that's the gun your mother handed to us, the police."

"Okay, then."

"And that is the gun that was left in your car?"

"That would be the gun." But if you pin Tony down, he won't submit without a quip. He added, "She hasn't got a gun like that."

Peters ploughed on, "No. Is that the gun that you were referring to as left in your car?"

"Yes."

The detectives took Tony right through the sequence of events for the shooting. When he got to coming down the stairs he got into trouble. Tony conceded that it was "dodgy" getting down his barstard'd staircase and then elaborated, without realising how he was blowing the gaffe, "Yes, very dodgy – especially with a gun. Much better freehand."

Peters perked up and asked, "I should think so. How do you hold the gun?"

Tony held up his right hand in a cradling motion. "Like that… I suppose." It was beginning to dawn on him that he may have opened up a can of worms.

"So right-handed?" Peters clarified.

Suddenly Tony saw the import of where the detectives' questions were taking him – his stairway banister is on the right-hand side! He began to fudge, "Yeah, okay then."

"So you are holding the gun in…"

Tony butted in and tried to draw them off the scent, "I don't know. What do you mean, 'when I was carrying it?'"

Peters confirmed what he was asking, "To get down the stairs."

"I don't know. I've no idea."

Peters had a gut feeling that he was on to something but he was not sure what it was. He asked, "Is there a banister rail to hold onto?"

"Yeah," Tony replied in a tone in which you can hear his heart sinking.

Peters carried on, "To get down the stairs and the missing bits?" Tony replied warily, "Yeah."

But they never asked what side the banister rail was on, and this line of questioning petered out as Tony managed to sidetrack them by drawing a plan of Bleak House. Having never been to the house neither of them realised the significance of what Tony had inadvertently revealed and they never played out the hand he had dealt them.

At trial his luck didn't hold.

A RIGHT TO KILL?

CHAPTER 5

MIDDLE ENGLAND FINDS A FOLK HERO

On the 24th August Tony Martin appeared before King's Lynn magistrates on the murder charge. He was heartened at the small group of supporters outside the court on his arrival. Ted Martin – Tony's cousin – and Helen Lilley had rallied the Wisbech locals to the injustice of charging an 'honest farmer' who was merely defending his property from the sort of theft that many of them had suffered. The protesters outside the King's Lynn magistrates court carried placards with the call "Support your local farmer" and there was even a sign erected near Bleak House reading "Tony Martin – Good Bloke".

Croker represented Martin but the hearing was brief with only the arresting officer DS Newton giving evidence about the bare facts of the case. Tony was remanded in custody for a week and taken to Norwich Prison. It was the first time he'd been in prison since 1962, when he was held as an illegal immigrant in New Zealand – he had jumped ship from the Merchant Navy – in Mount Eden Prison on the north island. Given the privation that he chose to live under when in Bleak House, it was not surprising that Tony adapted easily to the protective comforts of prison life.

Even before he was charged, the press had cast him as a man who had simply reached the end of his tether, harassed by thieves and ignored by the overstretched and incompetent Norfolk constabulary. *The Times* carried a report on the Monday describing Tony as...

'...dressing like a character from "The Last of the Summer Wine", he was known as a gentle and inoffensive man who was given to odd behaviour. Educated at a minor public school, he collected antique furniture and sometimes left his 300-acre fruit farm on a whim in order to attend auctions, only to return at night and start ploughing in the dark. He was known to be frightened, since he lived alone in the house, which is set back from a quiet country road and as such was considered a prime target for thieves.'

Stuart Mayfield was one of the first of Martin's neighbours to be quoted in the national press: "He was burgled twice within the past two months. They didn't get anything the first time, but on the second occasion they stole an antique chest of drawers. Most people are getting fed up with it all (the burglaries) and I said something like this was bound to happen. We have been broken into three times in the last few years. My sympathies are all for him, and others feel the same."

Stuart's wife Carole echoed her husband's sentiments by informing the papers that "Mr Martin had said he feared going back at night to find someone there."

The day after Tony was remanded to prison, the *Daily Mail* editorial read: 'Norfolk farmer Tony Martin accused of murdering a teenager who was said to have been trying to break into his home has just been refused bail. But the two men arrested on suspicion of attempting to burgle his house have been released without charge on police bail, until later this month. **Welcome to the wonders of British justice**.'

Later that month the same newspaper carried an article by another victim of the police's tender-hearted attitude to burglars who are attacked by their victims. Jon Pritchett neatly sidestepped the *sub judice* ban on a "live" criminal case by writing: 'It is not for me to comment on the details of Mr Martin's case, but I know what he is going through and what I want him to know is that I will do everything in my power to help him in the coming months.' Indeed, he opened his piece by saying his 'heart goes out to Tony Martin, the Norfolk Farmer…' Some five years previously Pritchett had also defended himself against burglars and been arrested. He then wrote what in various ways was to be written by hundreds of others who supported Tony Martin's case. In fact, it was the definitive mission statement of what was to become the Tony Martin bandwagon.

'I am old fashioned enough to believe that an *Englishman's home is his castle*. He has a right to defend his home, his family and his property against scum who come as thieves in the night to plunder and loot the treasured possessions it has taken a lifetime of hard work to acquire. If these yobs do not want to risk being shot then they should not break into other people's property and scare them half to death. Some do-gooders may say that my views are extreme. But I must tell them that in my part of Kent such opinions are commonplace. And if the law will not protect us, then we have to do the job ourselves.'

As a mission statement the only thing missing from it was that John Pritchett did not identify his particular neck of the Kent woods as Tunbridge Wells. Tony, though, rather liked the way the press had dubbed him "Norfolk Farmer" and he began signing his letters: "Tony Martin   Norfolk Farmer"

The local newspapers also piled in on Martin's side. In its August 25th, 1999 edition, the widely unread *Newcastle Journal*, headlined an editorial: 'Is it justifiable to shoot a burglar?' The question was really rhetorical, as the piece made it quite clear it was justified and, if it is not legally justifiable, then the law should be changed. 'Tony Martin has been accused of going over the edge. The decision to charge the 54-year-old with murder and with wounding another man has sparked a debate about the rights of property owners to protect themselves and their possessions.' Mr Dodd, North-East regional director of the rural pressure group the Countryside Alliance, admitted he had some sympathy with Mr Martin's position. 'I don't know the full facts of this case, but if this guy's been burgled before, he might have been threatened with a gun before. If the burglar had shot the farmer we would not have seen this in the papers.'

The esteemed *Bristol Evening News* printed a letter on September 17th written by Martyn Williams, 'I read with interest the article (Insight, September 11th) on reasonable force. In an increasingly aggressive society where much of the mindless behaviour comes from the young, it is time that reasonable force was specified in legislation and not left to the vagaries of the law of Henry II. I offer a salutary tale: If I was a wealthy man I would hire the best lawyer in the country to defend Tony Martin, the Norfolk farmer who shot the burglar. As it is, I can only regret the certainty that he will be presumed guilty and probably not proven innocent.'

The first politician to wade in on Tony's side was roly-poly Anne Widdecombe. As minister for prisons under then Home Secretary Michael Howard, Widders used to spend much of her time defending such practices as women prisoners being shackled to hospital radiators whilst giving birth.

On October 5th 1999, as shadow Home Secretary, she waddled up to the autocue at the Tory Party Conference in Brighton to say that the next Conservative government would "put the law in order". The blue-rinsers gave her a standing ovation after she abandoned both text and lectern and stomped around, on a creaking stage, thundering, "Victims are not only those who suffer from crime, but those who suffer from the law...I believe it is every citizen's right within reasonable and sensible limits to defend themselves, or their properties, against attack without then fearing a penalty at law. For too long, victims have been *just another statistic*. A great deal is said about the rights of criminals rather than the rights of victims..."

She went on, "Many police stations are many miles from the communities they serve, leading to high response times that, in turn, make crime, and the fear of crime, into a serious problem. Why should rural people have to wait more than twice as long as those who live in urban areas before they receive a police response to an emergency call?"

William Hague followed suite when, as part of his "common sense revolution", he promised: "In the next Conservative Government, when Ann Widdecombe is Home Secretary, I want every criminal in the land to look like Labour Ministers do when she gets up to speak – absolutely scared witless...

"Britain is a place where you should be rewarded for doing the right thing, but now you are penalised for it...If you believe in Britain as a country where the law is enforced and respected, but that now it is not respected enough, then come with me, and I will give you back your country. Whatever the rights and wrongs about the degree of force Tony Martin used, it's turning common sense upside down to consult a burglar about the liberty of his victim."

His last point was over the fact that under statutory provisions introduced by New Labour an injured victim has to be consulted when bail is being considered for the accused. This meant that Brendon Fearon's opinions on Tony Martin had been a factor in his second bail application.

While Tony was emerging as Middle England's folk hero *The Guardian* newspaper, or the *Social Workers Bible*, piled in early to peg him back. Patrick Holland dubbed him "an icon of malcontented Middle England". Tony was already receiving numerous letters of support, many of them asking how they could donate money to his defence. Around this time, Stuart Mayfield, then 48, threw himself into helping his neighbour. His farm is close to Tony's and he organised the harvesting of Martin's wheat crop and the picking of his apples; his wife also visited Tony in Norwich to tell him that his land was being looked after. Stuart also wrote to Tony advising him to instruct a professional lawyer and he recommended a friend of his, the cravat-wearing Nick Makin.

Makin's law firm M&S, in its corporate brochure, called "A Creative Approach", claims: "Sometimes clients want to do something that cannot be done. Rather than simply tell the client it cannot be done, our approach is to try to find an alternative way of achieving the same end for the client." Unbeknownst to Tony, Makin had handled the odd fraud case but his speciality was commercial litigation and company law.

Nonetheless, on August 28th, Nick Makin was formally instructed to act for Tony and, at his next court hearing on September 1st, the Legal Aid certificate was transferred from Paul Kenneth Bush and Co (Paul Croker) to Makin's firm, M&S. One of the first things Makin did was to set up the Tony Martin Defence Fund. He proclaimed to a local paper:

'Tony and his family wish to ensure that he receives the best possible representation at trial. In the light of the massive public support for Tony it has been decided to set up a defence fund to which people can contribute...This case has clearly touched a nerve with a lot of people. This case is not simply about Tony's fate, but also about the wider issue of the extent to which people are entitled to use force to defend themselves and their homes against intruders.'

The *Evening Standard* reported on the same day: 'A Tony Martin Defence Fund has been set up by friends and family to pay for the best legal representation.' On the following Friday, September 10th, the *Wisbech Standard* carried a more detailed story on the fund, mainly drawn from an interview with Nick Makin. 'The fund was hoping to raise more than a £100,000 to pay privately for a hand-picked QC. Makin assured the public that the whole fund was being independently audited by chartered accountants Pannell Kerr Forster. None of the money will be given directly to Martin or the solicitors.'

Pannell Kerr Forster received one phone call from Nick Makin asking whether they would be willing to audit the fund's accounts. They agreed but, as they later stated in a formal letter, "Nothing further was heard from Nick Makin. No books or accounts were delivered and therefore no audit took place." And there never was an audit of the fund.

Creative Makin did not receive money directly from the fund of which he was The Settlor. Instead Makin's firm opened up a client account for the fund, which was in the name of "Mr Nick Makin, Trading as M&S Solicitors". Behind this veil of respectability, Nick Makin, in practice, could and did receive money from the Tony Martin Defence Fund's account.

The Tony Martin Defence Fund was not called such in the document that established it as a legal entity. In the Declaration of Trust it was called the Tony Martin Support Trust. There was a reason for this: Legal Aid is available for indigent defendants and any money above £3,300 that the defendant has or has been given to him for his defence is offset against Legal Aid. Even before the Declaration of Trust document was drawn up, donations to The Tony Martin Defence Fund had exceeded the maximum amount allowed – £3,300 – before Legal Aid is cut back.

The problem for the Tony Martin Defence Fund was that donations were unlikely to cover the full cost of privately defending

Tony Martin, which eventually proved to be the case. The actual total accrued by the fund was £22,742; whereas the total cost of Tony's defence was £45,868. Creative Makin solved this particular problem by ring fencing the fund monies from anything covered by Legal Aid. The relevant clause stated:

"The Trustee shall hold the capital and income of the Trust fund [and] apply it…towards the conducting of the Defence including handling the publicity, cost of transport, legal and other fees not covered by legal aid…" Thus, the so-called Defence Fund was explicitly not "to pay privately for a hand-picked QC", which was what donors assumed when they contributed to it. The fund was actually used for ancillary matters such as travel, securing Tony's farm, paying for his safe-houses and so on. This is the reason why what the public thought was the Tony Martin *Defence* Trust was called the Tony Martin *Support* Fund. Or, perhaps, it should have been called "The M&S Expense Account".

Moreover, with the fund account being in Makin's name, it meant that he could bill all direct defence work to Legal Aid, while any other work on the case could be paid out of the fund. Makin's rate was £250 an hour and Michael Ballinger's £195 an hour. Makin billed the fund £1500 for his 6 hours travel London to attend the Appeal Court on 19th June 2000. On the same day he billed the fund £500 for "attending the press"and £62.50 for "waiting". He did not bill for attending the hearing as that would have meant using the fund to pay direct legal costs, thereby compromising its status. At his most 'Creative', Makin billed the fund for fielding a phone call from Peter Cadbury – who had donated £1000. If Makin had spent four hours on the phone appraising him of the situation, it would have wiped out Cadbury's original donation.

On May 9th, 2000, Ballinger billed the fund £16.25 for: "Telephone call from an anonymous person who said that Eli

Frankham was in a pub on Saturday, 29th April, stripped down to his underpants, ready to fight someone. He went on to say that Eli Frankham had had about ten pints but the police allowed him to drive. The observer's comments were that the police appeared to be too frightened to enforce the law on drink driving against him." Frankham was to prove a heavy hitter in the supporting bill to the trial.

Makin also billed the fund for briefing Max Clifford. According to Ballinger, M&S had contacted Max "in the first week because we were absolutely deluged by the press. We had no training in media relations and we felt it was in Tony Martin's interest to bring in an expert because lawyers would inevitably cock it up." Usually the diminutive Max works as a kiss 'n' tell pimp for the tabloids, so Ballinger's turn of phrase was fitting. Like all of his kind Max was notorious for keeping the lion's share of the spoils; yet on this occasion because he "identified" with Tony he donated his services gratis. So we have the spectacle of some backwater specialist in commercial law charging the Tony Martin Fund £250 an hour to talk to a big shot PR consultant who, while he normally wouldn't pick up the phone for less than a grand, was on this occasion working for nothing.

On September 1st, Tony appeared before Norwich Magistrate's instead of the scheduled King's Lynn – the venue was changed at the last minute because the police were concerned about threats to public order if the Barras contingent clashed with Tony's supporters. Makin's bail application was turned down and Tony went back to prison where he spent most of the time writing to well-wishers. However, six days later, a bail application to a judge in chambers was successful. Judge David Mellor ruled that Tony could have bail but on the condition that he lived at a secret address outside Norfolk and only came into the county with police approval. Hilary, Tony's mother, said, "It's wonderful news. It's what we were all hoping for. He wasn't born to be shut up and he wasn't coping well. I've just been praying that it would be good news, and now my prayers have been answered. I'm looking forward to seeing him."

On Sept 7th, Tony went to stay at a safe house in Market Harborough, which Makin arranged and was paid for out of the Defence Fund; he didn't visit his mother, although he did see his dogs. Even though he was out of prison Tony was very frustrated. In a letter to one of his supporters, he wrote, "It was like being in a straight jacket. I never felt free to discuss with other people the right decisions and options. Many people wanted to get hold of me, they could not."

Tony moaned about everything. To get him off their back, Makin and Ballinger asked Tony to write down everything that happened to him since he was born. He produced a 67-page "very private" testament, which M&S promptly mislaid. Tony still hasn't recovered his testament or forgiven Makin for losing it. He later called Makin "not only a charlatan but equally a shark".

The next day, on September 8th, a meeting was called by the Emneth parish council to debate the problem of crime and policing. Five hundred residents and Martin supporters packed out the village hall. The Rev Rachel Larkinson, who was the resident Methodist minister, took the chair, while local police chief, Superintendent Steve Thacker took the flak. Most of the audience had suffered the same sort of problems as Tony from local criminals whom the police seem to have been unable to arrest or even deter. Many had given up even reporting theft as policing was so bad. Naturally these people vented their fury at Thacker. A TV crew from regional news programme *Look East* were inside the hall and gleefully reported the ensuing bun fight.

The Rev Rachel splendidly took the proper line for a woman of the cloth. She asked them all to remember the "tragedy"of the young man's death. This prompted a farmer to shout at her furiously, "Let us never describe the death of a criminal as a tragedy." The audience stomped and cheered.

The Rev Rachel turned the other cheek: "Civilisation takes a step backwards if law is no longer a matter of common assent, but allows an individual to become jury, judge and executioner. We do not believe that stealing a sheep, nor even some valuable antiques, should be a capital offence."

Some wag in the audience piped up, "There ain't no sheep in Norfolk."

The Rev Rachel seemed to think that the laughter was for her as she graciously explained, "Countryside crime is not a new phenomenon. I was a young child when, 50 years ago, my new bike was stolen from the Fenland village where I grew up. The village bobby took the serial number, but it was never found." The audience were dumbfounded, mainly because many of them were all shaking their heads in disbelief. Even Superintendent Thacker thought this Christian attempt to calm the troubled waters a bit of what Fearon calls a "boo-boo".

Every time Thacker attempted to speak he was heckled so badly that he became visibly shaken with the intensity of contempt and anger that he provoked in the crowd. The complaints were not merely about inadequate police response times but also the attitude of police officers when they did arrive. They seemed to think that theft was something for the insurance companies to deal with, not them. Many people said that this was often the reason they had given up reporting crimes. To a cackle of jeers, Thacker replied, "I'm imploring you to report crime. My officers like to nick villains. That's what we do best."

Malcolm Starr, a local property developer who later became a figurehead of the campaign to free Tony, told Thacker, "You must have been living in a cave for the past five years. Your negative attitude makes us negative about you and that is why there is nothing constructive or positive to say to you."

Gillian Shepherd, an ex-Minister for Education under John Major and the then MP for South-West Norfolk, was also on the platform. She told the meeting that many of the letters she had received concerning the arrest of Tony Martin mirrored their grievances. She stated that victims of rural crime don't bother reporting crimes because they see "the police are over-stretched and the court system lets them down... But people", she warned, "will be tempted to take the law into their own hands unless they feel they can report crime without being intimidated, that the legal system is fair and the police have sufficient resources to make them feel safe in their own homes."

Given that virtually all the audience was present because they believed that taking the law into their own hands was the only answer, her warning made as much impact as a "keep off the grass" sign in Jamaica. Ted Martin, a cousin of Tony's, summed up the mood of the audience, when he said, "The only problem with what Tony did was he didn't shoot all three of them." Shepherd kept her mouth shut and her expression neutral. The meeting ended with an even bigger divide between those who are under the law and those who make and enforce it.

Meanwhile, a quite different meeting was being organised for the next morning. A Gypsy Court or *kris* was called for by a gypsy leader or *bandolier* who is from the same extended family as the Barras's. He asked for the Court because of what both Bark and Fearon had said happened when Martin ambushed them.

Both burglars had been released on bail, although Fearon was still in hospital undergoing surgery to have the pellets removed. However, they had both given their story to friends and relatives, who in turn had fed back what they said into the local gypsy community. The story they told was not what they had told the police, which had been ridiculously self-exculpatory. As against the lies they told the police, the truth that they told their friends swept like wildfire among the Newark gypsies, ratcheting up their fury about the murder of Barras.

What Fearon and Bark said was that they had *drummed up* (made a noise outside) and shone the car headlights on Bleak House before they broke in. As no one had appeared, they assumed that, except for the dogs, the place was empty. They hadn't gone on a *creep* (to burgle a property while the occupant is there). That was impossible anyway, as antiques – even smalls – are not capable of being stolen silently, like cash or jewellery, while the owner is asleep or unaware of the intruder's presence. The classic thief who creeps his victims is, of course, the cat burglar. In fact, Tony's farmhouse was such a tip that no one could move around it without making a racket. Nor had they planned to make the Bleak House burglary a *tie-up* job (one in which the occupant is over-powered and trussed up to expedite the theft). They had come to do exactly what Webster and his gang had done – turn over Martin for his antiques while he was away from the farm. The implication was plain as a pikestaff: Martin had set them up. He'd heard them, probably seen them, guessed what they planned, then hid until he sprung his shotgun ambush.

Early on the morning of the Fred Barras's funeral, at 6 am, the Newark gypsies convened their *kris* on a school football pitch that has a couple of crude shelters set back off the touchline for watching parents or teachers. Gypsy law is in the form of an oral tradition that loosely governs and regulates gypsy communities. It is distinctly separate from the encompassing non-gypsy system of law and order, although it shares some of the same values. Gypsies understand and have to come to terms with the claims of our legal system, while we are not even aware of the existence of theirs. Their law and the kris system are what gives a gypsy community its cohesiveness and distinctiveness from the local non-gypsy culture.

The Barras relation who called for the *kris* was not part of the five judges that heard the case against Tony Martin. But he did act as a kind of prosecuting council and said that it was now common knowledge that Martin had murdered Fred, that Martin was now free and was likely to escape proper punishment by the state's system of law. He pointed out Martin was already on bail, which was very unusual for someone on a murder charge. He summarised what Fearon had told his mother from his hospital bed, which had been by supported Bark who, while a *gaje*, spoke with "the ring of truth". Bark was also to be hounded out of Newark by the local gypsies because, under questioning after he was arrested, he revealed that it was Webster who told him about the antiques stored at Bleak House.

There were some fifty people present – including the area's champion bare-knuckle prize-fighter, Eli Frankham, who was to cause a rumpus at Martin's trial. A number spoke but no one argued against what the Barras *bandolier* wanted, a price put on Martin's head. The Barras spokesman stressed that this was an issue of honour and that, if they did not act, this cowardice would shame them all. After over half an hour of argument and discussion, the judges or *krisnitorya* went into a huddle and decided that despite the difficulty and danger such a course presented they had to issue such an order. The head of the *kris* announced the edict and ruled that a £60,000 bounty be put on Martin's head. This money was to be collected from the clan when it was claimed.

Curiously enough, after his conviction Tony slipped up in a phone interview in prison with a *Daily Mail* journalist and unwittingly confirmed Fearon's and Bark's account. It was printed in April 29th 2000 edition and the reporter – just a fact collector – filed a straight-from-the horse's-mouth article as he was unfamiliar with what Martin had previously said and was therefore unaware of the significance of what he told him. This was how Tony, all in direct quotes, was reported:

"It's also rubbish to say that I hate gypsies. I don't hate anyone. The only thing I hate is being terrorised.

"Just as I was thinking about going to sleep, I heard a car drive up outside. I thought whoever it was would circle around, perhaps get out and wander about a bit just to wind me up and then, because they knew I was at home, go away. It had happened before, but this time it was different. They stayed.

"Suddenly a feeling of absolute terror swept over me. It was hard to think straight, but it came to me that I couldn't just stay where I was. That I must do something. So I took my torch and went outside. It was pitch black. I couldn't see anyone, but I could feel their presence. When I turned back towards the house, I saw that a window had been pulled out from its frame. I could hardly breathe from fear.

"I retreated inside, a torch was shone in my face..."

The details in the article are muddled but, nonetheless, the description of the car pulling up outside was the first time that Martin mentions this. It is possible that he made this up just to give the reporter some fresh copy but the odds on such a possibility lengthen considerably when one factors in the fact that it tallies exactly with what Bark and Fearon said. It rather puts the lie to everything he told the police, the media, his lawyers, Middle England...

Tony slipped up in a similar, but less revealing fashion, around the same point in his interview with Peters and Newton. His story to the police and in court has always been that he woke up, went out on the landing saw a torch flitting around, then went back into the bedroom to get the gun. Early on in the interview, he described his sighting of the torch…

"Then, there's the landing and then the staircase…And I went out there and I see these lights, like car lights. Now these when I say these car lights, not from inside, and there seemed to be a lot of lights and err…at that stage, I'm afraid. I started *to become very frightened, fearful, terrified.*"

Neither Peters nor Newton picked up on his describing the burglars torch as car lights because they didn't know that the burglars had driven down and swept the car's lights around. Both Fearon and Bark in their initial statements denied doing anything criminal.

Later that morning Fred Barras' funeral took place at St Mary Magdalene Church, Newark. It was attended by 450 people who, with seven limousines carrying just his family, plus around 100 cars and lorries, brought the town to a standstill. Inspector Steve Ward said exasperatedly to critics of his accommodation to this: "I have had to close one street, make another one-way and make arrangements for them to drive through the market square which is a pedestrian area." Four of the lorries, flat and open at the back, were packed with floral tributes, which were estimated to have cost around £40,000. On one wreath from Fred's sister was the message: "You were a brother in a million. A brother who made us laugh and brother we will miss. Our love will always last." Twelve teenagers who knew him each carried a red rose. One of them, Lisa Doddin, 14, said, "He was always very funny and seemed to smile all the time – I am very shocked and will really miss him."

One outside observer described the atmosphere as "scary" but didn't know why. Revenge was in the air but they all knew how difficult it would be to locate Martin and exact retribution. Inside the church the Rev Richard Harlow-Trigg told the congregation that Fred was "a popular lad, happy-go-lucky and always game for a laugh. He was full of life – a young man who simply wanted to enjoy himself." He glossed over Fred's criminal record by saying that he did get into "scrapes" but he addressed the palpable anger of the gypsies. The Very Good Reverend said:

> "Fred's life was cut short on August 20th in circumstances that have been rehearsed too many times in newspapers and on TV. Everyone here knows he should not have been where he was. But he did not deserve to die like he did. Not surprisingly there is anger and recrimination, as well as sadness and mourning. We are not here to judge Fred, nor are we here to judge anyone else involved in this tragedy. But the thought of revenge must be cast out of any heart that harbours it."

Tony Martin actually saw the funeral on television and commented later, "I know they'd never believe me but during my time on remand when I was in a safe house I saw footage of the boy's funeral on TV. It was extremely emotional. Death is definite, it is permanent, and I found that a very moving moment."

Perhaps Tony's true attitude is best conveyed by what he said at the end of his final interview with detectives Peters and Newton. Peters asked him, "…how do you feel about the fact that there is a young lad that is dead and another that is injured as a result of your shooting them?"

Tony did not reply to the question but asked if he could have a word with his solicitor and the tape is stopped for three minutes.

When the interview resumed he gave his answer, "Well, I actually bitterly regret it, but I'm also… I find I was in a very… I don't know how to put it, in a very regrettable position. I don't know if that's the right way to put it, but that was the position I was in. I just don't know what else to say. I don't know what I've just said."

The news of the bounty on Martin's head had swept round Newark from the *kris* to the funeral and quickly reached the ears of the police. Norwich police were immediately informed. They took the threat seriously and, as they were unsure whether they could guarantee Martin's safety, they revoked Martin's conditions of bail. Martin was taken from the Market Harborough safe house to Norwich Prison. But as Keith Waterhouse wrote in the *Daily Mail*: 'Why couldn't they guarantee his safety? Isn't that what they're paid for? This is on a par with the local authority pocketing the council tax and then saying it can't guarantee to empty the dustbins.' Whether or not Waterhouse influenced the Norfolk constabulary we don't know but Tony was bailed again on September 17th, after Makin arranged an even safer house for him in Swadlincote, which was 9 miles away from the offices of M&S.

Tony took it easy in Swadlincote. He answered letters from his well-wishers. He took to riding an old bicycle, which he used to find local restaurants and pubs. He also travelled down to London. "I like going to Harrods because they have so many things from around the world." He bought another teddy from Harrods, a three foot one, in December.

Martin's extensive collection of teddy bears was removed from Bleak House by Helen Lilley, Roger Cotteril and Terry Howard, who is known as Badger. Tony, incidentally, is Toad. Badger, a horsy-faced man with a goatee beard, said, "The police kept an eye on us but I noticed there were 12-bore cartridges all over the house. Why were they there? Target practice?

"We were throwing all these teddies down the stairs. Tony

woulda' been horrified. Those teddies and his dogs were his kids. He used to talk about when he'd get the place fixed he'd arrange the teddies around the table as if they were his family sitting down for dinner. He used to say that they were compensation for all the toys he never had as a child. I got reams and reams of letters back from sending these teddies out. The teddies went all over Norfolk but I still have some. I was on the phone to him when he was in Swadlincote and I told him how we found homes for the teddies. I told him that my cousin Vicky had one and that she had a gorgeous body. I said to Tony 'just think of the teddy cuddling up to her naked body!' He didn't like that and he slammed the phone down on me."

"He's odd Tony, hasn't been right in the head for years. He used to think that the police and gypsies were in cahoots. But I remember it differently. Both me and Helen were approached by the CID. They were on his side. It was after he'd changed solicitors. They said to me that he should stay with Croker. Makin is a joke. He doesn't even do criminal work. One of 'em said to me, 'For god's sake tell Tony, get rid of Makin.' The police were just trying to help but the thing about Tony is, he'll still come out and say that the police are shite and they are only saying that because they want him convicted."

Tony also said about his sojourn in Swadlincote, "I just go out and go pruning trees, do something, somewhere. I get plenty of exercise gardening. I keep myself occupied. I get nice paintings out of magazines and get them blown up and put them in my room. I have got a picture of the battle of Trafalgar."

Meanwhile Max Clifford was drumming up more and more favourable media coverage. Martin could not give interviews but, as Max said, "the media can speak to his mother, his friends, people who know about him and who care about him. That is what I will be doing." And Max did. Martin's story ran and ran, nearly always along the lines of the good, honest, hard-working, middle-aged Norfolk Farmer who finally snapped under the harassment of the young, thieving yobs that were bringing England to its knees. Max even managed to work his own travesty of the facts into *The Sun*, "If three **armed** people broke into my house I wouldn't make them a cup of tea."

The pro-Martin publicity so incensed the Barras family they instructed a solicitor, Paul Gromett, who wrote a letter to *The Times*, which was published on September 28th, 1999. He wrote that he was approached because "the media coverage of the incident was extremely one-sided". As a result of this, a meeting had been arranged with senior policemen involved in the case, who satisfied the Barras family that the "prosecution was dealing with the case in a proper and conscientious way". Gromett then raised the engagement of Max Clifford and asked "whether the public thinks that the sort of campaign and placing of favourable coverage for the defendant in the media is a proper part of the legal process". He also notes that jurors who had been exposed to such a media campaign might be affected subliminally to favour Martin.

The purpose of engaging Max was precisely that, but there was the additional bonus that any pro-Martin publicity also attracted donations to the Defence Fund.

Tony basked in all the media attention, and he revelled in his elevation to folk hero. Whenever he was recognised on his forays out of the safe house, people would approach him, wanting to shake his hand and tell him that what he'd done was to stand up for them and that no English jury would find him guilty. The personal and media support understandably turned his head and also his habitual arrogance into hubris.

Apart from possessing a firearm without a licence, he assumed that on all the other charges he would be found not guilty and publicly vindicated for the action he'd taken. Consequently, he came to regard the trial as a platform to air his pet grievances such as police negligence, especially the lack of protection given to farmers like himself, the way in which criminals with long records are not kept in prison, the right of any householder to defend his home from thieves. His legal team, on the other hand, just wanted him to address the formidable case that the prosecution had assembled.

The conferences between Tony, his counsel, Anthony Scrivener QC, Makin and Ballinger were typically of the kind when two sides talk at cross purposes. Tony complained that "everything I commented on seemed to go in one ear and out the other...they ignored my vital input". He came to distrust Scrivenor who Martin said was a "devil's advocate". Tony's Asperger's seems to have kicked in here as he didn't mean that Scriv took on contentious cases to express unpopular or opposing views, rather than he defended people like Asil Nadir, IRA bombers, Winston Silcott and train drivers who crashed their trains... At the same time as the Martin trial, Scrivener was acting for the train drivers' union (ASLEF) at the Paddington rail crash inquiry.

Tony didn't like Makin and often turned sulky in his presence, so Ballinger became the legal team's factotum, which meant he bore the brunt of Tony. Ballinger subsequently moved to a City firm, Reynolds Porter Chamberlain, which is where Artnik contacted him. He has the sort of chirpiness and eye for a pound note that you find in auctioneers. He mentioned his fee very early on and followed it up immediately with an email setting out his terms:

"Further to our telephone conversation a few moments ago, I confirm our arrangements for next Friday.
We will meet at 12 o'clock. As discussed the meeting is to be on

the following basis:

1. You will pay me £150 for the interview, and will either pay me in cash or by cheque (payable to Michael Ballinger) at the beginning of the meeting.

2. The meeting will last no longer than one hour. If we go on longer this will be subject to a further fee to be paid immediately in cash.

3. I will not be in a position to discuss client sensitive or confidential information without Tony Martin's prior consent.

4. You confirm that the book is being written from an independent standpoint, with no editorial influence being exercised by the POW Trust.

There is one further condition, which we did not discuss, but please let me know if this is likely to be a problem. I would like to take a copy straight after the interview of any notes you take, and I would like your undertaking that any comment or quotes attributed to me will be entirely accurate.

Perhaps I could also ask for a complimentary copy of the book when published.

This interview is obviously given in my private capacity and not in my capacity as an employee of Reynolds Porter Chamberlain or as a former employee of M&S Solicitors."

At the end of 2003, when Artnik interviewed Michael Ballinger, he charged £150 an hour. At M&S, when dealing with the Martin case, he took what he could get. In the 'Customer Care' pack sent to Martin in jail, Ballinger charged £195 an hour, but when M&S was pressed by the Trustees for an *itemised* bill to back up an invoice they had drawn from the Tony Martin Defence Fund, the legal eagles had to think fast. Makin wasn't going to be held to account and barely itemised his part of the bill. Other than providing the date and number of hours, he billed the Fund for £2625 excluding VAT for just over 10 hours of 'time spent dealing with the press'.

Ballinger was more careful and knocked twenty pounds off his rate, charging a modest £175 an hour for his media relations work. In one item he charged £218.75 for 'travelling to Emneth to attend an aborted public meeting'. Makin also billed for the same trip. For dashing out a letter to a Mr Newberry, who was arranging a whip round for Tony, Ballinger charged the Fund £58.33. For the pleasure of talking to Helen Lilley over the phone six times in six weeks he charged £218.75. In all, he racked up £3990 excluding VAT from that invoice alone on April 13th 2000.

We met him outside the Lloyds building, which he called the "coffee percolator". He was clutching a blue court note pad and came over as slightly nervous at earning £150 on the sly. We all disappeared into the basement of a nearby Cafe Nero. He watched solicitously as his cheque was about to be written, "That's wonderful. Thank you..." But there was a slight change of his terms, "Err...can you make it out to my wife... She is doing the Christmas shopping." After pocketing the cheque, he leaned back confidently, swinging side to side in his swivel chair ready to hold court. Ginger-haired, plumpish, pompous and smug ... When the meter is running - as it was with us - every ten minutes or so he looks quizzically at his watch. Charles Dickens would have loved Ballinger.

He put the issue of the trial in a nutshell: "Well, a trial like Tony's is basically a political issue – if you get jurors who believe it is OK to shoot burglars you will be acquitted. If not..." He shrugged his shoulders in resignation. "It depends upon the political correctness of the jury. If you get a wishy-washy, liberal, sniffy, socialist, eye-washing jury, well, you will be convicted."

The worst stand-off between the defendant and his legal team was over where Tony fired the shots. He had always said that he never left the staircase, which is impossible. He fired from just inside the breakfast room with some possibility that the first shot came from the hallway. The evidence on this was definitive: the "holders"placed where Barras was shot, and the spread of the shot established how far Martin was from his targets. Crucially, the ejected shotgun cartridges that littered the floors of Bleak House plotted Tony's movements into the room. The forensic reports from both the prosecution and the defence were conclusive. In the face of this overwhelming evidence Tony would not budge. "I have to accept bullets don't go round corners but I didn't leave the stairs."

Even after discussing this with his own firearms expert, he stuck to his guns.

Tony wanted the case run on his terms and that is what he got. However, M&S did achieve something: they persuaded him not to use the witness box as soapbox. Ballinger explained that it took an awfully long time to get a detailed witness statement from him but "we did eventually... and we continually kept bringing him back to the point. He'd never heard the word pontificate before and he rather liked it. *Thou shalt not pontificate* became the 11th Commandment." And Tony did not pontificate, not that it did him much good.

As the trial date approached the legal team began to get through to him that despite his confidence his chosen defence meant that the verdict was not a forgone conclusion. On the back of this Makin even managed to persuade Tony to submit to a psychiatric examination. Tony was vehemently against the suggestion, "Just because I am a loner...eccentric...that doesn't make me a nutcase. That's another thing that's wrong with this country – too many doctors inventing fancy names for illnesses that people don't have. It's just a way of getting dole money..."

By mid-February, the defence was of the view that it desperately needed a way of beefing up Tony's case for self-defence. It would have helped, for example, if Tony had some mental affliction that made him more likely than the normal person to panic. Eventually, he agreed to be examined but he was on his best behaviour and gave the psychiatrist, Dr Anthony Maden, nothing which could have helped him be diagnosed as abnormal. Tony had decided that he was going for broke. It was guilty for murder or acquittal and because he was so confident of it, as Makin and Ballinger became, he could not be persuaded by friends or family to prepare a manslaughter safety net by playing up to the shrink.

The instructions from Ballinger to Maden showed that M&S were not only dealing with an extremely difficult client but also trying as best they could to cope. The instructions included under 'Purpose:' 'to ascertain that Tony's personality is such that he would be more fearful than most other people and as a result his finger may be more twitchy...'

It listed under 'Things people find odd about Tony Martin:' 'he lives in a house which most people would regard as unfit for human habitation... the prosecution portray Tony Martin's attitude toward didicois and criminals as extreme. He referred to them as "perverts". This is not a word usually used in this context, but Tony Martin says that he describes a "pervert" as anyone with a perverted sense of values and categorises criminals, didicois and homosexual as perverts.

'The prosecution make much of comments Tony Martin has made about Hitler. He is currently reading "Mein Kampf". As far as we can make out the admiration for Hitler is not so much because Tony Martin is a paid up Nazi, but because Hitler's methods for dealing with thieving gypsies (shoot the bastards) was far more effective than the methods used by the Norfolk Police and the

English legal system (give professional criminals a slap on the wrists and then set them free to go and terrorise other people with their crimes).

'We have on occasion found Tony Martin detached from reality.' Makin continued, 'One might expect someone who faces a murder charge with an automatic life sentence if convicted to be more concerned about winning the case than anything else. However, he does seem to be more concerned about this than about winning the case. Whenever we show him photographs or videos of Bleak House for the purpose of discussing forensic evidence in the case, he only ever seems interested in the fact that the police have moved items during the course of their investigation.

'As you will find out when you meet Tony Martin, once he starts talking, it is difficult to stop him. You will never get him to answer a question as he will go off at a tangent and talk about something else. He is very opinionated and never listens.

'Tony Martin does show his emotions. He regularly breaks down in tears, particularly when his mother is mentioned because it upsets him that his mother is being put through so much anguish as a result of this trial. If someone says something to upset Tony Martin (and the police regularly did so inadvertently) he will get into a huff so that rational conversation with him is impossible.'

This was a frank and open briefing, but it was asking for trouble to add: 'Please bear in mind that we are not psychiatrists and do not understand complex medical jargon. We would ask that your report is in plain English that laymen can understand.' It was as if Tony's cocksure attitude had rubbed off on them.

Maden kept it plain alright: after his two hour interview, he diagnosed Tony as not suffering, despite being an eccentric and a loner, from any personality disorder.

Nonetheless, for the first time, Tony began to face up to the possibility of being convicted and this concentrated his mind on the need to tidy up his financial affairs. Makin had also been making a lot of noise about there being problems with Tony's Legal Aid certificate and the costs his firm were incurring, so it made sense to bury his cash. He decided to buy some land with £83,000, which in November he had put into a newly-opened account at his Barclays bank in Wisbech. The money had been building up in a personal investment account, where for years he had been depositing profits from the sale of crops and apples harvested by contractors on his land . Tony liked to negotiate such deals in cash and now it was time for the money to be sunk back into the land.

On February 21st 2000, he transferred £83,131 from this Wisbech bank to a Barclays account in Swadlincote which he had opened while in the nearby safe house. On March 22nd, he tried to withdraw £87,000 in cash but the bank could only give him £15,000. He collected the remainder in cash – £72,000 – on March 28th. He then entrusted this money to one of the Trustees of the Support Fund, Stuart Mayfield, who in turn handed it over to Malcolm Starr. After his arrest, Tony became increasingly reliant on Starr to help manage both his business affairs and his campaign. Malcolm bought some arable farming land outside Wisbech on behalf of Tony but not in his name.

While this was going on the police were spending £20,000 a month to preserve Bleak House as a trial exhibit; Middle England was donating money to the Martin Defence Fund and, through their taxes, paying for his Legal Aid bill, which Tony could have comfortably met with the money he had just spent on his new land.

A RIGHT TO KILL?

CHAPTER 6

TRIAL BY JURY AND GYPSY

THURSDAY 6TH APRIL

The pool of jurors for the Martin trial arrived at Norwich Crown Court on April 6th, but two days had been set aside for pleadings and direction concerning the admissibility of evidence that the Crown proposed to call. This meant that after the twelve were selected and sworn in they would be excused until the following Monday, when the trial would begin.

Makin arranged with the police for a change in safe houses for Tony Martin. He left Swadlincote and was settled into another secret residence in Norwich. A police escort was arranged to drive him to and from court.

When the police collected him on Thursday morning, he had a large carrier bag stacked with papers and notes. Uniquely for a defendant, especially one facing a murder charge, he also carried one of his teddies. The cops in the police car did not say anything but they did exchange glances. His trial teddy was smaller than most in his collection at Bleak House, but Martin felt reassured by having one of his "children" by his side. Not so much as a good luck charm, more as a symbolic companion. Many of Martin's teddies had been farmed out to local fans in a diaspora instigated by Badger.

Norwich Crown Court was completed in 1988 and is a typical redbrick building of the period. It is in the shape of an "L" with the public entrance at its corner. The flagpole outside the entrance only flies the lion and unicorn flag when a High Court Judge is in residence. It was flying at Martin's trial as the case was being heard by Mr Justice John Owen, who had been appointed a Justice of the High Court in 1986. Owen was never one of the hatchet-men of the High Court, he preferred the rapier to the chopper to kill off an argument. Owlish in court, his beady eyes and sharp claws came with a strong liberal streak: in 1990, he developed the Common Law to allow rape charges to be brought against husbands when the partners were not living together. Martin's case was to be his last big criminal trial - he retired a few months later.

The barrage of snappers and rubberneckers who awaited Tony Martin's arrival were to be disappointed. In a security overkill, the police unit responsible for security had decided that it would help thwart any would-be assassin looking to collect the £60,000 reward posted by the gypsies by blanketing Tony's head as he left the vehicle to enter the court.

Tony submitted to the indignity of this, which he felt made him look like a guilty man ashamed to be seen by the public, but what he especially disliked was the way it messed up his hair. Although less than particular over his personal hygiene, Tony is quite vain about his silver, leonine locks. He was given the celebrity treatment in the holding area beneath the courts. However, teddy attracted some raised eyebrows. One female warder asked him boldly, "What's that?"

He looked at her indulgently, "It's what it looks like, I would say. It's a toy teddy bear." Then with a twinkle he added reassuringly, "He doesn't bite."

She was young and didn't like his superior air. "Down here, Mr Martin, the only people who bite are us," she snapped. Tony, startled by her aggressiveness, momentarily froze. He was directed into conference and told that his barrister would be coming down to talk to him soon.

At 9.30, Scriv with his junior, James Stobbard, both carrying their wigs and wearing their gowns, and Nick Makin, who was still wearing his waistcoat and red cravat, came down to the interview room for a conference. Martin was dressed in a navy-blue, double-breasted suit that he would wear throughout the trial together with a light blue shirt and his old school tie. Cokethorpe School caters for those parents who cannot abide state schools but don't like the fees of the private ones. Its fees are relatively modest as is its academic record. But Tony has a number of Cokethorpe's blue and white striped old school ties, which carry the outline of a peacock. This is why he keeps peacocks at Bleak House; in his own mind it attaches him to the landed gentry rather than the free holding yeomanry of rural England.

Tony always felt uneasy with Scriv, a looming 6'4" and with left-wing politics, whereas Tony is 5'6" and right-wing. Scriv explained that there were no last minute notices of additional evidence from the Crown but there were a number of procedural matters to be hammered out in front of the judge, Mr Justice Owen. But first Tony would have to enter his plea and a jury would then be selected before being sent home until Monday. Scriv was his usual confident self, "You've got nothing to worry about, Mr Martin. The truth will prevail...it usually does in my experience, despite what people say."

"Let's hope it does, Mr Scrivener, but I am worried that things'll be missed. There are a number of potential witnesses..."

Scriv is renowned for his sparkling after-dinner speeches and his ability to handle difficult clients. He had long got Tony's measure and how to cut it short – which is never to let him hold the floor. Indeed, Scriv always earmarks that as his own domain. "Mr Martin, every stone that was there to be turned has been. I can assure you of that. At the heart of this case is the simple proposition that a man has the right to defend himself from intruders. That's what you did, Mr Martin, and that is what you are going to convince the jury you did... just as empathically as you have convinced everyone who knows you... Nick will come down and see you and you can instruct him on anything you think we should know." With that he swept out...

Tony was called into the dock. He came into the court, looked at Justice Owen before bowing out of good manners. As he sat down, a middle-aged woman in the ground floor gallery where the general public sat stood up and approached the dock, holding a single red rose. She leaned towards the dock officer on Tony's right, there were a few words, then the officer took the flower off her and, after a cursory inspection, handed it to Tony. The card read "Stay strong Tony." He stood up courteously, smiled and bowed to her. He felt his spirits lift.

The clerk of court addressed him and told him to stand while the charges were read out. On the first four charges – murder, the attempted murder of Fearon, of wounding him and the possession of a firearm and ammunition with intent to injure life – he spoke clearly and authoritatively, "Not guilty." His voice never changed when he pleaded guilty to possessing a firearm without a firearm's licence. He then sat down and watched as the jury were sworn in. Six men and six women, mainly middle-aged but some quite young, almost student-like types.

Justice Owen explained to the jury that the court had to consider some other matters and they were to be excused until 10am Monday. He warned them not discuss the matter with anyone, not even their family. The jury filed out.

Tony broke off the stem of the rose until it was suitable for his buttonhole, then he settled back.

MONDAY 10TH APRIL: DAY ONE

Trial Opening

On the Monday morning, there was the same conference with Scrivener and Makin, then the woman with the rose appeared... So he had another fresh rose in his lapel when the jury filed in. The crown prosecution rose...

Prosecution Case

Tony wasn't sure about being prosecuted by a woman. Rosamund Horwood-Smart QC had a strong, broad face and, as much as he could make out beneath her gown, appeared of heavy build. "Good-child bearing hips..." He listened to her as she outlined the Crown's case against him...

She explained to the jury that they would be hearing the case against Tony Martin, referred them to their copy of the indictment and took them through the charges. Her job, she told them, was to prove the case for the Crown and to make them sure – to prove beyond a reasonable doubt – that the defendant was guilty. As they must already know, the burden of proof was on the Crown. It was not the defendant's job to prove his innocence. Under our system of law, the defendant – in this case Tony Martin – enjoys the presumption of innocence...

It was the usual preamble that any counsel can reel off in their sleep. Rosamund then outlined the case against Martin and ran through the witnesses whom she would be calling to substantiate it. She told the jury about this eccentric farmer who lived alone on his almost derelict farm with only three Rottweiler dogs for company, which he kept in a nearby, run-down cottage. On the evening in question one man and one teenager had burgled his home and

Martin had lain in wait for them, then gunned them down with a pump-action shotgun that he held without a licence.

She told the jury, "Over the years Mr Martin and his family have undoubtedly been the victims of crime. And he was burgled in May, some three months before the murder. When he reported the burglary, which he did shortly after midnight on May 13th, he told the police operator, Mrs Wood, that the burglars had left some furniture outside and that they may come back and, if they did, he would 'blow their heads off'. Mr Martin was well known for his strong views which he made clear to officers attending the May burglary. When officers visited his house to take details, Mr Martin was vitriolic about criminals and the police alike.

He made his views public at a Farm Watch meeting which had been organised in his area and attended by a number of his neighbours and friends. During the meeting, he had said, 'Out there you are on your own and you are the law. The police are a waste of time.'

"He attended a police surgery on local crime a year before and PC Douglas Cracknell, who was there and is to give evidence, said Mr Martin told him that the burglars, especially Gypsies, 'should be surrounded by barbed wire and machine-gunned'.

"Two or three days before the incident with which we are concerned, he told a neighbour that he was worried about burglars and 'light-fingered pikies'. He said if he caught the bastards he would shoot them."

She told the court that, because of Tony's obsession with burglars, he took a number of "security measures that turned his farmhouse into what you may think was a fortress. He lashed ladders to his roof and one was even attached to a tree. Were they a series of look-out posts?" she asked rhetorically. "He made his house an obstacle course for burglars. He booby-trapped his stairs, taking three steps out of the bottom and the top…"

She referred the jury to their exhibits folder and the picture of Bleak House's staircase, then said, "You can see the booby trap at the top near the landing. The top three stairs have been removed." Then she continued. "The ground floor windows and doors of his home had been fitted with iron bars, he regularly slept fully-clothed, wearing his boots and with a gun under his bed in contemplation of something happening, ready to confront any intruders."

As she spoke, Tony sat expressionless; but he was already coming to dislike Ms 'Whorewood-Smartypants'. He didn't like her tone of voice, which was icy and unrelentingly hostile. What stung most, though, was her disdain. "This is not a Sheila I'd wanna meet on a blind date, even with a shotgun in my trouser pocket," he said to counsel later.

He had a notepad and pen but it was all happening too fast for him to make coherent comments. He wrote comments like: "Booby trap. Wrong"…and circled comments like "wrong" with his biro. Disliking her, though, was also a way of hiding from the formidable case she was building up.

Horwood-Smart said that Mr Martin knew guns and had used them all his life as a farmer. "He was a man that knew the power, force, and damage that a shotgun could inflict. He had the gun, eventually recovered by the police, for one particular reason. He had that gun to use, if and when the occasion arose... to shoot any intruder who had the temerity to come onto his land and into his home. Police found rounds of ammunition all over the house and its outbuildings. Was this so he would be prepared for intruders from wherever they came?"

She told the jury that the gun was eventually recovered from the home of Mr Martin's mother and it was found to be well-oiled and in good working order. Mr Martin told police in an interview that he had found the gun in his car with a note explaining that 'he might need it', but could not remember when this happened. He admitted not having a firearm's certificate for this gun, and claimed he had never fired the gun before and did not know how many cartridges it held.

"You will hear from a ballistics expert who will tell you that the gun had been well-maintained and had not been stored under a bed for we know not how long.

"He told the police that he had gone to bed that Friday evening at about 9 pm, having put two dogs in the cottage and having left a third, Bruno, to roam the grounds. Mr Martin was upstairs in his bedroom, having fallen asleep reading from the 15-watt bulb that was in his bedroom. The only other lighting in the house was from another 15-watt bulb hanging from a flex in the hallway. He was used to living in darkness or near-dark conditions.

"Earlier Fred Barras, Mr Fearon and a third man, Mr Darren Bark, aged 33, had set off from their homes in Newark with the intention of burgling Martin's home, which they thought was derelict but contained antiques. All three had a string of previous convictions. Barras and Fearon first tried to break into a cottage in the farm grounds. They heard growling. Little did they know it had been turned into a kennel by Martin for his Rottweilers. They were confronted by two of Mr Martin's dogs. Fearon also became aware of another big dog growling in the dark behind them which was Martin's third Rottweiler, Bruno. They gave up trying to burgle the cottage and backed off towards the farmhouse, where they forced a window and entered the downstairs hallway.

"They moved towards a dresser. Fearon remembers Fred Barras being close behind him just before he put his bag on the floor. He heard a noise and shone his torch towards the stairs and saw a man standing there, halfway down."

This piece of her opening was the only mistake that Horwood-Smart made in a magisterial overview of events. Fearon originally did say that in the light from the flash of the gun he saw a man standing halfway up the stairs. However, when he had recovered, he was taken by the police to Bleak House to reconstruct events; he then realised from the layout of the place and where the holders were he must have seen the man in the hallway entrance not the stairs. Horwood-Smart corrected this later.

She continued, "Fearon then heard Barras shout 'He's got me' as he heard a loud bang. He made his way to a window and he heard a second shot and his left leg went numb. He heard a third bang and felt pain in his right leg. He heard Barras screaming, 'He's got me. I'm sorry. Please don't...Mum!"

Tony stared impassively into space but some of Fred Barras's sisters, who were sitting at the back of the court with their mother and father, sobbed quietly as they heard how their brother had been killed.

"Mr Martin said that he was awakened by noises. At first he thought that Bruno had got into the house. Then he saw flashes of light downstairs. He said he returned to his bedroom and retrieved the gun. He loaded it until it was full. He did not know how many cartridges it held. You will hear that there is space for four cartridges plus a further cartridge in the gun, making five in all. He returned to the landing, negotiated that gap at the top where the three steps were missing, and went halfway down the stairs. At that point a torch was pointed at him and he took aim and fired a shot below the height of the torch and he continued to fire until the gun was empty. He stated that all the shots were fired from the same position, halfway down the stairs.

"Mr Martin told officers repeatedly that he thought he was in danger. He told them that he had at no time warned the intruders or given them the chance to surrender. You will hear from ballistics experts who later estimated that the men were shot at a distance of approximately four metres and consequently Mr Martin could not have been on the stairs. Some of the shots may have hit both men."

She told the jury that Fearon frantically smashed his way out through a window and hobbled to a nearby farm. "Barras followed Fearon out of the window. The teenager would have died within two minutes but it was not until the following day that his body was found. Barras was wearing rubber gloves and a chisel was found nearby. Fearon was badly injured and approached the cottage of Martin's neighbours, the Leets, who called an ambulance. He and the getaway driver Darren Bark were arrested. They are currently serving jail terms over the bungled raid.

"Meanwhile, Mr Martin took his gun and drove around the property looking for the burglars, passing only a few metres from Fred Barras's body. He then went to the Leets. Neighbour Paul Leet said Martin had driven into his drive after the shooting and told him he had taken a shot at three intruders in his house. He told him he didn't know if he had hit them but they had run off. Mr Leet said he told Martin to phone the police but he did not reply and drove off.

"Mr Martin drove to his mother's house and left the pump-action shotgun in her lavatory and that was the gun that was used in the shootings.

"Mr Leet's wife Jacqueline later saw the injured Fearon staggering into the yard of their cottage." Horwood-Smart read from Jacqui Leet's statement: "'I saw a man dragging himself along the road. He was moaning. He came to the window but it's all a blur really I think it was sheer terror.'" Mrs Leet dialled 999 while her husband tended to the man, whose legs were bleeding severely.

Mr Leet told officers that Martin's attitude both to the police and to travellers was 'not very good'. Martin, he said, felt that the police did not give his property enough protection.

"His life was not in danger. He fired at Barras and Fearon from downstairs, not in self-defence, but in accordance with his professed views that the only way to stop thieves was to shoot them. In acting as he did, he was intending to kill or cause serious injury and that is why he is charged with murder and attempted murder."

Horwood-Smart then began calling witnesses to substantiate her opening speech. PC Douglas Cracknell, the officer who was approached by Tony at a local police surgery on crime, was one of the first to be called. Martin had explained to Cracknell how burglars should be surrounded by barbed wire and machine-gunned. When Scriv cross-examined the officer, he got him to admit that he had not believed the remark was said seriously. Scriv also asked him if there was a shortage of police officers in the area. The constable said: "I would be a fool to say there wasn't."

TUESDAY 11TH APRIL: DAY TWO

The local eel-catcher, William Spalton, who drove past the injured Fearon on his way to the Leets', also raised a chuckle in the courtroom. Horwood-Smart asked him where he worked. He replied, "Everywhere you might find eels." When she asked him about what he was doing driving home so late, he replied, "You could say I'd had a hard day at the office."

More ominous was his answer as to why he didn't stop for Fearon: "I did see a chap in the middle of the road looking a bit sorry for himself. I thought he was wearing black and red trousers but I soon realised it was blood. He signalled me to stop but I know the area – you don't stop unless you know somebody. It occurred to me that he could have taken the van off me. It isn't much but it's what I've got.... I phoned the police after I heard Tony had shot two of them, just to let them know I was in the vicinity. Then I heard that one of them was dead. You see the people you are up against. If you leave your mate dying in the undergrowth you must be pretty hard."

The Leets gave evidence and Paul upset Martin when he described him not as a "friend" but an "acquaintance". Martin squirmed uneasily in the dock, he was beginning to feel that even people he thought were his friends didn't see things quite the way he did. Paul Leet also said that they had been burgled twice in the last six years.

Horwood-Smart then established the finding of the corpse and the injuries sustained by Fearon. It wasn't until Wednesday that the two ambulance men both confirmed, along with the Leets, that when Fearon was asked whether anyone else was with him he had said there wasn't.

That Tuesday, fellow-farmer David Gathercole also gave evidence, relating how Tony had behaved at a Farm Watch meeting in Emneth at which the problem of rural theft was the issue. "He sort of said, 'Do you know the best way to stop them?' And everybody went quiet and Mr Martin said, 'Well, shoot the bastards.' Although a number of us were thinking this, no one else actually said it. I am sure it is a normal topic of conversation among the farming community."

DPC Jim Welham gave evidence on what Tony had said when he had visited Bleak House in June to follow up his reporting of the May burglary. "I came into the farmyard and saw a man wearing a green beret, sunglasses and overalls and I asked if he was Tony Martin. He asked who I was. It was obvious I was a policeman. When he accepted that I was a policeman he just became abusive over a long period of time...everything from police pensions, early retirement, ill health, police management. Anything you could think of. He particularly besludged gypsies and criminals of all sorts. That's one of the things I can particularly remember. We looked at a field of the far side of his house. He said he would put barbed wire around it, fill it full of gypsies and machine gun them all."

Welham described that the next time he saw Tony was at Terrington Police Station when he arrived demanding to speak to a member of the CID. He showed contempt for the uniformed officers and announced "I don't deal with uniform men".

Scriv made no impact on Welham at all.

Helen Lilley gave evidence regarding Martin's arrival at her place after he left the gun at his mother's. She came into court, wearing a voluminous tent-like dress, and exchanged glances of recognition with Tony. She spoke about the area's reputation for crime. "When people come to the area the first thing they want to say is that crime is high here." Although she was to claim the exact opposite to Artnik...

"If you are in business in the town, it is not the thing you want to talk about." She told the court that Tony would usually visit her once or twice a day. On the night of the shooting, "He appeared to be stressed. He said there had been an incident and said the police would be coming. I made him a cup of tea and left him to sleep on a sofa." Her son-in-law Roger Cotteril was called to describe how he discovered the body after Lilley had left the stand.

DC Buxton gave evidence on his interviews with Fearon and Bark and detailed the convictions of the three burglars. Some of the jury looked startled as he read out Barras's sheet: convicted of burglary, handling stolen goods, two assaults against policemen, seven thefts and six frauds. He had twice been sent to young offenders institutions and at the time of the shooting last August was on bail for yet another offence. He committed his first assault when he was only 13. His "career of crime" began when, at 14, he was placed under a six-month supervision order for obtaining property by deception. Other crimes, including common assault and theft, followed, and he spent months in young offender institutions (including Glen Parva). He had racked up 29 convictions since he was 14.

As it was over two years, his criminal record was actually worse than Fearon's or Bark's. Fearon, 33, was 13 when his record began. At the time of the trial he had 33 convictions. Bark, 33, did even better than Fearon, he had 52 offences to his name – 20 convictions for theft and five for assault, his conviction for conspiring to burgle Bleak House, for which he was serving 30 months, plus other time added for breaking the parole on his last sentence. Between the three of them, they had 113 convictions at the time Martin was tried.

In his interviews with police officers, Bark told officers he had visited the village with a gypsy who had pointed out the house and said that in a previous burglary antique furniture worth £5,000 had been stolen. Both Bark and Fearon admitted in their interviews with police that they were 'knockers', which is thief-speak for burglars who knock on their intended victims doors to test whether the place is empty before breaking and entering. It was not clarified in court, although it was the case: none of the three had a conviction for burgling a home while the victim was present, then stealing by stealth or by overpowering him or threatening him into submission. Yet all had convictions for violence.

They had met while in prison but gave conflicting accounts as to how they had come to be at Bleak House. Bark claimed that he had been shown the place by one of the May burglars, while Fearon said he'd been told about it recently by Bark and had cased the place a four or so days prior to the raid. Only Fearon gave evidence at the murder trial. Fearon limped into court leaning heavily on a walking stick. He had come from HMP Stocken where he was serving 3 years for the Bleak House burglary. He still had his earring, but in prison he had grown a pigtail and turned his moustache into a goatee beard. He wore a black coat with black jeans that were held up by striped braces. His Prince of Darkness air was rather punctuated by his inability to read the oath. He had to repeat it after the usher.

He described how they had gone to Bleak House equipped with holdalls, a torch and gloves. Barras had a screwdriver. He told the court that he and Bark had only taken the 16-year-old along for a ride to "keep him out of trouble" but he was ashamed now as he "took the little lad there to get killed". He said he had found the 16-year-old drinking with a group of his friends. He added, "Fred said 'Let me come for a ride.' I thought it would keep him out of trouble. We were just going to look at the house and see what the outcome was when we got there. I was told that Martin's house was empty but contained valuable antiques. The purpose was to look at the place - nobody was going in."

The plan, he claimed, was to burgle a cottage on the property, which he had believed was empty and full of antiques, but he denied he had wanted to break into Bleak House. He said that when Bark dropped them off at Martin's farmhouse they were confronted by a Rottweiler dog, belonging to Martin, on a dirt track outside. Fearon told how Barras had been terrified as they stumbled in the dark among trees at the farm. The dog was snarling as it chased them. In the dark Barras had clung to his friend in fear. "He was crying and clinging on to my shoulder. I don't think he liked dogs," said Fearon.

In the dark, he and Barras had "found themselves against a wall" and "his elbow had smashed a window", he said. They had climbed into a room then tripped over cans, bottles, wood and rubble. They only ended up at the main house, he said, accidentally, as they were trying to escape the threatening Rottweiler. Though he had a torch around his neck he said it was difficult to see in the dark.

Describing the shooting Fearon said: "I saw a flash and I thought it was a torch but then I heard Freddy saying 'He's got me'. He was shouting 'He's got me. Mum I'm sorry.'" As Fearon spoke Barras's sisters began quietly sobbing again. Fearon continued, "I saw another flash and my leg felt numb. I seen an old man standing in the stairway. I went through a window. It had bars in it but I ripped it out. I just went mad and ended up looking for somewhere to get out. There was another flash.

"My legs went and I fell down. I came back up. Fred was still at my shoulder shouting and crying, then I got shot in the other leg," said Fearon. He said he remembered eight or nine loud bangs but had since been told some of them may have been the shots repeating in his head. He said he was certain he definitely heard three very loud blasts. Fearon said he climbed out of the window and staggered through a field, believing Barras was behind him, and that he managed to get help at a nearby bungalow.

Horwood-Smart asked him if he had told the ambulance attendants that someone else had been shot. "I told him I had been shot and another lad had been shot," he replied.

Scriv tore into Fearon describing his account as rubbish and lies, and suggested the thief had deliberately targetted the house and even gone to check it out weeks earlier. Fearon denied this. He said he had gone there because he had been told the cottage was deserted. Scriv put to him that they had gone there thinking that it would be easy to rob an "old man's house". He denied that.

Some of Mr Martin's silverware had been found in two holdalls, which Fearon had taken to the house and left behind, though he denied stealing. "Do you have any explanation for how this silverware got into your holdall?" asked Scrivener.

Fearon replied, "The farmer put them in to explain his actions."

Scriv asked Fearon about the noise he and Barras had been making. Fearon admitted they were noisy as even with the torch there was so much clutter it was impossible not to be. Scriv put to him that he shone the torch in Martin eyes, which is when he first saw him. When he denied this, Scriv said scornfully that he lied to the ambulance men about no one else being shot and he also repeated the same lie to the police when he was first interviewed in hospital. Fearon replied: "I was just coming out of sedation. I just wanted to put all the blame on me. I thought, 'You took the little lad there to get killed.'" It was probably the only truthful and heartfelt thing he said in the witness box.

Evidence was called from a forensic scientist that Fred Barras' blood showed traces of cannabis and alcohol close to the drink driving limit. His urine also proved positive for traces of amphetamine that had probably been in his system for some time.

There was then a voir dire – a trial within a trial – over whether the first interview by Peters and Newton with Martin was admissible. The problem for Martin's defence was not that he had made any incriminating admissions in the first interview but he had colluded in the ignorance of the interviewing officers over there being only one burglar in the farmhouse. This went further than Martin not telling the truth. It meant that in the words of the caution he had "not mentioned when questioned something which he later" relied on in his defence.

The caution that is given: "You do not have to say anything, but it may harm your defence if you do not mention when questioned something which you later rely on in court. Anything you do say may be given in evidence."

During the first interview, then, Martin was under a statutory obligation to tell Peters and Newton that he heard at least two burglars. His story in later interviews and, of course, in court was that when he was on the landing he heard them talking to each other. If Horwood-Smart had been successful, Justice Owen would have directed the jury that Martin's omission put in doubt the truthfulness of his answers to police questions and supported the prosecution's case. The issue was decided in the absence of the jury.

Tiernan gave evidence as did Newton.

Horwood-Smart made Dr Tiernan go through his check-ups on Martin at King's Lynn, eliciting with consummate ease the fact she needed to make clear.

"Did you find any clinical signs of depression when you examined him?" she asked.

"No."

"Were you of the view…that he was fit to be detained and interviewed?"

"Yes." In a few minutes she had finished with him and passed him over to Scrivener for the tough stuff.

"Where are the original notes you made of your visits to King's Lynn police station on the 21st and 22nd of August last year?" posed Scrivener as he was passed the paper from which Tiernan was reading from on the stand.

"I left them at home. I haven't been home since 5 am yesterday morning, I've been on call in Norwich," he replied wearily, in no mood to have his professional standards dragged through the mud by a quick-witted lawyer. Scrivener had little option but to press him on the bare facts and propose "extreme examples" and hypotheses. Tiernan wouldn't budge an inch.

"I've known people in custody refuse food and fluid all weekend and still be fit for interview on Monday morning."

Tiernan spoke clearly, looking directly at the troublesome QC. Both doctor and barrister had had enough.

What turned the issue, however, in the defence's favour was the fact that Martin had told Newton and Peter that he did not want to discuss the matter 38 times.

Owen ruled:

" I think the fact that he refused to answer, as you have elicited, Mr Scrivener, 38 odd times, I think that is perfectly fair. That he said it was a nightmare, that he did not give any details. I think all that should be known by the jury. That is my feeling. What I am not prepared, however, to say would be fair is to say that that is in some way some evidence of his guilt, because I am not, I do not believe it is."

The jury returned and they were taken through Martin's arrest and the evidence of the custody sergeants who had been responsible for Martin whilst he was held at King's Lynn police station. PC Growther told how Martin had refused all food and fluids until well into Saturday and that he was extremely quiet. As standard procedure dictated, they called for the medical examiner Dr Dermott Gerard Tiernan. Tiernan's conclusion that Martin could be examined on the Monday after a day's rest was read out to the jury.

WEDNESDAY 12TH APRIL: DAY THREE

Tony's neighbour, pig farmer Peter Huggins, was called to give evidence. He had been at the Farm Watch meeting in Emneth Hungate some six months before the shooting. Huggins told the court, "There seemed to be an extreme worry among the farming community about what was going on and the inability of the law to do anything about it. Tony Martin spoke at the meeting. He felt it was a waste of time calling the police. He was basically saying that it was time we started to take the law into our own hands."

But Huggins said how he met Tony a few days before the shooting. "He asked me if I had seen any light-fingered pikies lately. He also seemed to have got the idea that someone was after him. He had had some previous break-ins and he had the feeling that he was being targetted. He said what everyone would say, 'If I catch them at my place I will blow their heads off."

Scriv asked if that meant people in the area were in favour of mass murder. Huggins replied, "No, it is the kind of thing I would say myself."

Ballistic expert Brian Arnold was sworn in after Huggins and he took the jury through the working of the Winchester pump-action shotgun that Martin used. As he began to show the jury the gun, Ellen Barras left the court in tears.

The gun was 4ft in length and nearly 7 lbs in weight. Arnold explained that the magazine took four 12-bore cartridges and one in the breech, making five in all. He showed how it was loaded and how the pump action worked. He used dummy ammunition to show how the Winchester was loaded. The Winchester required the shooter to use the magazine release lever for the magazine to drop and the cartridges to be inserted. It is relatively easy to do but it would require a familiarity with the gun. Arnold estimated the range at which Barras and Fearon were shot was 15ft. He said that it was impossible to establish the sequence of shots, but it was assumed that the first shot had hit Barras in the back, probably as he knelt down to put something in one of the holdalls, while the second and third shots hit them as they scrambled out of the open window frame.

He said that when he received it the gun had no rust on the inside of the barrels. But in the two months it was in his possession rust did develop. From this he concluded it had been regularly

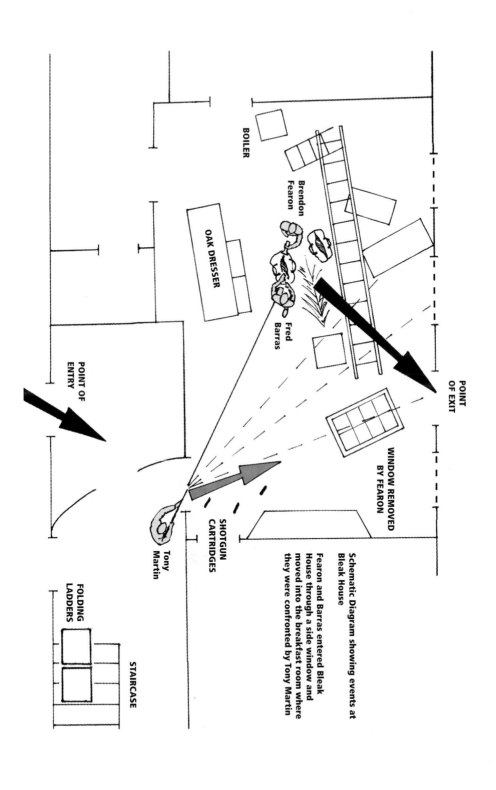

BOILER

Brendon
Fearon

OAK DRESSER

Fred
Barras

POINT OF
ENTRY

POINT
OF EXIT

WINDOW REMOVED
BY FEARON

Schematic Diagram showing events at
Bleak House

Fearon and Barras entered Bleak
House through a side window and
moved into the breakfast room where
they were confronted by Tony Martin

SHOTGUN
CARTRIDGES

Tony
Martin

FOLDING
LADDERS

STAIRCASE

top **Dresser and holdalls in the breakfast room of Bleak House**
bottom left **Window ripped out by Fearon
in the breakfast room of Bleak House**
bottom right **PC Steve Matthews, holding
the Winchester pump-action shotgun**

Bleak House Staircase. Tony Martin claimed he walked down these stairs carrying a shotgun weighing nearly 7lbs in his right hand. He maintained this despite the fact that the bannister was on the right hand side, and that there were obvious obstructions at the bottom of the staircase.

top **Bleak House as it looked in 2003, under police guard**
middle **Bleak House in the 1980's**
bottom **Fearon and Barras' entry point**

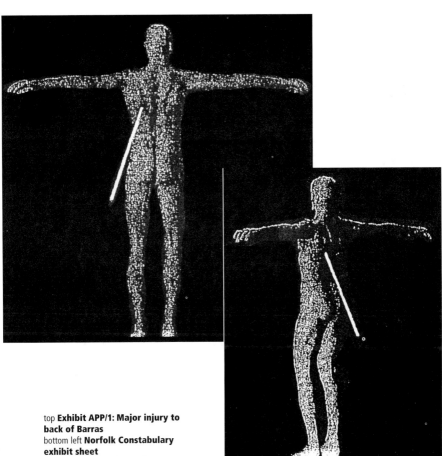

top **Exhibit APP/1: Major injury to back of Barras**
bottom left **Norfolk Constabulary exhibit sheet**
bottom right **Frederick Jackson Barras police mugshot**

Death of
Frederick Jackson BARRAS
at
Bleak House, Emneth Hungate

Major injury to back of BARRAS

Exhibit APP/1

top **Paul and Jacqui Leet relax at home**
bottom **Rusting farm machinery litters Bleak House Farm**

top **Martin in jovial mood at The Phoenix Chinese restaurant in Wisbech**
bottom **Outbuilding on Bleak House Farm**

top **Some of Tony Martin's teddies saved from Bleak House by Badger**
bottom **Otto, Martin's only remaining Rottweiler**

top **Martin aged 6 months**
right **Martin aged 3 years**
bottom **Dad Walter, Mum Hilary and older brother Robin
with Martin aged 5**

top **Martin's uncle Andrew Fountaine,
founder of the National Front**
left **Martin looking dapper in the blazer
with chrome buttons that women
could not resist!**

The Philisophical Musings of Prisoner No. BH9000 while at HMP Gartree

1 The Police and the Criminals make us look like fools

2 Churchill described this country 'This Sceptred Isle' I would describe 'This Scuppered Isle'

3 People think I have a free life. Far from it. It had become increasingly risky to leave the property. People are very angry. **Greed Kills.**

4 Police are putting people at risk. That is a crime. To (do) nothing is a crime. People say I am a hero. No I am not a hero

5 I always make do. But on this occasion everyone else is to blame for this. I am a totally innocent person. The blame lays with the police and the criminals. They are in cahoots.

Defendant's reaction to previous burglary:

'If they return I'll blow their heads off'

30th. September, 1999

Price £1.50

FIREARMS NEWS

Tony Martin Case

Bear up, Fayed tells sad Tony

HARRODS owner Mohamed Al Fayed moved to lift the spirits of jailed farmer Tony Martin with a Christmas gift – a giant toy bear.

I'LL BEAT FEARON THANKS TO *THE sun*

The case saturated the local and national press

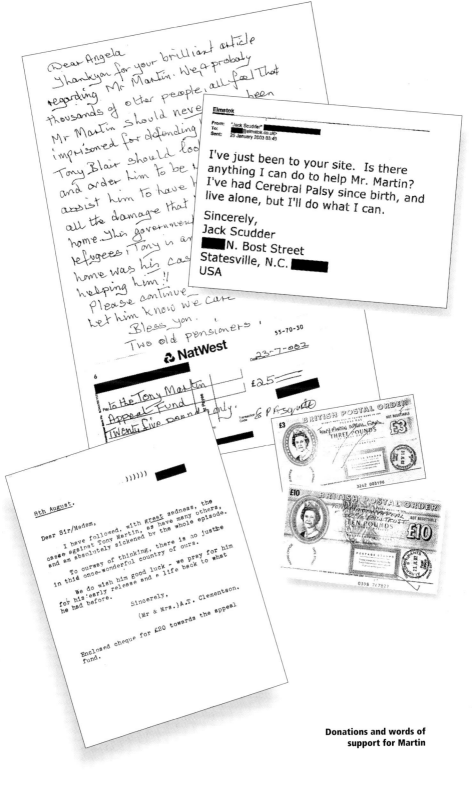

Dear Angela
Thank you for your brilliant article regarding Mr. Martin. We & probaly thousands of other people, all feel that Mr. Martin should never have been imprisoned for defending ...
Tony Blair should look ... and order him to be ... assist him to have ... all the damage that ... home. This government ... refugees, Tony is an ... home was his cas ... helping him!!
Please continue ... Let him know we care
Bless you.
Two old pensioners!

Elmstok

From: "Jack Scudder"
To: ▮▮▮@elmstok.co.uk
Sent: 26 January 2003 03:49

I've just been to your site. Is there anything I can do to help Mr. Martin? I've had Cerebral Palsy since birth, and live alone, but I'll do what I can.

Sincerely,
Jack Scudder
▮ N. Bost Street
Statesville, N.C. ▮
USA

NatWest   55-70-30
Date 23-7-002
£25
to the Tony Martin Appeal Fund
Twenty five pounds only   G P Risqu[...]

8th August.

Dear Sir/Madam,

I have followed, with great sadness, the case against Tony Martin, as have many others, and am absolutely sickened by the whole episode.

To our way of thinking, there is no justice in this once-wonderful country of ours.

We do wish him good luck - we pray for him for his early release and a life back to what he had before.

Sincerely,

(Mr & Mrs.)A.T. Clementson.

Enclosed cheque for £20 towards the appeal fund.

£3 BRITISH POSTAL ORDER £3
THREE POUNDS
3242 003196

£10 BRITISH POSTAL ORDER £10
TEN POUNDS
0398 767827

**Donations and words of
support for Martin**

Business Premium Account Statement

BARCLAYS

Account name A P MARTIN ESQ BUSINESS ACCOUNT
Account number ▓▓▓▓▓▓▓▓

A B MARTIN ESQ

WISBECH
CAMBS

Statement for 29 Feb – 29 Mar 2000
Statement sheet 65 (issued on 30 Mar 2000)

Balance from 28 Feb 2000	87,002.95
Total payments	87,000.00
Total receipts – incl. interest	145.45
Gross interest received	181.81
Tax paid	36.36
Net interest received	145.45
Balance as at 29 Mar	148.40

Current Interest Rates
Interest is calculated and tiered so your rate changes whenever your account moves into a different tier. Current gross rates are:

£0 – £1,999	2.100 %
£2,000 – £24,999	2.300 %
£25,000 – £99,999	2.700 %
£100,000 – £249,999	2.850 %
£250,000 – £999,999	3.100 %
£1,000,000+	3.250 %

Transactions in date order

Date	Description	Payments	Receipts	Balance
	Balance brought forward			87,002.95
20 Mar	Gross interest £181.81 less tax £36.36 = net interest paid £145.45 For the period 13 Dec 1999 –		145.45	87,148.40
22 Mar	Cash withdrawal at Barclays Swadlincote 2	15,000.00		72,148.40
28 Mar	Cash withdrawal at Barclays Swadlincote 2	72,000.00		148.40
29 Mar	Balance carried forward			148.40
	Total Payments/Receipts	87,000.00	145.45	

22 Mar	Cash withdrawal at Barclays Swadlincote 2	15,000.00
28 Mar	Cash withdrawal at Barclays Swadlincote 2	72,000.00
29 Mar	Balance carried forward	
	Total Payments/Receipts	87,000.00

top **Bank statement showing Martin's withdrawal of £87,000 from his Barclays account. He used the money to buy land but did not declare it on his legal aid form.**
bottom **The withdrawal took place less than two weeks before Martin went on trial for murder.**

That this House expresses its grave concern that Brendon Fearon, one of the burglars who broke into Tony Martin's house, is now suing for civil damages in respect of the injuries that he sustained during his criminal acts, including his loss of sexual enjoyment and an ability to practise martial arts; expresses further concern that Brendon Fearon's case is now being funded by the Legal Aid Board depite the willingness of his solicitor to take the case on a no win-no fee contingency basis; urges the Government to look urgently at changing the law so that criminals who break into properties leave all their civil rights outside that property; urges the Government to reform the rules governing legal aid so that it cannot be claimed in such case s; and further urges the Government to note that 83 per cent. of those surveyed by the Freedom Association believe that an intruder should have no case against a homeowner who takes direct action against them.

TERESA GORMAN MP
Billericay & District
House of Commons
London SW1A 0AA

28 July 2000

Dear Paul,

re: MR TONY MARTIN

What are you doing to get this man out of prison? Even the Prime Minister seems to agree it was a bad decision to put him there in the first place.

I read in the papers that Mr Tony Martin has been transferred for his own safety to Gartree Prison where his privilege of having a TV in his cell has been denied him for a month.

Can you imagine the horror that Mr Martin is going through just for protecting himself and his property, in the dark, from burglars, and accidentally killing one of them. How can he possibly be convicted of murder when it was obviously not premeditated?

My constituents are shocked at his treatment and demand a retrial. Meanwhile, since he is not a danger to anyone, he should be sent to an open prison.

Teresa

Mrs Teresa Gorman MP

The Rt Hon Paul Boateng MP
House of Commons

HOUSE OF COMMONS
LONDON SW1A 0AA

Peter Sainsbury Esq
The General Secretary, The POW Trust
295a Queenstown Road
Battersea
London. SW8 3NP

Friday 1st August 2003
Our Reference OK/NCB

Dear Mr Sainsbury

Re: Tony Martin

Please find enclosed letters which I have been asked to forward to Tony Martin

I have received an enormous number of letters expressing support for Tony Martin expressing great concern about the way in which he has been treated.

I have also been asked by many people how they may go about helping Tony and I have taken the liberty of providing them with your contact details. I hope the offers of support and help are not proving to be too overwhelming!

Every Best Wish.

Henry Bellingham, MP
(North West Norfolk)

Support from the Commons
top **Henry Bellingham's Early Day Motion**
middle **Letter from Teresa Gorman to Paul Boateng**
bottom **Letter from Henry Bellingham to Peter Sainsbury**

top **'Prince of Darkness' Brendon Fearon**
right **Letter from Fearon to Martin, written to aid his 'rehabilitation'**

Dear Tony.

I write regarding your paper reviews that I have been reading. I must stress that your influential sincerity to the papers was overwhelming, I feel that you will gain your sense of truth in time. As you and I know what happened that fateful night. I understand that it wasn't justified but reconciliation will not occur until you face up to your doings as I myself have done so.

I was there that night, as you well know. We was not there to take your belongings merely to escape your dogs and didn't mean to be intruders.

However, whatever the reason may have been for us being there that shouldn't have led to a little boy dying as there is no making amends for that little boy (Fred). we at least have that chance.

I have since been visited by the victim support group in relation to my feeling, about you gaining parole in the future. I was therefore forced to think about how remorseful you may be, judging from the cold words of your distorted truth in the paper reviews my thoughts are not overly optimistic.

What is so sad is that you haven't even stressed your sorrows for taking a human life and given the little boy's family a second thought as they have received a life sentence which there is no going back from. (So sad).

My feelings are with you. I hope you feel remorse as its the only way forward.

Yours sincerely

F Estreou

B.J.Fearon

26. 6. 03

Anthony E. Martin
"Highpoint" Stradishall
Newmarket Suffolk

Dear Peter. Thank [...]
comment on the secret lette[...]
depends on the source of th[...]
end as it more than app[...]
quite right about Dew[...]
statement that I am [...]
to say the least. As [...]
come clean and tell [...]
views or is he [...]
does he base his v[...]
and say I understa[...]
B.B.C. and on tha[...]
the point I read [...]
public comments [...]
work for the B[...]
Equally he m[...]
draw attention to [...]
is all I can say he will [...]
up with Admiral Lord Nelson. You [...]
politically correct brigade may replace [...]
Trafalgar square with [...]
he is doing a good [...]
Should [...]

my experience with Makin as he continually strips
the knife in me. He is asking for what he is going to
get. Of course I have to be carefull about libel. He
has proven to be totally incompetent. I can't see how
I owe him this money, and have proof [...] on two
occasions I did not owe him any money. Anyway
thank you for helping me and Peny Daring. Yes I
say I could write all day. I will leave it with Sandra
relating to the Law Society. I am out of my depth at this stage

Best wishes

Tony

Norfolk Farmer

patient for my release. The cat will
soon be out of the bag and the Genie free.

Best wishes

Tony Martin   Norfolk Farmer

P.T.O.

Martin frequently put the world to rights in his correspondence with Peter Sainsbury. He always signed off: Tony Martin, Norfolk Farmer

top **Tony Martin, Norfolk Farmer, in his orchard at Bleak House**
bottom **Martin holds court in a London restaurant**

DECLARATION OF TRUST

DATE

PARTIES

(1) NICK MAKIN of M & S Solicitors Home Farm 5 Newton Road Heather Leicestershire

LE67 2RD ("THE SETTLOR"): and

(2) STUART MAYFIELD (3) PAUL COMBY ("THE TRUSTEES")

PART 1 – OPERATIVE PROVISIONS

1.   **DEFINITIONS AND CONSTRUCTION**

In this Deed, unless it appears there is another intention, the following definitions and rules of
construction shall apply:

1.1   The "Trust" shall mean the Tony Martin Support Trust constituted by this Deed.

COPY

7 August 2000

Invoice No. 4895

RE: Appeal

Description		VAT	AMOUNT
To our professional charges for work done and advice given in connection with the above			
Our fees		5,514.90	31,513.74

With Compliments

NICK MAKIN
M & S SOLICITORS LTD

Total fees	31,513.74
Total VAT @ 17.50%	5,514.90
Total Amount Due	37,028.64

VAT No.

Tony Martin
8P Oartree
Bowfield Road
Market Harborough
Leicestershire. LE16 7RP

M & S Solicitors Ltd., Home Farm, 5 Newton Road, Heather, Leicester, LE67 2RD.

top **Ballinger outside the Lloyds building**
bottom left **Declaration of Trust to set up the**
Tony Martin Support Trust (Defence Fund)
bottom right **Bill for £37,000 from M&S to Martin**

HSBC 〈X〉

62 Market Street
Ashby de la Zouch
Leicestershire
LE65 1BE

MR NICK MAKIN
TRADING AS
M & S SOLICITORS
CLIENTS ACCOUNT RE:
TONY MARTIN DEFENCE FUND
BUSINESS NO-NOTICE ACCOUNT

Sort Code: ▮▮▮▮
Tel: 01530 503700
Fax: 01530 503799

SHEET 011	ACCOUNT NO. ▮▮▮▮▮▮▮	PAID OUT	PA
30MAR00	BALANCE BROUGHT FORWARD		
06APR00	CR	PAID IN AT HSBC BANK PLC ASHBY-DE-LA-ZOUCH	
13APR00	CR	PAID IN AT HSBC BANK PLC ASHBY-DE-LA-ZOUCH	
13APR00	CR	PAID IN AT HSBC BANK PLC ASHBY-DE-LA-ZOUCH	2
13APR00	CR	PAID IN AT HSBC BANK PLC ASHBY-DE-LA-ZOUCH	
13APR00	CR	PAID IN AT HSBC BANK PLC ASHBY-DE-LA-ZOUCH	
' 'R00	CR	PAID IN AT HSBC BANK PLC ASHBY-DE-LA-ZOUCH	
18APR00	CR	PAID IN AT HSBC BANK PLC ASHBY-DE-LA-ZOUCH	
18APR00	CR	PAID IN AT HSBC BANK PLC ASHBY-DE-LA-ZOUCH	
20APR00	CR	PAID IN AT HSBC BANK PLC ASHBY-DE-LA-ZOUCH	
20APR00	TFR	TRANSFER	8,840.39
27APR00	CR	PAID IN AT HSBC BANK PLC ASHBY-DE-LA-ZOUCH	
27APR00	CR	PAID IN AT HSBC BANK PLC ASHBY-DE-LA-ZOUCH	8
27APR00	CR	PAID IN AT HSBC BANK PLC	

top **Bank statement showing Makin's £8,840 invoice leaving the Tony Martin Defence Fund account**
right **M&S brochure outlines their "Creative Approach"**

A Creative Approach

We aim to find commercial solutions to our clients' problems. Sometimes clients want to do something which cannot be done. Rather than simply tell the client it cannot be done, our approach is to try to find an alternative way of achieving the same end for the client.

top **Afternoon Tea at the Ritz, left to right: Tony Martin, Valentina Artsrunik, Sally Farmiloe-Neville, Peter Sainsbury**
bottom **Tony Martin and Valentina Artsrunik in Knightsbridge's San Lorenzo restaurant**

Dig deep to help Martin

Supporters asked to help pay for farmer's legal bill

SUPPORTERS of jailed farmer Tony Martin are being urged to put their hands in their pockets to help fund his legal aid bill and save his farm from being sold.

Businessman Malcolm Starr, one of the trustees of a new support fund which has been set up to raise money for the forthcoming appeal, said: "If we cannot raise the necessary money then Tony will have to sell his farm and that would devastate him.

"It's bad enough being in prison but that farm was his life and if there's nothing there for him when he comes out I don't know what he will do.

"We want to protect his property for him."

Martin's 350-acre farm at Elmeth Hungate has been looked after by friends since he was jailed for life six months ago, for the murder of 16-year-old burglar Fred Barras.

application for legal aid by his new team of solicitors, Saunders and Co, was refused.

The bill to fight the appeal which is expected to be heard before the end of the year could be as much as £200,000.

Saunders and Co have replaced M and S Solicitors sacked by Martin a couple of months ago, who had become increasingly unhappy with way the trial had been conducted.

"We do need all the help we can get," said Mr Starr.

"We are conscious that some people donated money to an earlier fund and thought this was for an appeal but this new fund has been set up for the sole purpose of paying the legal costs."

Donations can be made to Lloyds-TSB Bank plc, 3 No Brink, Wisbech, Cambs, P 1JT, account no: 1000153, code 30-99-77.

A new website concerning Tony Martin, former of Westry, March, has also been set up. Anything on the website will

above left **Starr opens fresh defence fund for Martin's appeal case**
above right **Martin's signature on a Legal Aid form, including a very modest evaluation of his assets**

top **Malcolm Starr, the landlord of the Hare Arms, Tony Martin**
bottom **Malcolm Starr, Tony Martin, Peter Sainsbury in the offices of the POW Trust**

top **Tony Martin takes to the lectern at the UKIP conference**
bottom **Martin imparts his wisdom to the younger generation**

maintained.

Scriv established that if it had been oiled, then just stored and not touched that it might not develop rust. Arnold agreed that was possible. He also agreed from the angle of the wounds that Martin had fired downwards, especially the shot that killed Barras

THURSDAY 13TH APRIL: DAY FOUR

The interviews conducted by Newton and Peters with Tony Martin after his arrest were read out to the jury, then Peters also gave evidence on the incident that led to the revoking of Tony's shotgun licence. The court was told that five years earlier, Tony discovered a man, Mark Aldin, in his orchard and set his Rottweiler dogs upon him. Peters agreed with Horwood-Smart's summary of the incident. "Mr Martin disturbed a Mr Aldin stealing apples from his orchard. When asked to leave he became abusive and aggressive. Mr Martin went back into the house and got his dogs. He went out with a shotgun and thought he saw Mr Aldin trying to run his dogs down. He shot at the vehicle and hit the rear wing."

The court was told of Tony's personal armoury when his shotgun certificate was withdrawn: a 12-bore side-by-side shotgun, a .410 single barrelled shotgun, a .22 rifle (this can be held under a shotgun licence), and a smaller calibre shotgun. Tony initiated an appeal against losing his gun licence but did not pursue it. Horwood-Smart said, "The Chief Constable was advised that if pursued the appeal was likely to be successful."

Later that day the jury trooped off in convoy to Bleak House. Jurors were issued with yellow hard hats and a torch identical to the one Fearon had used. Everyone had to attend...ushers, clerk of the court, counsel, solicitors and Tony, as well, in a separate police van. They saw for themselves Martin's virtually derelict farmhouse, his yard full of rusting machinery, outbuildings, barn and the cottage where his three Rottweilers were kept. Outside they saw three "outpost" ladders that had been lashed to branches of a 50ft oak, these could be accessed by another two ladders standing against the farmhouse.

The farmhouse was enveloped with poisonous giant hogweed, ivy and moss, and the jury were shown the spot just outside where Barras was found dead. Inside, even in daylight, Martin's home was gloomy because the windows were covered by the enveloping undergrowth. Every cartridge on the floor was marked out with a small flag, as was the shot damage to the exterior door and the wall. The jurors were directed along a prearranged route to approximately where Barras was shot and where the "holders" were found; court warders then helped jurors scale a ladder to the landing where they examined Martin's bedroom. After two hours on the property, the convoy drove back the 54 miles to Norwich Crown Court.

FRIDAY 14TH APRIL: DAY FIVE

Trial by Gypsy

At 7am on Friday morning three gypsies set off for Norwich Crown Court from Walpole St. Andrew, a small village just outside Wisbech in Cambridgeshire. Driving was Eli Frankham, a towering 6' 5", 21 stone bare-knuckle boxing gypsy. Riding shotgun was his cousin Dave who, like Eli, was a large man in his early thirties though noticeably fatter than his pugilist cousin. Their younger nephew Peter Chilton, a thick set, slow witted gypsy lay sprawled across the back seat bleary eyed at the early start.

"What's the fucking point of getting to Norwich so early?" said Chilton through a yawn.

"Cos we have to queue up for passes and if we get there at nine, we won't get in, mush. I'm not missing me chance to see that basta'd in the dock. Anyway I promised Ellen we'd be down."

He hadn't promised Ellen, Fred's mother, anything, but he knew she'd be pleased that the extended family had shown their faces. Eli had his own way of showing the courts that the gypsy community would have its say. They took a pit stop just outside Dereham to grab some tobacco and cans of Coke to keep them fired up until they pulled into Bishopgate, Norwich. It was 8.15 and even Peter Chilton had perked up a bit. Eli extracted his massive frame from the car with the usual difficulty.

Eli picked out a familiar face in the queue waiting for passes to the No1 Court where Martin was being tried. The 50-year-old woman was a gypsy from Newark. He couldn't remember her name but he'd talked to her the previous September when he'd gone up for the *kris* and Fred's funeral.

"Hello, when they giving up the passes?" said Eli as if he'd known her all his life.

"Not 'til half nine but you gotta line up" She replied, craning her neck up to look at Eli.

"I've met you before, round Newark – you're a Frankham aren't you." She said after looking him up and down.

"Yeah, I'm here for Freddie," sniffed Eli. "Look, I've brought a couple of Fred's mates down to see it all for 'emselves, could you spare us tickets when you get 'em? Only I've gotta pick someone else up a bit later and I won't 'ave the time." He said tapping his wrist, even though he didn't have a watch on.

"Course I will," she said.

"Cheers!" exclaimed Eli already heading back to the car.

"I hope they hangs him!" she called after him as he sauntered back to the car.

"Done," he said. "I've got some old bag gettin' us 'em." They found a café to sit in until just before ten.

Eli Frankham was no stranger to the courtroom. In 1998 he was sent down for fifteen months for violent disorder and unlawful wounding of the landlord of the Princess Victoria pub in Walpole St Andrew. On July 18th 1997, Eli was barred from the Victoria for almost causing a bar brawl. Shortly after that Eli roped Peter Chilton and another clan member Eddie Dolan into sorting out landlord Ian Madder who'd had him thrown out. Eli led his lynching gang back to the pub and meted out some rough justice to the unfortunate pint puller. Ian Madder was forced to the ground under the nose of the landlady Carol, Madder's sister, and pelted with pint glasses and ashtrays until his head was gashed open and he was left unconscious. Locals at the pub were stunned by the violence of the act and many of them chose to testify against the gypsies at trial the following year.

Eli, never one to let others do his dirty work, went around the witnesses intimidating them one by one. At first he would offer them a bung of £3000, then he'd threaten to smash their faces in if they refused. One of the witness, who has now left the area, said, "When we refused it was clear we were in for a rough time. Every day Frankham or Chilton shouted at us to the effect that if we gave evidence, we were as good as dead. They said we would end up six feet under." It was all to no avail – the witnesses ignored the threats and testified against Frankham and Chilton who were found guilty and imprisoned.

After hanging back at a safe distance from the police that now guarded the court entrance, Eli, with Dave and Peter in tow strolled up to the old gypsy who had earlier procured them the court passes and went inside to take their seats in the public gallery.

"Hello, hello, hello," joked Chilton as they strode into the lobby of the Court, which was awash with police officers. Eli was the tallest man in the crowded lobby and easily spotted a family friend, gypsy Wayne Dolan. Wayne's great aunt was one of Fred's grandmothers, Mary.

"Y'right Eli, I thought you might turn up, y'right Dave!" said Wayne cheerfully.

"Yeah all right, wouldn't a missed this for the world." Eli replied.

They pushed through the swing doors into the public gallery, "Y'sit opposite 'em, they sit over there" Eli said pointing to jury benches that ran along the opposite side of the oblong courtroom. Eli sat down with Wayne on one arm and Peter and Dave on the other. Horwood-Smart and Scriv stood deep in conference in the middle of the room. To the left of them sat the dais on which the judge's bench stood with the aged Justice John Owen sitting at it. Then Martin came up into the dock. Eli gave him the evil eye but Martin did not notice.

"Ah…Jury watching…" Eli sighed "Don't you just love it?" he said turning to Peter. Wayne leant over and pointed with his arm outstretched,

"Yeah, look at her" he said, singling out one of the jurors, a plump woman who was fidgeting nervously in her seat.

"What? That freak?" said Peter. The female juror was now intently observing the gypsies who were huddled in whispered discussion at the back of the public gallery. That settled it for Eli: "Yes, she's the one!"

"I'm going to give her the eye!" The juror sat, transfixed. Shortly afterwards, the session was interrupted when the jurors were asked to step out of box whilst a point of law was discussed. The break allowed Justice Owen to question Sergeant Newton on the bounty that had allegedly been put on Martin's head by the gypsy court. Owen ruled that the jurors need not be warned directly about this threat. Owen instructed the court clerk to call the jury back in.

The jury duly resumed their seats, but something was different. Now they were all scanning the public gallery for something. Justice Owen informed the jury that they were to be "vigilant" when they left the court and call the police if they felt in any danger. Eli smothered a laugh, fixing the woman juror once again with a piercing stare. Some gypsies actually believe that with enough concentration you can hex someone's mind.

But concentration is not Eli's strongest point. Too many punches to the head had rather loosened up his grey matter. He signalled to the other two and they left the court before Martin came into the witness box. Their exit did not go unnoticed by the Norfolk Constabulary.

Defence Case

Tony took the oath in a confident and authoritative voice. The court was packed as he stood in the witness box. He was looking forward to setting the record straight. Horwood-Smart had other ideas.

Scriv took him gently through his account. On all the critical points, it differed only marginally from the interview that he gave to Peters and Newton. However, it included much more detail about his family, Bleak House and the constant battle with theft. Stories of the latter came thick and fast at the beginning. On one occasion in 1979/80, Tony claimed to have confronted a burglar who was carrying a pillowcase of swag that he'd stolen from Bleak House. "…I was younger then and it was a bright night and I chased him down the lawn, round the back of the orchard. He dropped the loot…and he disappeared…" Asked what impression it made on him, Tony replied, "Well, I felt dirty. I was confused. I spent a week or two feeling; was it somebody I knew? Or who was it? I didn't know."

After a couple of other similar incidents he agreed that he had started feeling unsafe in his own house. Then, after recounting the theft of some Windsor chairs that belonged to his auntie Gladys, he came visibly close to tears. The litany of theft went on and on.

Scriv then digressed slightly and in relation to the time his shotgun licence was revoked he asked what Martin used the guns for?

"I used it to…for pigeons."

"What, shooting at pigeons or disturbing pigeons?"

Tony replied, "Disturbing them. I'm not a very good shot."

After describing a few more thefts, Scriv took Tony through the problems of the high incidence of burglary in the area and the unsatisfactory police response. He then took him to the Farm Watch meeting in which he made remarks already referred to at the trial.

Scriv asked him, "Are you someone who puts their views forward quite forcibly on occasions?"

"I'm not frightened of making an opinion. I think it's more helpful all round, you know."

Scriv then asked him whether he made the remark attributed to him of shooting burglars.

Tony replied, "No, I don't think I said that at all."

"Did you say it in jest or anything like that in jest?"

Tony answered, "I actually can't remember what I said there but basically I was getting… the point was coming through to me that I weren't going to get any police help anymore…" Tony slewed away from the question, but denied making the remark.

Scriv moved on to the aftermath of that burglary. Tony went through his visit to King's Lynn police station to inquire how the investigation was getting on but Scriv didn't ask Tony what was said as he knew he would deny what the police had reported.

Of course, Scriv had been given a hand by Tony that he could not play. Tony had denied making the "round up the gypsies and shoot them" remark on various occasions to different people, none of whom had any reason to lie. Scriv's instructions from Tony were that he did not make this remark. Consequently, Scriv had been dealt the thankless task of putting to these witnesses that they were mistaken, had misheard or were lying. But even with Tony he judged it better to let sleeping dogs lie, albeit he knew that Horwood-Smart would waken them.

Scriv moved on to the evening of August the 20th, asking Martin what time he came home after leaving his mother's.

"Well, I'm not sure but it was getting late enough. It was getting dark. The nights start to pull in at that time, you know, harvest time. They start to pull in fast... I wouldn't like to say. Maybe half-past nine, maybe nine. I don't know."

He then explained that he went up to the bedroom and fell asleep wearing his working clothes.

Scriv led him, "You were woken up and what did you hear?"

"Just a horrendous noise. Noises that I can't say I've ever heard or understood before." He was asked to describe them... "Well, I'll try; but I don't really think anybody could understand the noises – you'd have to have a tape recording of it but I just felt I was in a horror movie and there was this continual banging noise. It sounded like somebody coming up the stairs. I heard another kind of noise, which...I've got a solid fuel boiler out in the garage and if you overfill it and it gets too hot you get airlocks and this bang bang with a slithering noise. There were so many noises. I know it could not have been the boiler because the boiler wasn't on..."

After Tony lay there, then got up, he described seeing "...a bright light coming up the staircase. I became fearful and it sounded just like them coming up the staircase and I thought 'I don't know', so I went back to the bedroom… I stood there because I expected people to follow up and come that way and nobody did. It got to the situation where I got visions of people coming through the door - which they didn't – and I had this terrific thumping in my body, the beating of my heart. I mean I could hear it and I felt like the whole room was like it and I knew I'd got a gun there and I thought 'This is crazy'. I picked the gun up, loaded it, stood there, waited, thought about it. I was still getting this terrific banging. There was a noise downstairs so I went outside on the landing…. The torchlight had gone then. This terrific bright light, I mean, it was just like…it was as bright as this (he indicated the court lights), brighter, really bright… the noise was still downstairs."

Martin told the court how he went down the stairs and, with Scriv leading him, described how a light was shone at him… "I assume it was a torch."

Scriv asked, "Now where were you, where do you believe you were when the light was shone at you?"

Tony: "I'm sorry?"

Scriv: "Where do you think you were when that light was…"

Tony: "Well, I had the impression I was on the staircase." He then repeated the familiar account of the light hitting him in the eyes and his being frightened. "Lots of things go through your mind, you just become blind, terrified, vulnerable." Martin told how he started firing and that he didn't know how many shots he had let off. He then turned back and went into the bedroom.

When asked where he fired the gun in relation to the torch, he said, "Well, the light was coming from down in what I call a well or a long dark tunnel and I thought I was firing down at the bottom. I mean I call it a doorway but it's not a doorway because it's all bricks, isn't it, it hasn't been finished off. Basically fired right down at the bottom of the doorway."

Next Tony described going back downstairs, getting a torch from the car and coming back into the breakfast room... "Well, because... I was utterly amazed and I saw this window being pulled out of the wall. I know it wasn't secure but it was reasonably... I mean, it wasn't like a normal window cemented in... and I saw it lay there, so I just assumed they'd gone out that way. I got in the car because I felt safe in there. I don't really know what happened after that. I just decided I would drive round to see if there was any car around or anybody about."

Tony described going to the Leets and his version of the conversation he had with Paul Leet he remembered as: "I think, roughly, I said, 'Have you seen anybody about?'. And I said to him, 'Well, you won't believe it but I've just found some people in my house.'"

"Did you say you'd used your shotgun, you'd shot? Scriv asked.

"I told him, 'Yes.' I think I did."

Scriv then took Tony through the history of the gun he used that night. Where had it come from? "I found it in one of my cars," replied Martin.

"When? Before or after the May raid?" Scriv responded.

"No, I had the gun a long while before that."

"How did you find it?"

"It was in my car... there was a small note... It was just something... it just said, thought I might 'find it useful'. It was somebody who knew Arthur Garner many years ago, and that was it. The letter's probably still in the house, if you have a look for it, with lots of other things..." Martin replied, with an almost imperceptible shrug of the shoulders.

Scriv then asked him, "did you know at the time in fact that that gun was of a type which had been banned unless you had a different type of certificate?"

"I didn't know anything about those sort of guns," said Martin

After taking him through leaving the gun at his mother's, going to Helen Lilley's and being arrested, Scriv handed him over to the steely mercies of Horwood-Smart.

She took him staccato like through some aspects of his life and Tony answered straight to the point without having a clue what point she was working towards.

"Generally do you like people?" she began.

"I find people very interesting," he replied.

"Friendship important to you?"

"Very much so."

"Relationship with you neighbours, important?"

"Very much so."

"Family?"

"Very much so"

"Your animals?"

"Very much so."

"Last summer – what were the most important relationships in you life?"

"I don't know."

"Animals or people?"

"Both."

"Which?"

"Both"

"Any in particular?"

"No." She then backed off and took him through his history at Bleak House. She took him through his DIY bodging and his love of plants. It was all fairly innocuous and clearly designed to disarm Tony.

"So hogweed grows some eighteen foot or so high – a wonderful handsome plant?" Horwood-Smart leant forward slightly as she spoke.

"It is a handsome plant."

"Well over three times my size?"

"Double." But nothing like your girth, Tony thought.

"So all round your house was a canopy of plants?" she asked.

"Yes, it got like that. Yes."

"And over your house ivy grew?"

"Yes. Planted on the north side," Tony stated for the record.

"After the ivy and hogweed, there was the willow tree, all left to take nature's course."

She moved in, "So outside generally, would it be fair to say you let things be? Things grew as they wanted to grow and where they wanted to grow."

"Yes, I suppose you could say that to a point" Tony replied.

She now came to her point, "In amongst all that you had erected a number of ladders?"

"Yes."

"Why was that?" she asked.

Tony felt tricked. "Well, that would be about 23, 14 years ago, when I was taking a great deal of interest in the garden and I'd have this magnificent oak tree growing close to the house and one of the branches grew right across the front of the house which shaded it and another one was just touching the slates on the roof and I thought, if you don't do something about that…slates on a house like those kind of slates are difficult things to repair, so they'd got to come off unfortunately. I'd like to have left them, but you couldn't do it."

"Any reason why the ladders are in some of the branches which face away from the foot of the house?" She glanced downward at her notes, allowing him time to reply.

"I can't actually say. I don't actually know where the ladders are at the moment up there. There is no particular reason. It's just that they've been put there to cut the branches off…" Tony replied.

Using the same technique of lulling Tony into a false sense of security she then moved on to comments he'd made about gypsies. She turned back to PC Cracknell's evidence.

"You told him in no uncertain terms what you thought about policing, did you not?"

"I had discussed it with him."

"You discussed your views about thieves generally?"

"There was discussion about it," Tony answered warily.

"You expressed your views about gypsies, travellers?"

"No, I didn't."

Horwood-Smart shifted to the other people he'd made similar remarks to, "You have expressed those views to a number of people, have you not?"

"Not about gypsies," he replied, feigning indignation.

She reminded him of what his neighbour Huggins had reported him as saying, "The phrase 'light-fingered pikies' are they not your words?"

Tony went for broke – or was it bankruptcy? "I have never used that word in my life."

"A description that they should be rounded and put in a field…" she continued.

"I'm misquoted."

"The precise description – a field with barbed wire round it, gun turrets at the corners?" she intoned.

"That isn't what I said."

"And that they should be shot?"

"I didn't say that either."

"Wasn't it your considered view, Mr Martin, that the only way to stop thieves was to shoot them?"

"No."

The jurors faces told the way the verdict was going. But Tony was convinced that he could say everyone was lying except him and be believed.

She moved onto the ammunition pointing out that after a thorough police search there were no cartridges found in the bedroom but a great deal of ammunition distributed round the house.

"Well, I actually got the impression they were spent cartridges" Tony commented.

She was not going to give Tony any wiggle room and she stated coldly,

"You know there were collections of cartridges found around your house."

Tony conceded but, as is his want, not completely, "So I understand."

She tightened the screw, "Boxes placed conveniently around the house? One of them in the hallway?"

"I don't recollect."

"Those boxes could only have been placed there by you, Mr Martin" she said decisively.

Tony could not let the conclusion stand: "I understand what you're saying. The boxes there…as far as I know I'd used up my own cartridges…but I had brought boxes from my mother's and father's house, and my brother's house, with business papers and there may have been boxes of cartridges in there. What with the…as the jury will know having been to my house, it's rather unorganised. Over the years things have got pushed around, broken out of boxes, dogs run around, it's not very difficult to break open a box of cartridges. I picked them up and put them back in boxes but the boxes have got broken so they won't stay in properly. I've put them back in cardboard boxes and with the dogs running in and out and me bringing tools in from the farm – in there for the winter time – it's got like that. That's why it's like that."

Horwood-Smart let him waffle away while she peered down at her notes, preparing her next question. When Tony petered out, she switched to the gun…

"placed in your car by a well-wisher?" she stated, repeating his own words.

"I wouldn't say a well-wisher, but it just had been put in there." Tony knew how lame he sounded.

She then moved onto the issue of a shotgun licence.

"You knew, as a former holder of a shotgun licence, that it was a firearm, not a shotgun?"

"I thought it was a shotgun."

She put the obvious, "It was a shotgun that held more than two cartridges?"

"I'm sorry, I didn't know that."

Horwood-Smart does not go in for the histrionic reactions that some barristers use but she could not resist a feigned surprise,

"You didn't know that?"

"I thought it was a shotgun," Tony kept to his furrow.

"Are you saying you never examined it?"

"I am saying that I understand what you're saying is that a firearm is like a 2.2, a single shot. Is that right?"

She nodded. "I don't know" he replied.

"That's what you're saying, you don't know?" she asked incredulously.

Tony couldn't think of anything to say and paused. Justice Owen leaned to his left, unable to resist doubling up on Horwood-Smart:

"What is being suggested to you is that whilst you can have a shotgun with two cartridges…"

Tony had to come to heel, "Yes."

"Right," she said. Her manner was like a schoolmistress who intends to pin down an evasive pupil's account.

"If it has more, if it has a pump action particularly, then it becomes a firearm?" she reminded the jury by way of a question.

"No, I didn't know that."

"Well, that is what you are being asked," she commented wryly.

"Sorry. Well, I thought I'd already answered the question."

She moved on. In a slightly exasperated voice, she asked, "For how many years did you have a shotgun licence, Mr Martin?"

"I don't actually know but it was sometime between August and…"

"1984, wasn't it," she asked looking down at her notes.

"Sorry?"

"1984."

"What? When I had a shotgun licence?"

"Yes."

"Probably."

She moved on to how and when he acquired the Winchester shotgun. She reminded him that in his interview, he had said that he had never even loaded it until the evening of the shooting. He agreed that he had neither loaded it nor fired until then.

"And that is your position?" she asked.

"Yes."

"Can you explain why it is well-oiled?"

Martin was backed into another corner… "I expect the previous owner – whomever had it – had it well looked after. But I noticed when I had looked at it from time to time it actually was getting rusty on the outside of the barrel."

Smartypants reminded him that the ballistic expert had said it was "in good condition".

Tony thought he saw a way out, "I think he was talking about internally. I'd never inspected it internally."

"Well-oiled?"

"Yes."

She asked deadpan, "How long had the gun been in your possession?"

"Well, it was somewhere between…sometime after…when the milk float incident, until August," Tony floundered.

"Are you saying you never oiled it, never looked after it at all?"

Tony floundered on, "No, I never bothered about it. I think you will find there is rust on the outside of the gun actually." She queried why he ignored the fact that the expert had said the inside of the barrel was clean.

"Well, I don't know whether he was talking about that. I assumed he was talking about the mechanisms where the firing takes place or how that works in there."

She asked him if he remembered the expert saying that rust appeared on the inside of the barrel in a short time.

"Yes, I did," he answered curtly.

She repeated that it became rusty quickly.

"I'm a little confused here. When you are talking about rust are you talking about the inside of the barrels?" he inquired.

She confirmed that that was exactly what she was talking about.

"I wouldn't have thought a gun, if it was kept in storage, would rust inside but you are supposed to clear them up to stop pitting. So you're saying before the gun was fired there was no rust there. I don't know."

She put the obvious, "You had been maintaining that gun, hadn't you?"

"No, I hadn't."

"That gun was your armoury against thieves?"

"No, it wasn't."

She then tried to establish when he acquired the gun. At first Tony edged and evaded but she pushed him into a corner again, "When was it?"

"Several years ago," he answered.

Horwood-Smart backed off again and took Tony through about 5 or 6 minutes of innocuous questions about his habit of changing cars before she asked suddenly, "What was the cartridge doing in the Nissan?"

Tony hadn't been lulled into a false sense of security this time but he did not anticipate the line of attack. He floundered again,

"Well, I've listened to that and I don't know what that was doing there. I can only assume that... the jury have been to my house they might find it quite untidy. It was much more untidy. I probably spent a whole day taking the newspapers out of my house and out of the hallway and I used my car as a large wheel barrow and took them down to the bottom of the drive to the small field... I've got a bit of machinery...I had a big fire there and maybe there could have been one of those cartridge shells was picked up then with newspapers and maybe it was put down. Unless I picked up some boxes with some stuff in there and I had to sort out what was what..."

He saw the look of sceptical disbelief on her face and he stopped the verbal walkabout. Ballinger had made Martin obey the 11th commandment of not pontificating but perhaps he should have been reminded of the Rule of Wells – when the well is poisoned, stop drinking.

"I don't know. Other than that I don't know," he wittered into silence.

"An unfired cartridge?" she asked, her tone even more sceptical than her look.

"Oh… an unfired cartridge, sorry. Ummm… well there again it could be the same thing."

Next she questioned him on the top of the staircase and the three missing treads that Martin described as requiring "one great leap for mankind".

"But were you, Mr Martin, well used to making that leap with the Winchester repeater gun?" she asked.

"No."

"It's quite a heavy gun that, isn't it?"

"It is."

"It needs a five pound pull on the trigger?"

"Well, I don't really understand what that means. Only I understand what you mean but what it amounts to I don't know," Tony replied.

"You used that gun. You have pulled that trigger, Mr Martin?"

"Yes."

"It's quite a heavy gun," she asked.

Tony answered directly, "It's a very heavy gun. I thought it was."

"Are you saying that you, that night, negotiated the staircase, holding that gun?"

Tony just said "yes", but then she took him through the whole sequence in which in his working boots, on a staircase that is uncarpeted, he went down the stairs without alerting the intruders to his presence.

After that Horwood-Smart moved to the issue of where Tony fired the gun. He confirmed twice that it was halfway down the stairs. She asked, "Mr Martin, was that an honest belief or was that a lie to the officers who were interviewing you?"

He replied, "No, that was the impression I got. That was the question I was asked and I tried to help them as best I could."

"Have you by any chance changed that story afterwards since it has become scientifically clear that you could not have fired the gun from halfway down the stairs?"

Tony replied, "Well, I can only go on the impression of what it was like and where I was at the time and what I visualised and how I felt things were."

"And?"

"Well, it's the impression that I had of where I was in the dark."

She put to him, "You remember you were asked about this many times by the officer?"

"Yes."

"And you were quite clear as to where you were?"

"Yes," Tony said wearily.

"And that was not right, was it?"

"So it appears," Tony replied, his voice sounding resigned.

"You were not standing on the stairs at any time when you fired that gun, were you?"

"I got that impression that where I stopped on the stairs, that is where I fired from."

"You were at least in the doorway of that room, if not inside the room itself, Mr Martin?"

"No, I don't see it like that."

"You don't ..."

Tony interrupted her, "I don't remember it like that, shall I say."

"Is it because you don't wish to remember it?"

"No. There have been discussions about this and I have to accept that bullets don't go round corners and I don't understand it but I definitely got the impression that I fired from the middle of the stairs. I didn't want to leave the stairs. It was the safest place to be."

This was not safest thing to say to Horwood-Smart, Queen's Counsel. She took him through his sequence of events by which he went out to the top of the stairs holding the Winchester. Then she put to him, "Up there, at the top of the staircase, holding a loaded shotgun, you were in the safest place in the house, were you not?"

Tony rejected her proposition, "It didn't feel like that... I came down the stairs in the end because I didn't know whether I was going to have a heart attack. I didn't know whether I was going to have a thrombosis because I've already had one. I didn't know whether I was going to pass out because I had feelings that I was going to pass out. I had feelings at times when I couldn't move and in the end I came out of the bedroom."

She put another scenario to him – he heard two people outside. "No."

Heard them trying to break in. "No."

Forcing the window. "No."

Breaking one pane. "No."

Breaking another pane. "I don't know," he replied, exasperated.

Forcing the window open.

"No."

Next she asked, "Was that slithering sound the ivy being pulled away from the window?"

Tony answered, "I've never heard ivy being pulled away from a window."

"Are you saying that there wasn't ivy growing over your window?"

Tony replied, "Well, according to where they came in – which I found out later - there was a little bit of ivy but there wasn't that much because that was a window that I used to periodically pull the ivy away from so it would let some light into that room, because that house... It was a very dark house when I got it because there aren't many windows on the north side. The north side didn't have windows. It was kept cool because there used to be a dairy there years ago before the war."

Even though her point about the ivy was speculative, Horwood-Smart was almost certainly correct about the origin of the slithering sound. Liars often use some real feature of an event to add credence to their embellishments. Tony did it also with the torch lights that he continually says were extremely bright. Fearon's torch was nothing like as bright as Tony claims but as with the ivy sound he is transposing the light from the car to the torch to add realism to his account.

She continued her scenario, breaking up each action into a question. Was he already downstairs when the two burglars moved from the entry room, across the hallway at the bottom of the stairs into the breakfast room? "No"

Did he see them moving across that little hallway to reach it. "No."

Was he there with his loaded gun? "No."

Did he go behind them and shoot them? "No."

"Like rats in a trap?"

"No!" he answered, letting a little emotion show.

Horwood-Smart then put the ballistic evidence of the ejected cartridges to him. She pointed out to him that he fired the first and second shots from the entrance to the room. "No."

In fact, Horwood-Smart missed the most likely proof that Tony shot from actually inside the doorway entrance. As soon as a shooter fires a shot from a pump-action shotgun, he immediately reloads. This would be even more likely with someone holding, as Tony was, the gun "cowboy style", to use Detective Peters phrase. The first ejected cartridge on such a scenario would definitely mark where the first shot was fired. This cartridge was inside the breakfast room.

She put to him that he shot them "when by the flickering torch you could see where they were?"

"No."

She put to him that he was not a frightened man that night but an angry man. Tony denied that, "I was a very frightened man." She then returned to the unlikely scenario of him holding the gun and the hand rail at the same time as he crossed the gaps in the staircase, which would have meant he was in a position where it would be impossible to fire a weapon.

"This is what they're saying." Tony replied.

She retorted, "It's what you agree with, isn't it?"

Rosamund Horwood-Smart put to Martin that he must have known he had hit someone, that he must have heard the cries of Barras, that it seemed odd that he didn't reload but still carried the gun around and, most of all, that he had not told the truth.

She took him through his behaviour after the shooting: driving around his garden, then out on the road still hell-bent on revenge, being "a law unto himself". He rejected all her accusations and inferences.

It didn't matter. Tony was already utterly discredited.

But she wasn't finished. Horwood-Smart also raised the problem that in his first interview with the police Tony had colluded in their information – gleaned from Fearon – that there was only one burglar in Bleak House. She reminded him that he'd told the police officers the day after the shooting that he did not want to talk about his experience.

As obtuse as ever Tony replied, "I did talk about it the next day to the police officers."

She reminded him of what he had said, "A horrendous experience and you didn't want to speak about it."

Scriv jumped up to stall any further questions and said to her, "I thought that we had an agreed version of what happened?" She replied that they did have an agreement. Scriv said dryly, "Well, can you keep to it."

Tony then butted in from the witness box, "Well, I'd got myself into what you call a…is it a surreal situation. I mean I just can't…"

Scrivener then interrupted proceedings and asked to make an application in the absence of the jury. The upshot of this was that Owen allowed Horwood-Smart to question Martin on his answers to Peters, but ruled: "I am not going to allow any comment saying that the jury can make a statutory conclusion supporting the prosecution case, but I said throughout I cannot see any reason why it should not be asked."

The jury came back in and Horwood-Smart asked Tony if he'd known from the questions put to him by Peters that the police believed only one burglar had entered his farmhouse.

"I was aware of that, yes," Martin replied dutifully.

She put the question again just in case Martin pretended that he didn't understand what was being put to him. Martin affirmed that he knew the police had been lied to. Horwood-Smart homed in on the obvious, "Why did you not tell them what had happened?"

Martin answered as if it was clear as day, "I did not know who was there."

Deliberately allowing her exasperation to show, Horwood-Smart tightened the noose, "Why did you not tell them what had happened?"

Martin locked horns with her, "I got the impression that the police did know what had happened."

Horwood-Smart looked at him contemptuously, "And that is your answer, is it?"

Martin, knowing that he had been bushwhacked by her, went into walkabout mode, "You're saying that Fearon made a statement to the King's Lynn police and you're asking me that... You said to me that I knew that what they told the police was not correct about the man walking up the gravel, the driveway, saying that I walked out of my front door..."

Justice Owen decided to block off Martin's segue into obtuseness, "I do not think we got into detail like that at all." The unimpressed tone of Justice Owen pushed Martin into apologising.

"I am sorry," he interjected. "I was being asked what the situation was and I was told that..."

Justice Owen decided to nail Martin, "No. All that is being said is that you were aware that Fearon had been seen and had not told the truth." And, as if taking to a recalcitrant child, "Right?"

In the face of determination from the bench to keep to the point, Martin decided he'd better keep to it, too, "That is what I was told, yes."

Justice Owen pressed on, "So you were asked..."

Martin, though, knowing that his answer had got him closer to where he did not want to go decided to confuse matters again, "Sorry, My Lord, I'm not deliberately..."

Justice Owen ploughed on, "Then, if you were asked, why did you not say..."

Martin blinked and started to look confused...

"Are we in more difficulty again?" Justice Owen sighed.

"Alright. Why didn't you say, because it was clear to you that they (the police) didn't know there was a second person there..."

Martin always ready to be pedantic again interrupted, "I didn't know there was a second person there."

Justice Owen knew that he was digging a hole for himself but carried on digging nonetheless, "Why did you not say: 'Well, I gained the impression there were two or even three there?' Owen looked away and stared into the middle-distance. "That is the only real point," Justice Owen concluded.

Martin felt that he had trailed enough red herrings over this one to put anyone off the scent and just replied meekly, "I can't remember what I said at the time."

Horwood Smart, knowing that Justice Owen had had enough of this particular trail, intervened now: "I do not need to ask you any more about that…"

She did not really ask Tony any more questions, she merely put to him that most of his evidence had been lies. He denied each accusation.

Tony's defence called four more witnesses, one was John Allen, who was an area sales manager for Omex Agriculture Ltd. He confirmed the amount of theft of agricultural equipment in the area, but did not add much to the case.

An old friend, Richard Portham, and a new friend, Stuart Mayfield testified to Martin's sound personality and confirmed the atrocious levels of crime in the area. The final defence witness was a gift to the defence. She was a staff member from the Glen Parva Young Offenders' Institution. She remained anonymous because of the bounty put on Martin's head by the Newark gypsies. The female witness recounted how she had met Fred Barras at Glen Parva, shortly before the Bleak House shooting.

"He was boasting about a big job he was gonna do at a Norfolk farmhouse. It stuck in my mind because the boys don't normally talk about crimes they are about to commit," she said softly. Martin had been told it was coming but he huffed and shuffled his papers when she said it, as if with those words she had vindicated his defence.

MONDAY 17TH APRIL: DAY SIX

Rosamund Horwood-Smart QC: Closing Speech

Horwood-Smart summarised much of what she had put to Martin: "Members of the jury…the evidence that the Crown has presented to you proves beyond a shadow of a doubt that Mr Martin is guilty of all that he is charged with, including murder. It is understandable that some of you may feel sympathy for Mr Martin's predicament and circumstances, as a hard working farmer plagued by thieves. He was a victim of crime and he became disgruntled with the ineffectiveness of the police at investigating reports of theft made by him and other farmers in the area. But Mr Martin allowed his resentment to fester into a hatred of those he viewed as mainly responsible for these thefts and burglaries – light-fingered pikies, gypsies.

"And do you remember him giving evidence and denying saying that or even using the term, 'pikies'. Was his neighbour Mr Huggins lying when he told you that is what Mr Martin said to him, when he spoke to him two days before the shooting? Were the police lying who told you that he would like to herd gypsies into a field and machine-gun them? Was the policewoman whom he spoke to when he reported his May burglary lying when she said that if the thieves returned he would blow their heads off? Was his Farm Watch associate lying when he told you that is what Mr Martin publicly advocated at one meeting?

"Mr Martin developed an irrational hatred for light-fingered pikies and he turned his farm into a fortress for fighting them. He lashed ladders to trees around his house to use as look-out posts, he bolted and barred most places of entry, he booby-trapped his stairs, he had three Rottweilers patrolling his land and he acquired an illegal pump-action Winchester shotgun. Mr Martin was a man that knew the power, force, and damage that a shotgun can inflict. He had that gun for one particular reason. He had that gun to use, if and when the occasion arose, to shoot any intruder who had the temerity to come in to his property, into his home, on to his land. We say he was a man who was waiting for intruders... And when they came he did what he said he would do, he shot them. This was not a blind shooting. Nor was it a shooting done out of fright. Mr Martin shot out of anger.

"Nor did he shoot from the staircase. He was not on the staircase when he fired the first shot – the scientific evidence proves that. Even Mr Martin accepts that you can't fire bullets round corners. He fired from the entrance to the breakfast room. The evidence of the ejected cartridges and the ballistic evidence of the spread of the shot point to him being some 4 to 5 metres from his victims. At the entrance to the breakfast room. That is the evidence, the objective evidence. Yet, Mr Martin says he was on the stairs – 'the safest place' to be was how he put it to you. Why did he lie? We say he lied because he was downstairs. He saw those burglars cross the hallway and enter the breakfast room, then he ambushed them. He shot them like rats in a trap.

"He shot them with a gun that, as the firearms expert told you, was well-oiled and well-maintained. Yet, according to Mr Martin he had not used or even loaded that gun in the several years it had been in his possession. According to him, it lay under his bed!! And I will not go into his absurd account of how he acquired it. In the two months that Mr Arnold the firearms expert had it in his possession, it developed rust inside the barrels. Again Mr Martin lied to you. Again you must ask yourselves why. Why did he lie? He lied because that gun was his armoury for fighting thieves. He kept that gun well-maintained and oiled as he did not know when he was going to need it. And when he did need it, that gun was in tip-top condition.

"He was never upstairs when the torch shone in his face, if it ever did. You saw the stairs when you visited Bleak House. Ask yourself if it is possible for a 54-year-old man, who he told you is not very strong since he developed thrombosis, could step over that 3-tread gap at the top of his stairs, holding that Winchester in his right hand (she pointed at the exhibited gun), which is on the side of the hand rail, then negotiate the gap at the bottom of the stairs with the aluminium ladder bridge, without stumbling or, at least, alerting the intruders? Possible! Ask yourself why he is lying.

"Mr Martin was a man who was prepared to be a police force, investigating force, jury, judge and, if necessary, executioner. All the evidence, including Mr Martin's evasiveness, illogical and lying answers in the witness box, lead to only one conclusion: he had waited while Fearon and Barras broke in, then as they stole from his possessions he shot them, as I have already said, like rats in a trap. But he did not use not merely disproportionate and unreasonable force, he has lied and lied again to cover up the way he deliberately ambushed these burglars. He murdered them just as surely as they broke into his farmhouse."

Anthony Scrivener QC: Closing Speech

Anthony Scrivener followed her with a closing that was short and sweet. Tony Martin had been a victim of crime. Time and time again, his farmhouse had been raided by thieves and he had become desperate at the way he felt the police had left farmers like him to fend for themselves. He did not lure these burglars into his house nor did he know they were coming. He was no vigilante who set out to administer rough justice by setting up these thieves, then gunning them down like rats in a trap.

Justice Owen: Summing Up

Mr Justice Owen reminded the jury of how they should decide their verdict... "So how do you decide? Well there are various rules which, please, you must accept. The first is you decide on the evidence. You do not decide on emotion. You do not decide on sympathy... You are here to decide on the evidence which you have heard and unlike many" – Owen's thoughts drifted outside Court Number One to the gathering press – "you have heard it all."

He then launched into a long, rambling summation of the case that, as far as Martin's case was concerned, was a bit like the curate's egg. The good bits, though, definitely outweighed the bad bits. Nonetheless, it was not a summing up that either by content or tone of voice cued the jury up to find Martin not guilty. True, it was loaded in his favour, but the unfolding of the evidence had already damned him. Perhaps the worst that could be indisputably said against it was that it was muddled and boring. And it spilled over into day seven of the trial.

TUESDAY 18TH APRIL: DAY SEVEN

In the morning, he directed the jury on the law as regards the various charges, the most important being that even if Tony had not set out to kill, but he fired intending "to cause some really serious injury" he was guilty of murder. "The person who murders does not have to intend to kill. It would be sufficient to show that he intended to cause some really serious injury."

Most judges in such circumstances do not use "really", so Owen is seen to favour Martin.

He then directed them on the possibility that they might find that Martin had only intended to cause physical, albeit not serious, harm. If this turned out to be the case, they could bring in a verdict of manslaughter. He then explained the criteria for assessing that, but again leant over backwards to favour Tony. The issue of self-defence he explained clearly and succinctly: did Tony believe he was in danger of being attacked and was what he did in the face of that threat reasonable?

The jury retired at 12.30 and deliberated until 4.30, when they went home.

WEDNESDAY 19TH APRIL: DAY EIGHT

The Verdict

The shrewd money was on a verdict sometime on Wednesday. The body language of the jurors…the way the trial had gone, it looked a good bet.

It meant an early start for Eli Frankham, Peter Chilton and their cousin Dave Frankham. They set off from Newark at 8 am, so that they would be at Norwich reasonably early. No sooner had they pulled into the car park on Bishopgate at 9.30, they met one of Fred's cousins. He told them that he had already been briefing the press about the *kris* and that Martin was "a dead man".

This time Eli had to bung the old gypsy woman twenty pounds to get three tickets. She said, "But they's a lot of people want them today. It be verdict today, see." She had eight urchins in the queue.

"I had to give her twenty quid!" Eli said in disbelief as he got back in the car. He added, "We'll have to be a bit lively…it starts soon." They piled into court to await first Owen, then Martin, then the jury.

The three moved onto a bench at the very back of the gallery, more or less as Owen was preparing to send the jury out to continue their deliberations. But the gypsies' presence did not go unnoticed. Scriv clocked them early and leant over to his junior, Stobbard, who turned to Martin's solicitor Makin, who sat on the bench behind. In turn, Makin alerted the clerk who approached Justice Owen.

"A important matter has been brought to my attention. The court will rise for a short adjournment." He asked the jury to retire to their jury room while the issue was dealt with, then everyone rose. Owen left the court. Before another word was spoken by counsel, the gypsies were marched out of the court by the ushers with some burly police officers in attendance. Outside, their passes were confiscated.

Eli protested, "You can't do this. I've got the right to…I'm related to Fred Barras."

The usher quietly explained that matters had been brought to his attention, which he believed to be of such seriousness that he had decided their presence would interfere with the course of justice. They could, of course, protest to the Lord Chancellor's office…

The expulsion caught the reporters in court by surprise, but it wasn't long before some of them were flocking around the three expelled tearaways, conjuring up copy about curses, hexes and the "evil eye". Eli played it cool, he wasn't going to get in trouble for jury nobbling again.

"I was only jury watching, everyone does it," said Eli

"I'd just seen it on telly and thought – that looks interesting," Peter Chilton piped up.

Inside the court the jury were brought back in. Owen carried on as if nothing had happened. The jury were sent out to continue their deliberations.

At 12.30 the jury reached their verdict, finding Tony not guilty of attempted murder and possessing a firearm with intent to endanger life. Owen now directed that he accept a majority verdict of up to ten to two. They returned three hours later and found Tony guilty of murder and wounding with intent both on a ten to two majority. Flanked by two dock officers, Tony stood to receive the verdict. He remained impassive.

On the other hand, relatives of Barras in the gallery shouted out in delight; from the way the jury had decided on the lesser charges they had become pessimistic about getting a guilty verdict on murder. Owen glanced sternly at those responsible for the interruption but did not rebuke them. The usher merely muttered, "Order, order, order in court…"

Tony sat down at the urging of the dock officers. Owen took down some notes, before asking Tony to stand again to be sentenced to life, for murder, and to 10 years for wounding with intent. Tony again said nothing and remained expressionless.

Owen, ever courteous, addressed Martin and the court, "Sit down, would you." Tony did.

He later joked, "Streuth, he had me going up and down like a jack-in-box. I began to wonder what it was doing to my old blood clots in the legs."

Owen continued, "The outcome of any trial depends on the evidence before the Court and, in my opinion, rarely are generalisations justified. However, it seems to me that this case does serve as a dire warning to all burglars who break into the houses of other people. The law is that every citizen is entitled to use reasonable force to prevent crime. Burglary is a crime, a householder in his own home may think he is being reasonable but he may not be reasonable and that can have tragic consequences. A trial also serves to emphasise the fact that householders also have a responsibility."

Owen was careful not to compliment the jury on their verdict. But he did thank them for their attentiveness and the obvious care they gave to the matter. After some other remarks concerning the threats made to Tony's life, which were a disgrace to any country that tries to live by the rule of law, he turned to the last outstanding matter, having a firearm without a certificate.

In direct contrast with his tone on the matter in his summing up, he said, "In the wrong hands, a repeating shotgun is a fearsome weapon. You should not have had that and I am quite satisfied in my mind that had you applied to have a licence which would have enabled you to have that firearm, it would have been refused."

As Tony was taken down, one of Fred Barras's sisters shouted,

"I hope you die in jail." Tony was driven to Norwich Prison. Outside the courthouse, Ellen Barras, with her daughters and estranged husband, read out a statement to the press: "We are aware that Fred had failings and would have expected him to be dealt with and punished in the criminal justice system. He was not given that chance. Fred was fun-loving and always happy, with no mean streak. He was a devoted and loving son and brother. Please remember that he was just 16 and the baby of our family. We are all devastated by his loss."

Fred senior was not that devastated, as six weeks later, wearing a balaclava and armed, he tied up a woman security guard and held a gun to her head during a £400,000 raid on a clothing warehouse. In June 2002, he was sentenced to 14 years.

CHAPTER 7

APPEAL – PALM TREE JUSTICE!

Once upon a time, when Britain ruled the world, all manner of civil servants were posted around the Empire burdened with the onerous task of bringing British Justice to the 'natives'. These emissaries of civilization found that English law books and practice were of little use in societies that placed more faith in consulting chicken entrails. As a consequence they put their legal training to one side and muddled along using common sense and the customs of the country. One compensation was that more often than not these lands were in hotter climes than our own, so they could find themselves working in tepee and baggy khaki shorts, sitting in the shade of a palm tree while being served iced tea by dusky maidens in colourful sarongs. Back in Blighty this kind of law-making was affectionately known as "palm tree justice".

With the demise of Empire, the concept looked like it was doomed to be a colonial anachronism that would live on only in the memories of those who had dispensed it. However, in 1966, an Oxford Professor of Jurisprudence, Dr John Morris, hijacked the term and applied it to judgments where the Court of Appeal departed from the established rule of law and decided cases by principles of their own choosing. Generally, these principles were sourced from public opinion. At its most extreme this new form of palm tree justice meant that legal disputes were decided by public opinion or, more often, by influential pressure groups working through the media and only ratified by our higher judiciary.

This development had some worrying side effects, not least that the judiciary was usurping parliament as well as disregarding the integrity of common law, but also had the consequence of freeing those prisoners who attracted public sympathy or, better still, widespread support.

After Martin was sentenced to life imprisonment, the murder squad's headquarters, which were based in Norwich, was bombarded with hate mail and deluged with anonymous and even named callers blaming the constabulary for this latest travesty of Blair's Britain. An officer said it felt like the American Embassy in Saigon just before they pulled out and left it to the Viet Cong. Someone said we better lease the helicopter again in case they storm the building. They blamed us for his conviction! But Tony Martin had a fair crack of the whip. The investigation was conducted with impeccable respect for his rights.

The squad may well have acted scrupulously in its investigations but the fact was that Tony Martin went down for murder, which his fan club not only felt was unjust but also believed was the fault of the police for putting him in the situation where he'd been forced to defend himself.

Indeed, Justice Owen seemed to agree in his sentencing comments: "...there has been another aspect of the evidence and that has been complaints by farmers, including Farm Watch, about the number of burglaries in the country areas of Norfolk... one does not hear what has been done to attend to those difficulties, nor does one hear the extent of the difficulties, but I believe it is right to say that those complaints should be brought to the attention of the Chief Constable."

In his circumspect but very unusual comment, Owen hinted that Tony Martin took the law into his own hands partly because those paid to enforce the law had failed in their duty. This was the context in which Tony's legal team ran self-defence as an answer to the murder charge.

Owen's comments gave the press the green light on how they would report Tony's conviction. The editorial line had generally been pro-Martin from the moment of arrest – now the support came in spades, with the Norfolk police getting it in the neck along the way. Malcolm Starr had taken over the reins of press management from Max Clifford and, despite having no experience at the job, was no less effective. It was also a lot cheaper for the journalists. Pro-Martin stories, anecdotes and leaks were carefully channelled down the phone line to those journalists who wanted to reflect the disgust of "all right-thinking people" – i.e. their readership – at this grotesque miscarriage of justice.

Richard Littlejohn in The Sun, 22nd April, was the most forthright exponent of Tony's cause. The Sun ran straw polls on the Martin issue throughout the case and, at one point one poll was running 30-1 in the farmer's favour:

"Britain is united in the belief that there has been a serious miscarriage of justice… Front-line coppers are frustrated and angry at the attitudes and priorities of their senior officers. The top brass seem interested solely in advancing their own careers by sucking up to The Guardian readers in the Home Office and pandering to their obsession with the politics of race and sex and the rights of criminals…

"…Anyone who dares disagree with them is smeared as an extremist or part of the dreaded forces of conservatism. But they are the real extremists, on everything from the promotion of homosexuality in schools to their determination to scrap the pound. They pose as liberals, but in reality they are crypto-fascists."

Littlejohn makes a habit of going over the top but usually to a purpose:

"...the prosecution and the police went out of their way to demonise Martin as a bloodthirsty eccentric... the New Establishment believes there is no difference between the rights of burglars and the rights of householders."

Everyone in the country is governed by the due process of law and has rights, including burglars. One right that burglars enjoy is that the law protects them from angry and revengeful householders. And your typical burglar is often younger than 16. The legal doctrine that checks vigilantism is "reasonable force". Justice Owen again opened a window on his own views when he said that the Martin trial did "serve as a dire warning to all burglars who break into the houses of other people...while every citizen is entitled to use force to prevent crime, it must be reasonable force."

What degree of force is considered "reasonable" is what, in the circumstances, the jury decides is reasonable. This is why cases that are similar in circumstance can produce entirely different verdicts. What is defined as reasonable force is what any particular jury says it is. Some judges offer a jury guidance but there is no set standard, and all Owen told the Martin jury was: "...should he have shouted, should he have fired one shot and so on. These are arguments which will best be considered by you and are required to be considered by you and certainly not by me."

This is how trials of a defendant arguing self-defence are, in practical terms, decided. Judging whether an action is reasonable or unreasonable, then, is different in kind, not degree, from judging whether a fact or evidence is true or untrue.

In the United States, a criminal who breaks into a property with intent to steal is considered fair game and, in most jurisdictions in that country, what Tony Martin did would have been deemed justifiable homicide. Between the Wars our law was not dissimilar. In 1924, the Lord Chief Justice ruled:

"in defence of a man's house, the owner or his family may kill a trespasser who would forcibly dispossess him of it, in the same way as he might, by law, kill in self-defence a man who attacks him personally".

In the wake of the Martin trial, Norfolk's Chief Constable Carry-On Kenneth, as Tony dubbed him, advised those who found themselves in Tony's position:

"If you hear a burglar, the best thing to do is scream."

A MORI poll commissioned by the Daily Mail taken in the 48 hours following Tony's conviction and sentencing found that seventy-five per cent of respondents sympathised with Martin, but only four per cent sympathised solely with 16-year old Fred Barras.

Predictably, soon after the results of this poll were announced, Anne Widdecombe waded in again. Ever the tireless chugger for Middle England's causes, she took the opportunity to earn some brownie points by preaching what would earn her a standing ovation at the next party conference. Widders commented, "Whatever the wrongdoing in this case, we must not let it obscure the genuine concern that people do not feel able to take reasonable and sensible measures to defend themselves. I think it's quite right to say 'have a go' as long as one is responsible about it."

She argued that it was reasonable for householders to use force to defend their property and that, short of killing, the law should countenance them to do so. She said, "In a case where there's a dead body on the floor there would have to be a trial. But if you go down to what is far more common, which is people hitting a burglar over the head, then my view is that it is unacceptable that a person is at risk of prosecution. There needs to be a much greater presumption on the part of the police and the Crown Prosecution Service that force is reasonable in those circumstances and, therefore, there won't be a case to answer."

The then-Conservative Party leader William Hague made similar pledges about a future Conservative government. He said that the Martin case had "lit a touch paper that has led to an explosion of anger". He trotted out a raft of policies: new guidelines to the Crown Prosecution Service on exercising "greater restraint" when dealing with cases of self-defence, and "a strong presumption that in future the state will be on the side of people who protect their homes against criminals". It was all very predictable – local elections were in the offing.

He was accused of fostering a "lynch-mob mentality" but what rather soured his political opportunism was Tony's comments from Bullingdon Prison, Oxfordshire, where he had been relocated because of death threats. He told the Daily Mail, "…what William Hague said about people who defend their homes against intruders will have the law stacked in their favour under the Tories is admirable, but this huge increase in rural crime hasn't just happened during this Labour Government. It was increasing while the Conservative Party was in power, too."

The final nails in the coffin of the Tory pledges were the disclosures that the last Tory government looked at the law on self-defence but "decided we had other priorities" and the discovery that, in 1991, Hague had himself voted against proposals to abolish mandatory life sentences for murder. Labour made hay with all this.

Meanwhile the Hague-Widders bandwagon got bogged down in the intellectual and legal critique that it attracted and, in

December 2000, a Tory spokesman sheepishly announced that they were no longer planning to change the law in respect of self defence.

In fact, Justice Owen recommended that Tony Martin serve a minimum of 9 years of his life sentence before being considered for release on licence; the Lord Chief Justice reduced this tariff to 8 years. An 8-year *recc* for a lifer is roughly equivalent to a 14-year fixed sentence. Owen would almost certainly have passed a lesser sentence if he'd had to take into account Tony's history of break-ins, the poor police response to his complaints, his general anger over rising crime and his shaky mental health. However, making a psychological plea of mitigation to a judge prior to sentencing is quite different from doing the same thing to a jury to acquit or convict on a lesser charge.

If Tony's pre-trial psychiatrist, Dr Maden, had diagnosed some kind of personality disorder, say paranoia, then Tony could have been presented as someone who would scare more easily than the ordinary person. Without psychiatric back-up, though, pleading self-defence was really an all or nothing strategy – murder or acquittal. It left the jury with hardly any middle ground to rest on a manslaughter verdict.

An alternative defence – provocation – was thrashed out with Tony. This involves claiming that the killing was the result of a sudden and temporary loss of control in the face of something said or done, which any reasonable person could see themselves doing likewise. As a defence to murder it is a bit like diminished responsibility: it denies murder but admits to manslaughter. Ballinger said, "Heat of the moment, lost control… We could have plea bargained for it. I am sure the prosecution would have entertained the idea… But Tony wanted to run with murder or nothing." Self-defence is just that: guilty or not guilty, it does allow the jury to default to manslaughter.

Tony had obeyed Ballinger's 11th commandment in court and a lot of good it did him. Now in Bullingdon he pontificated with a vengeance to the press over the phone. Meanwhile Max was in London drumming up even more Martyr-Martin articles, Hague and Widders were still on the bandwagon and Nick Makin and Michael Ballinger were drawing up the grounds of appeal…when a member of the jury decided to take over the circus.

A Norwich based commercial radio station, Broadland 102.4 FM, had received a phone call allegedly from one of the female jurors who spoke off-air to a presenter. The station refused to reveal the details of the phone conversation publicly but the Press Association put them out over the wire. Makin thought he had retrial material and whipped up a media frenzy, claiming that the juror was intimidated into voting guilty because of fears of reprisals. One of Makin's soundbites for the press: "We suspected there was a degree of intimidation or an intention to intimidate by these people going to the court. We are asking witnesses and jurors to contact us if they did feel intimidated by these people. Mr Martin should have had a fair trial and that may not have been the case."

Max immediately issued a denial that he was behind the woman's claim but he quickly fed into the national press that the caller had told the radio station that the trial had "changed her life", and how she felt "frightened to leave her house". She claimed that the jury was intimidated or, as the media had it, nobbled.

A spokeswoman for the station said the woman caller who claimed to have been a juror had not spoken of being "intimidated, pressured or nobbled". The spokeswoman for Broadlands said, "We want to clarify what was said because we feel that it has been misreported in some respects and want to set the record straight. I have read the transcript of what the alleged juror actually said and what was reported on air and at no point were the words 'intimidation' or 'pressure' or 'nobbled' mentioned at all."

Nick Makin wrote excitedly to Martin with news of the 'dramatic development' concerning the jury. 'We do not have concrete evidence at the moment' wrote Makin, but M&S 'are appealing to the public to let us have concrete evidence of this. If the story does prove to be correct, then obviously this will have a substantial impact on an immediate appeal.'

The Lord Chancellor's Department was informed but was not impressed, "There has been no formal complaint from jurors of any intimidation. There is nothing to investigate at present."

Eventually Scrivener made an application to the High Court on June 19th 2000 for the Registrar, an official of the Court, to write to each juror and ask if he or she had been intimidated or influenced in any way by outside pressure. The delicacy of this operation – a jury's deliberations are considered sacrosanct – was such that the press were ordered not to report what the jury were asked. In the event no jurors claimed that their deliberations were influenced in any untoward way. As Mr Justice Tomlinson had ordered "if there is not (any untoward influence) it can be forgotten" and, once it was discovered there was no improper influence, it was forgotten.

However, at the same time as Scrivener made this application, he made another one for legal aid for the appeal. Justice Tomlinson queried Martin's finances.

Scrivener replied, "We filled in a form, I believe." He paused. The Legal Aid position had by that stage become indefensible.

Tomlinson ruled, "Mr Scrivener, for reasons which it is not necessary to address at this stage, we think it would be better if that application is made subsequently rather than today."

By mid-June, M&S were in a tailspin over Martin's buried assets. The reason they had been discovered was that Tony, as always, was lazy about covering his tracks. On May 10th, Ballinger wrote to the Court of Appeal seeking confirmation that Legal Aid had been extended to cover the appeal. The judge dealing with the matter – Master Mackenzie – said that he could not confirm anything until Martin's Statement of Means was properly completed. Martin did this on 16th May 2000 with the help of his legal eagles. Nonetheless, as Makin was later to point out in a letter, although they assisted him 'it was he (Martin) who provided the information'.

On the form Tony had admitted owning a £30,000 house on land worth another £80,000. In fact, Bleak House at the time was worth upwards of £750,000. Nor did he declare that he owned another farm near Bungay, some tied cottages in the March area and that he had recently bought further farmland nearby Bleak House for £87,000. He filled in the document to the effect that he had no income or savings or other property, but under "Further Information" he referred to the Support Fund run by M&S: "No one has paid fees in respect of these proceedings but there is a discretionary trust fund from a public appeal over which I have no control at all that has made contributions towards expenses. I have no guarantee of future contributions. Further information can obtained from my solicitors."

The Legal Services Commission, which oversees these matters were not nonplussed, they just held their noses. They contacted M&S... Ballinger was put on the case and he discovered, after talking to Martin's accountant, the facts about the £87,000 in cash that Tony had drawn out of the bank to buy land just before the trial. When Ballinger confronted Martin, he waffled away about how it was money he owed his mother and that, with the trial coming up, he had decided to repay it. Typically Tony hadn't told Hilary about this and, when Ballinger queried it with her, she told him that this was the first time she'd heard about it. And more of Martin's monies came to light: the farm was making a substantial profit, which he'd concealed and there were other investments, including a joint £70,000 investment with a monthly pay out for both Hilary and Tony.

His Legal Aid Certificate was revoked for work on the appeal. M&S were not happy bunnies. Makin went back to prison to rub Tony's nose in the dirt.

For once Martin came clean – he admitted he'd lied about giving the eighty-seven grand to his mother but he refused to tell Makin where the money had gone. He did agree that Makin could tell the Legal Services Commission that they could now take the £87,000 into account. However, as Makin was now pressing upon him his liability to fund M&S's unpaid costs, he virtually instructed them to stop working on his appeal.

In fact, they had already submitted an appeal on April 28th on the grounds that Owen misdirected the jury on various issues of law. This was backed up by other minor grounds. For example, Owen pointed out, in response to Helen Lilley's claim that Tony was kind to her grandchildren, that as Hitler and Stalin were said to be kind to children this didn't take the jury very far. Any criminal lawyer would regard such grounds as clutching at straws, but clients like it, which is good for business. Initially, Tony was optimistic that the appeal would succeed but when his Legal Aid con unravelled he became more concerned about having to fund his own legal costs than challenging his life sentence.

His legal eagles did, though, come up with some new evidence on which they could ask for a re-trial. Nick Makin found the elusive bag of cartridges that Martin had said were in his bedroom and he'd used to load the Winchester. The police had not been able to find them, albeit they had thoroughly searched and photographed the bedroom.

Ballinger was rather boastful of this example of M&S's Perry Mason style of defending Martin. When he was asked why they had not searched the bedroom before the trial, he replied, "It first became an issue during the trial as…" Then he said in his mock prosecuting counsel's voice, "He said he got them from the bedroom and, there is no bag!!" The police had searched from top to bottom and not found it, now, 'Should we go and have a look there?' And we thought, No. It is not going to make a blind bit of difference. The jury either likes him or they hate him. But when it comes to an appeal ground! we can say, *Aha. New evidence, we better have another trial.* It was tactically better to find those things afterwards." His aghast expression showed they would never plant them. "I mean we didn't…"

Scrivener's notes on the matter made interesting reading: "The house had been thoroughly searched by Norfolk police over many weeks. I had personally been to the house before trial and into the bedroom where Mr Martin said he had a bag of cartridges and I did not suggest a search should be made. There were statements from police officers who searched the bedroom. I was very surprised when out of the blue Mr Makin telephoned me to say he had found the cartridges."

While all this was going on, the cavalry thundered over the horizon in the rather large frame of Peter Sainsbury, the General Secretary of the People's Opportunity for Work Trust (POW). This charity assists the "socially excluded", which seems to be life's waifs and strays as well as those recently released from a spell at Her Majesty's pleasure.

POW doesn't do therapy, so there is no counselling to help offenders address their offending behaviour. Sainsbury has neither a social science degree nor any training in penology, so as far as the therapeutic debate is concerned he sounds a bit simple-minded. His sole idea seems to be work. "We get them working and if they don't, won't, shirk or refuse work, we get rid of them. The way I see it is if they are working, they're too busy to be a nuisance."

Whatever the merits of Sainsbury's approach he exudes bonhomie and goodwill, which he spreads liberally. Someone once compared his style of praising everyone to that of Thatcher's first Home Secretary Willie Whitelaw. On one prison inspection, Willie was famously shown around a Lifers' Wing and, as some of the inmates attempted to buttonhole him with their grievances, he just strode past saying, "Splendid, splendid. Keep up the good work."

Afterwards one of his aides asked him if it was wise to make such an insensitive remark and Whitelaw replied, "What else can you say to people who have got themselves locked up for life?" Sainsbury has more than a touch of the Willie Whitelaws.

When Tony Martin was convicted, one of the lawyers who worked for POW had a look at the case. He picked up that Martin had been defended by two local solicitors who did not practise criminal law, the jury had come in 10-2, the conviction looked shaky, Martin was clearly an oddball but the public were sending donations to fund his defence. Yes…this was right in POW's bailiwick: Sainsbury set the POW machine into action, writing to Martin who responded enthusiastically.

POW quickly exposed the antics of M&S and began to press Martin to change solicitors. They briefed a hotshot London criminal solicitor named James Saunders. Saunders' charges at the time were £200 per hour; his main assistant on the case was £150 per hour – Makin was £250 and Ballinger £195. As Saunders reviewed the papers that POW sent him, he went ballistic at M&S's invoicing practices. Eventually, with Martin's agreement, he reported them to the Law Society for their alleged financial shenanigans. Tony shilly-shallied on dumping M&S but in August

2000, a week after they submitted a bill of £37,028 for their work on his appeal, he sacked them.

Despite a bombardment of accusations from Saunders, Makin stood his ground, especially over the thirty-seven grand. His trump card was the case papers and he refused to hand them over until his firm was paid. Saunders took the dispute to the High Court by which time an additional ground of appeal had been filed: "The solicitor acting for the defendant failed to prepare the case properly and failed to advise the defendant properly as to the various defences available to him." Actually, the strongest ground was Tony's mental health, which counsel at this hearing claimed "jumped out of the papers".

Really what jumped off the page, given Martin's crackpot manner, was that M&S had not hired a psychiatrist for the original murder trial who could have found some kind of personality disorder that would have allowed him much more latitude in the use of reasonable force. M&S did not know the ropes in this area. They clearly were not practised in sourcing sympathetic expert witnesses. They played it by the book, overly confident of acquittal, but inexperience here is not incompetence.

There were more hearings at the High Court over the case papers and a further attempt was made to obtain Legal Aid, although the panel of judges were completely dismissive of the latter. In September 2000, after a legal dogfight, Martin's new counsel, Michael Wolkind QC, failed at an attempt to secure the case papers that Makin still clung onto (as security on his unpaid £37,000 invoice). The Appeal Court were understandably reluctant to ignore the fraudulent Means Form that Martin had filled out for the original trial. Michael Wolkind tried his best to sidestep the issue but Lord Justice Kennedy was having none of it.

At one stage an exasperated Kennedy told Wolkind, "The position is quite simple as it seems to me. There is that sum of money withdrawn. Your client is in a position to tell the Court where it is and to pay in the court, on the face of it or not to pay into court, but pay to you some £37,000."

Peter Sainsbury paced up and down the corridor outside the court chamber, thinking about all those donations and the publicity... Justice Kennedy, however, was adamant and impressed upon Wolkind that, if Tony didn't come clean about his £87,000 withdrawal and pay Makin, then his appeal would have to go ahead without the papers.

"If he does", Justice Kennedy hammered home, "then progress can be made with the criminal appeal. If he chooses not to do that you are not going to get the information that you require."

As Martin was still more concerned at casting himself as a victim of circumstance, Tony's mother stepped in: Hilary paid £37,000 to Saunders (to be held as security until the end of the Appeal) and M&S handed over the case papers. In fact, after legal adjudication on M&S's bill, the £37,000 was whittled down to around £8,000.

The grounds of appeal were prepared and Martin was interviewed by a psychiatrist and a psychologist, both of whom submitted reports that were adduced in evidence. Three fresh ballistics expert were also commissioned to produce reports.

There were seven grounds of appeal at the hearing in October 2001 before Lord Chief Justice Woolf, Mr Justice Wright and Mr Justice Grigson. Wolkind led for the appellant and Horwood-Smart for the Crown. Martin was present at the Appeal, having been transferred to Pentonville. Woolf delivered the judgment. He noted in his preamble that "Because he was being burgled, at the time, there was considerable public sympathy for Mr Martin and media interest in his case. There were also suggestions that the law was in need of change."

Woolf quickly dismissed any criticism of Owen's directions on the law of self-defence but he considered the claim that the way the defence case had been prepared and presented had denied Martin a fair trial. As this overlapped with another ground – that the new forensic evidence supported self-defence – these were dealt with together. The forensic evidence from the ballistics experts argued that Martin could possibly have fired the first shot from the stairs. Indeed, this had been agreed as a possibility by both defence and Crown experts in their reports at trial.

Scrivener did not run with this at trial, nor did he cross-examine Fearon about his first statement in which he claimed that when the first shot was fired he saw Martin on the stairs. Instead Scrivener kept to the version that Fearon switched to when he went with the police to the farmhouse to reconstruct the events of the shooting. The reason Martin's counsel didn't put this was that the positions of the spent cartridges would have put Tony in hot pursuit of the burglars.

If he had fired the first shot from the stairs, then the three cartridge cases found by the fireplace meant he had not racked the pump-action after he fired the first shot – which in itself is so unlikely as to be absurd – but negotiated the bottom gap in the staircase holding his unprimed Winchester, entered the breakfast room, then racked the next cartridge into the breech, ejecting the shell of the one he'd fired on the staircase, then let off two more around that position. And here we have to factor in the astonishing marksmanship of being on the stairs and hitting Barras at a very acute angle without a single pellet touching the entrance to the breakfast room. But even if we do, the fact is that this is not someone in fear of his life and firing in self-defence. Thus, Tony would have been going from the frying pan into the fire.

The staircase scenario was a disaster for Martin at both trial and appeal. Dr Arnold, the Crown's ballistic expert flagged the danger to Martin's defence team when they asked him about the issue of all the shots being fired from the staircase.

Dr Arnold replied definitively, "Well, two couldn't have been. And you have three cartridge cases close together with the implication being that they were fired close together."

The self-defence scenario could only run if he fired all three shots when he was at the entrance to the breakfast room. Which was why the defence team ran with this at trial. In such a version, Martin's own recollection of being on the staircase was a kind of amnesia in which his memory had been distorted by the shock of what occurred.

Woolf put it: "Such an approach would eliminate the element of pursuit and so support the defence of self-defence... We find it impossible to say that the tactics that were adopted by leading counsel on behalf of Mr Martin at trial were inappropriate. On the contrary, in the circumstances they were fully justified."

The panel of justices then dismissed the claim that the defence at trial had been flawed and that the new forensic evidence shed new light on the issue of self-defence.

What this judgment did was simply to uphold what the Crown presented at trial and what the jury's verdict upheld: Martin, "having been disturbed by the approach of the burglars, had lain in wait for them and shot at them at short range with the intention either of killing or seriously injuring them".

In fact, Horwood-Smart ran the Crown's case a lot higher than this. She ran the scenario that Tony set up a "rats in the trap" ambush. Later on in the judgment, Woolf summarised this case:

"Martin was cross-examined on the basis that his evidence and the account he had given in interview was untrue; that he had heard the two men approaching the house and had readied himself so that by the time they entered the breakfast room he was downstairs, lying in wait in the hall and his gun already loaded; and that he had stepped into the breakfast room with the intention of killing."

The jury's verdict and the Appeal Court's review of the evidence validated what the Crown presented. Martinistas refused to face up to this legal reality.

In terms of the issues at trial, a jury keeping to its oath of coming to a verdict on the basis of the law and the evidence had to find Tony guilty. It is difficult to see how he could clear even one of the two hurdles that a defendant running self-defence faces. If he set up an ambush, then he clearly falls at the first hurdle, that in his head he believed he was acting in defence of his life. If he sprang them like rats in a trap, then he also falls at the other hurdle, reasonable force.

The implicit position of Martin's camp was that, despite what the law was and whatever the evidence proved, the jury should have acquitted. However, a defendant looking for such a verdict still has, if not some hurdles to clear, then at least some hoops to jump through.

The nature of a jury trial is such that juries can ignore the oath to render a verdict according to the law and the evidence. Juries occasionally do give defendants the benefit of their discretion ignoring both the law and the evidence. The legal profession calls these verdicts perverse. Non-lawyers might think of them as grass-roots verdicts. Juries have acquitted civil servants who have broken the law by leaking documents; they have acquitted protesters who have broken the law in pursuit of some cause; they have acquitted defendants who turn the tables on criminals and kill them in a blatantly unreasonable way.

Fundamentally this was Martin's case. He asked for a verdict that upheld a man's right in certain circumstances to take the law into his own hands. He claimed his circumstances were exactly those where most right-thinking jurors should give him the benefit of their discretion.

Perhaps the Martin jury did sympathise with Tony's plight and wanted to find him not guilty. Certainly, their deliberations lasted quite a long time, given that it was a fairly short trial. And they wobbled with their verdict, coming in at 10-2. It might be that the reason they turned against him in the end was that if a defendant was looking for a grassroots verdict it was unwise to behave as Tony did in the witness box. Defendants angling for such a verdict need to build on the sympathy of the jury, and not, as Tony did, take it for granted. He didn't play the game: he didn't show a shred of fake compassion for Barras, he insulted the jury's intelligence with much of his evidence, he didn't give them something better than the torchlight in the eyes as a belief that his life was in danger, time and again he was outwitted by Horwood-Smart... In short, Tony blew it because characteristically he couldn't be bothered to act and lie better.

After dealing with the criticisms of the trial and the forensic evidence, the panel then moved onto the new psychiatric evidence presented by Wolkind that supported self-defence and diminished responsibility. First they summarised the original Maden report for the defence at trial, which concluded that Martin was mentally stable. Then they moved onto two new reports that were commissioned by the defence for the appeal. Both found that at the time of the offence Martin was suffering from a long-standing paranoid personality disorder, which substantially diminished his mental responsibility for murder. It was suggested that he also suffered from a mental illness – depression – which exacerbated his paranoia.

The weightier of the new reports, by Dr Joseph, found that because of these disorders, when faced with a threatening situation Martin would think he was in more danger than the average person and would have been more likely to take disproportionate counter-measures. His finger on the trigger would be more twitchy than others. Moreover, his depression and the emotional arousal excited by the shooting may well have resulted in genuine amnesia about only firing from the stairs.

In response, the Crown also commissioned two further psychiatric reports. One was actually by Maden, whose second report mirrored the findings of his original assessment prepared for the trial of April 2000: 'an oddball but no personality disorders'. The second report was by a Dr Mackeith. He found no evidence of a paranoid personality disorder or a depressive illness but did identify various psychological problems, which under the law were not abnormalities that went to diminished responsibility.

Woolf noted that the four "distinguished experts" had been heard by the court and their reports studied. "This court is not required to choose between their respective opinions on the issue of diminished responsibility." The two defence experts' evidence was "credible" and Martin was "entitled to rely on it", especially as "the negative terms" of Maden's first report for the defence precluded such evidence being called.

A lawyer against palm tree justice might well in the face of this decision put it to the court that a hallowed principle of English law is that when a fully-informed defendant opts for a particular defence he can't, if convicted, appeal on the basis of a different defence which "might have stood a greater chance of success". Martin explicitly rejected diminished responsibility. We know from Ballinger that Martin "wanted to run with murder or nothing". He also rejected provocation, which required pleading to manslaughter. In law, the court cannot allow the appellant to switch horses on appeal. Nor should it cherry-pick the two defence psychiatrists over the two Crown ones.

As Justice Owen noted in his summing up at the Martin trial, Drs. Arnold and Renshaw "had co-operated, and of course it is always sensible for experts to do this. If they are experts, you do not expect there to be any wide divergence, but if there is it is better that should be known and dealt with by the experts. Who are we say to say if there finishes up a problem?"

But there are never anti-palm tree lawyers in the Appeal Court. The fact that Woolf was planting psychiatric palm trees meant that Martin was going to get a result.

The court then went on to deal with what defences the psychiatric evidence could go to: (1) self-defence; (2) diminished responsibility.

To accept that the new psychiatric evidence went to self-defence meant they would have had to set Martin free. (Self-defence does not admit manslaughter.) And they weren't going to set him free, that's for sure.

Woolf worked some pretty deft logic-chopping to make the new evidence inadmissible and irrelevant to self-defence. The next task the panel faced was to arrive at a compromise verdict via diminished responsibility, and get there by a reasonably respectable route. This was tricky. What they seem to have decided was that if they were going to pull a rabbit out a hat, they might as well do it quickly and blatantly:

Thus, the judgment concluded:

"For these reasons the fresh medical evidence has no bearing on the jury's rejection of Mr Martin's contention that he was entitled to be acquitted on the grounds that he was acting in self-defence. The position as to the fresh evidence relating to diminished responsibility is different. Here the evidence is admissible and relevant. The jury did not have the opportunity of considering this issue. Although the issue was never raised at the trial this was because the evidence was not then available to Mr Martin. Mr Martin is entitled to rely on the evidence for the purposes of his appeal. (R v Weekes [1999] Crim. LR907) The conviction for murder must therefore be quashed."

Woolf then substituted a verdict of manslaughter by reason of diminished responsibility because "the jury must have been satisfied of facts which proved him guilty of the other offence, namely manslaughter by reason of diminished responsibility".

This is Alice-in-wonderland reasoning: If I say something it means what I want it to say. The integrity of this judgment was further compounded by the way Woolf and co. calculated Tony's sentence for manslaughter:

"...we have to assume the opinion expressed by Dr Joseph supported by Miss Craissati is correct. It however remains the position that Mr Martin used a firearm which he knew he was not entitled to have in a manner which was wholly unjustified. There can be no excuse for this though we treat his responsibility as being reduced for the reasons explained by Dr Joseph."

A sentence of 5 years was handed down. This meant if Martin was paroled, he would be released in under a year.

The Justices didn't have any reason to assume that the "opinion expressed by Dr Joseph supported by Miss Craissati is correct" – they arbitrarily assumed it. And this was in direct contradiction to what they claimed was their purpose when they outlined the issues posed by the new psychiatric evidence:

"This court is not required to choose between their respective opinions on the issue of diminished responsibility." Yet, this is precisely that they did. Two psychiatric experts said there was nothing going to mental illness that ushered in diminished responsibility; two others declared the opposite.

Why did they go with Joseph? As the Judgment noted in its preamble Martin's plight had attracted considerable public sympathy and media interest, it had also provoked calls for the law to be changed. Who knows how the realpolitik of democracy worked in this case. Perhaps Lord Irvine – Lord Chancellor at the time – dropped a hint. After all, the Blair government was nothing if not obsessive about the tabloid issues of the day. Perhaps the Justices were intimidated by the vision – and smell – of the Countryside Alliance dumping a lorry-load of pigshit on the steps of the High Court if nothing was done. Perhaps it was no more than a conclusion that the Common Law needed to beef up the interests of the householder when faced with intruders.

Of course, it was ironic to see the second highest court in the land bringing in a grassroots verdict by the back door. Believers in the High Court's commitment to the rule of law might also have felt that their faith was shaken. But there was no hidden agenda, no backhanders, nothing truly sinister – this is just how the law works in a democracy. If Tony had been an unpublicised Joe Bloggs, he'd still be serving life…but the law, like everything else, isn't perfect.

A RIGHT TO KILL?

CHAPTER 8

SHRINKING TONY BACK TO SIZE

When someone is charged with murder, the law requires that the accused is psychiatrically examined by both defence and prosecution. Tony was examined for the Crown soon after he was arrested by a Giresh Shetty, a Consultant Forensic Psychiatrist, who now works for the NHS in Norwich. Shetty had been Medical Director, of Ashworth Special Hospital and was mildly criticised in a 1999 report of a government appointed inquiry into irregularities there. It concluded that he was 'not robust enough to tackle the poor performance of many of his colleagues'. He was robust enough to find that there was nothing wrong with Martin. As did Professor Maden. There were no psychiatric issues at trial.

Martin ran his 'all or nothing' defence: not guilty by virtue of self-defence or guilty of murder. For the appeal, a fresh round of psychiatrists were called. The defence recruited Dr Joseph and Ms Craissati who both diagnosed a long-standing paranoid disorder and depression. The Crown now called in Maden and Mackeith hopefully to rebut Joseph and Craissati, which their reports predictably did. They diagnosed Tony Martin as odd but with no paranoia or depression.

Same man: different diagnoses, even contradictory. If Martin had a broken leg and one doctor identified it as such and the other one said he was fine we would be clamouring for the latter to be struck off. However, if a psychiatrist identifies depression and another psychiatrist says the opposite nobody gets excited. This sort of thing comes with the psychiatric territory. Moreover, these diagnoses are done by psychiatrists who have neither known nor observed Martin for any considerable period of time, say, during a long term stay in a ward. The reports were done on the basis of two or three hour interviews, sometimes supplemented by Martin filling out a questionnaire. The anti-psychiatry camp would also see it as significant that before conviction when Tony was determined to show he was not a nutcase the defence psychiatrist found nothing amiss; whereas after conviction the defence psychiatrist and psychological profiler both found pathological mental conditions.

Even distinguished psychiatrists accept that a personality disorder such as paranoia is not the mental equivalent of, say, measles. They also accept that some defendants facing a murder charge will – for obvious reasons – cheat in their responses to questions. Many would claim that there are safeguards built into their method of diagnosis that measure the honesty of the subject. Yet, they also know that there have been numerous research projects in which students fake mental symptoms and trick psychiatrists into diagnosing spurious mental conditions. Similar studies show that mental patients who shop around with the same symptoms are diagnosed differently by different psychiatrists.

In the past, eminent theologians spent many distinguished years arguing how many angels could dance on the tip of a needle. Modern British psychiatry does not believe in angels but it does believe that what departs far from "the normal" is evidence of either a personality disorder or a mental illness. Tests are then developed for detecting and even measuring what is now being defined as abnormal. Rather than thinking the abnormal is no more than uniquely different, the assumption is that it is pathological. You don't have to be a subscriber to "The myth of Mental Illness" (Thomas Szasz) to accept that psychiatry is not rocket science.

Mathew Parris of *The Times* took some fanciful clinical psychiatrist to task in his column in December 2003: "...the waters of the clinical language psychiatric terminology are indeed muddy... because this rather flimsy science is such a swamp – roughly where medicine was in the Middle Ages when doctors offered their diagnosis in terms of four bodily humours: blood, phlegm, choler and melancholy. Our successors will one day laugh at much than now passes for science in the study of personality."

We all accept that some people are mentally ill or disturbed, so we are not talking astrology or palmistry here. While psychiatry has nothing like the rigour that its practitioners like to claim for it, it does grapple with a real phenomenon, although its hold on it is slippery. Anyone who meets Tony Martin quickly appreciates that he is odd. As he told Artnik himself, "I can assure you, most people who have had an association with me are never quite the same again." He clearly doesn't relate or connect like normal people do and a few people who know him well say he is a bit of a nutcase or a nutter, an oddball, a misfit or has a screw loose, to use popular parlance. But these people never talk about him being a depressive or paranoid – they might say he is obsessive, a waffler, arrogant, dogmatic, intolerant, distant, a loner, an extremist, weird and, the term he uses about himself, "eccentric"... But you don't hear anything that comes near the conditions diagnosed by the mental health experts, which the Appeal Court ruled would have led it to decide that manslaughter not murder was the appropriate verdict. Of the two reports it was the one by Dr Joseph that they relied on to pull their manslaughter rabbit out of the hat, whereas Craissati's psychological profile was mainly invoked to back up Joseph.

After Joseph was approached by Tony's solicitor, James Saunders, to examine him for the appeal, he noted that his fees were £80 per hour and that he would keep them as low as possible because he knew the defence was not legally aided. Even for the psychiatrist Joseph this was OK, he was as sharp as button, and a barrister to boot. For his report he interviewed Martin twice, read many of the case papers and even watched a TV documentary, "A Very British Murder", that was broadcast after the trial. Joseph doesn't do things by half, but he can be too clever by half as well.

He reported that during the interviews Martin was "unable to keep to the point when answering questions and tended to go off into extraneous detail". This habit of Martin's, underestimated by Joseph, was referred to in a variety of ways. "It was difficult to get him to keep to the point...Mr Martin talks about events in enormous and often extraneous detail and he is very difficult to interrupt...he threatened to leave the room when I tried to get him to focus on the questions I asked and he said he would not co-operate unless he could answer the question in his own way." To the layman this is the most defining characteristic of Martin: his habit of verbal walkabouts, waffling, rambling... Yet, it does not figure in Joseph's conclusions, in that it is not central to his diagnosis of paranoia or depression.

He attributed to Martin the odd comment "that he and his brother (Robin) were like chalk and cheese but basically they are the same"! Joseph made nothing of this contradiction. Anyone who knows Tony would recognise this as an example of the way he jumbles the meaning of words and phrases. One would have thought this would be significant to Joseph but he didn't pick up on it. Nor did Joseph mention the incident that was widely reported after the trial, how in 1987 Tony pulled a shotgun on Robin blowing out the windows of his snooker room in his luxury home. Martin claimed he was only protecting his mother from his playboy, crook brother who was trying to trick him out of some land that their mother had ceded to him. Robin's story was rather different – he'd beat Tony at snooker.

In looking at Tony's upbringing, Joseph mentioned the usual family difficulties such as when Tony once saw his father grabbing his mother's hair and how his father also blamed Tony for things that Robin did. He also reports that Tony said he had an autistic cousin and that twenty years ago his aunt's husband committed suicide, which was flagged by Joseph as his history of family psychiatric illness. Tony also told him about two sexual incidents that occurred when he was around 10 years old. The first one concerned his headmaster, Major Bailey, at his boarding school, Glebe House. The Major, Tony claimed, used to cane him on his bare buttocks, slap him around the head, then hug him. He told Craissati at the time that he knew that "was something strange".

The second incident concerned a boy around four years older than Tony, Rodney Turney, who was the son of a clergyman friend of his parents. He would sleepover at Tony's house and come into his bedroom. He would try to get in Tony's bed. Tony claimed that he used to double over the sheets of his bed and lie in his bed frozen with fear while Turney tried to thread his hand through the sheets and touch him. Craissati quotes Tony as saying that Turney "fumbled with the sheets for hours trying to touch him". On one car journey, he also tried to get his hand up Tony's trousers. Presumably they were short ones. As with Tony's account of the shooting, though, both experts took what he said at face value.

Joseph reported that Tony concluded that these examples of being molested were what ruined his life and left him unable to form any lasting relationships with women. Instead, according to Joseph, Tony became "emotionally attached to trees and he became fearful when talking about this... He said that he has a closer emotional bond with trees than people".

There is no report of any tree-hugging. But he told Craissati that his teddies were "very nice people" and Joseph that his dogs were not animals but like children to him.

However, what Joseph did not address, even though it was in the public domain, was that when the allegations about being groped as a child were brought to his mother's attention, Hilary ridiculed these claims, recalling that Tony was always badgering her to let him spend the weekends at Turney's home. Most laymen would not believe that Turney fumbled for hours trying to get his hand through the sheets and onto Tony's body. They would suspect, as do some of Tony's friends, that there was some kind of consensual sexual relationship, which Tony later became quite shameful about as he was vitriolic about homosexuals.

Tony also told Joseph that the sexual violation he suffered at the hands of Major Bailey and Roger Turney stopped him committing himself to the only woman with whom he had "…a serious intimate relationship. He had felt unable to commit himself to the relationship because of his previous experience of sexual abuse, but when Anne ended the relationship he said that he became depressed, which lasted for many years. At times he has wondered if he ever really got over his depression. He has had no further serious relationships, although a number of casual relationships with women, which he was unhappy about because he felt that he was violating them in some way."

Again Craissati was better on the detail: Anne Masters "…seemed to be the only woman who had really got to know him intimately and he reported feeling very perturbed by her comments 'you're the type to commit suicide' and on another occasion 'you don't have any friends'. Eventually he began to feel increasingly 'dirty' as a result of their sexual contact and he started to avoid seeing her. He described the relationship break-up as 'all my own fault', something he sincerely regretted as he felt that he loved her".

What Tony fed the psychiatrist and the psychological profiler was his version, which was quite different from what has been constructed from other people who were around at the time. Much of this was in the public domain when these reports were compiled but neither Joseph nor Craissati referred to them or even seemed aware of them.

The, supposedly traumatic, Anne Masters affair all happened in 1969, when Tony met a local trainee teacher – Masters is now a headmistress – seven years his junior. They started going out together and their relationship was sexual but they never lived together and whatever sex there was, was invariably a fumbled shudder in the front seat of his Lotus Elan. Tony doesn't like being touched, which has to be seen to be believed. If a woman goes to peck him on the cheek in a social greetings, he either backs off and holds his hand up to stop any contact or he goes rigid. Again the experts don't observe this but merely report him saying it. Anne quickly began to feel that for all his seeming charm and money Tony was a "weirdo". He was jealous, domineering and, even to an 18-year-old, manifestly insecure. She tried to break off the relationship but he became threatening and abusive. When eventually she broke off the affair she became frightened of what Tony would do, and almost in desperation, took up with another man.

Tony used to stalk her and found out about her new boyfriend. He climbed a tree outside her house, entered her bedroom and hid in her cupboard listening while she had sex then slept with her new boyfriend. The imagery of her having proper sex with another man devastated him.

A few days later, in January 1970, he hacked off his hair and began walking to London like someone on a self-flagellatory pilgrimage to the North Pole. He was picked up by the police, disorientated and suffering from hypothermia. He was sectioned under the mental health act to a psychiatric hospital in Cambridge and was there for three months. When he was released he went back to his mothers in Wisbech but he was now a man who was *Living with Strangers*, which was one of the two titles that he wanted this book to be called. The other title was *Victim of Circumstance*.

A couple of years later, Tony managed to get Anne into his Elan and showed her a handgun that he had in the glove compartment. It looked so antiquated that she said it looked like it belonged in a museum. To prove that it was lethal Tony calmly aimed it at wood pigeon nestling in a nearby tree and downed it with one shot. Anne never came near him again and Tony never ever went out with another women. The Lotus Elan, incidentally, is still in one of the outbuildings of Bleak House, abandoned with a rusty lawnmower sticking through the floor to remind him of the time he parked it drunkenly after a bender in Downham Market. His friends dread it when he gets out the old photographs of him and Anne together as he always becomes maudlin and tearful. When the announcement of Anne's marriage appeared in the papers some years ago, the old wound was reopened once again, the old tales relived. To this day Tony keeps his guard up where the opposite sex are concerned. "Succumb to a woman," Tony exclaimed in mock horror, in an interview with one of the Artnik team. "Ha...ha...ha...ha!" he reeled off with heavy sarcasm, "I've got a very strong mind, you've got to have keep women at bay."

Yet, he will tell everyone he meets of his promiscuous past in his "ladykiller" days, to use his expression. On different occasions five people from the Artnik office have interviewed Tony and early on in conversation, he has related to each of them the familiar claim that he used to be "very attractive to women and bedded so many he lost count". He made the same claim to Joseph and Craissati. To each of them he said that when he had sex with a woman it always made him feel dirty and he felt later that he had "violated" them. When one of the Artnik team asked him was it true that he crept into Anne's bedroom and listened to her have sex with her new man, he replied, "I've forgotten what happened. You'd better ask her."

To Joseph he said that after Anne he became depressed, which lasted "many years" and he "wondered if he ever really got over it". He then claimed that after "he had a number of casual relationships with women, which he was unhappy about because he felt that he was violating them in some way". Yet, a number of his friends disputed this. They pointed out that he has never been out with a woman. Terry 'Badger' Howard, the guardian of Tony's teddies, has known him since he got back from Australia.

He told Artnik, "One of the first things he tells when you meet him is what a ladies man he was when he was young. I've known him since his twenties and I've never seen him with a girl. Never. Anne Masters was before my time. But he's never had another girlfriend. EVER." He added sarcastically, "It didn't occur to me that he might be bent." But it did to my two girls, they have known him all that time and say he is 'a raving poofter'. But don't get me wrong, I've never seen him with a man either. It's all repressed. Repressed is what he is. He can't admit it but that is why they are all perverts. Homosexuals – perverts. Everyone he don't like is a pervert. Gypsies, criminals, homosexuals, blacks, you name it they're perverts. And if he's such a ladies man, why do we not read of him romancing one out of all these women who were writing to him in prison. Ask yourself that?"

This wasn't the sort of question that Joseph or Craissati could ask themselves as they interviewed Tony in the run-up to his appeal but it begs more than a few questions about their methods that they didn't get near to what everyone who knows Tony thinks about him. The closest Joseph got to the layman's interpretation was when he described one of Tony's digressions while talking about the burglary.

The psychiatrist thought that Tony's use of 'violate' implied that he feared the burglars would rape him and his report noted on: 'He did not want to express this overtly, but he went on to say that he does not like people touching him or him touching others. He said that he would have got married but he cannot show affection to people. The feelings are there but he cannot do it. He watches other people being friendly with each other, but if he does it he feels dirty. He feels that he has molested women when he has been out with them. He hates being left with children because he knows what can happen to them. He said, 'When you've been molested it makes you self-conscious. I worry that people think I might do something. When I was younger people thought I was queer.' He thought that meant he was homosexual or that he was odd. He said, 'The world is full of queers. When you've been molested you become very sensitive to people.'"

Craissati again culled the significant detail about his possible repressed homosexuality. As already described, Tony took up cycling in 1996 but had an accident in which he injured his pelvis. Badger described it, "He was going like the clappers, head down and he hit a parked car." However, after a couple of weeks of pain, Tony was admitted to Kings' Lynn hospital. In the hospital a doctor examined his prostate: "…he described his horror at having 'fingers up my backside.'" Neither Joseph or Craissati obtained his medical record for that admission to hospital. If they had, they would have discovered that Tony was thrown out of the ward because he racially abused a black nurse.

Tony had experienced "some traumatic events during his childhood, in particular physical mistreatment by a sadistic schoolmaster at his boarding school and sexual abuse by a family friend. These experiences, at a developing age, engendered in Mr Martin a deep distrust of the motives of others which has affected his ability to form meaningful relationships throughout his adult life. He is unable to form intimate relationships with women because he fears that by doing so he will violate them and he feels dirty and guilty…

Joseph went on to claim that "I am of the opinion that Mr Martin suffers from a longstanding personality disorder, the most likely category being paranoid personality disorder. The condition of his house is extraordinary and has to reflect a significant degree of mental disorder in its owner, even though Mr Martin tries to rationalise the state of the house."

Joseph concluded that Tony had experienced bouts of depression throughout his life, "which are likely to be due to his realisation that he is unable to form intimate relationships with others, and this has emphasised the loneliness and isolation of his life". Thus, the psychiatrist's reasoning is that the sexual abuse was the main factor in causing the paranoia that prevented Tony from forming normal emotional attachments. This affected his life so much that it led to him developing a depressive illness.

Having developed this theory, Joseph now applies it to the murder: "At the time of the killing I believe Mr Martin was suffering from an abnormality of the mind, namely a paranoid personality disorder arising from inherent cause, and depression which is a disease of the mind. The combination of these conditions will undoubtedly have affected his perception of events leading up to the killing and would have had a significant impact on his ability to exercise his judgement and willpower. In particular, as a result of his paranoid personality disorder, I believe Mr Martin would have perceived a much greater danger to his physical safety than an average person in that situation. He is more likely to have felt that his life was in danger and more likely to have believed that he was going to be seriously harmed or violated, perhaps sexually, by the intruders.

"On that basis, it is my opinion that if Mr Martin intended to kill or cause serious harm at the time of the killing, then his mental responsibility was substantially impaired at that time. He is more likely to have believed that his life was in danger than a person who does not have a paranoid personality disorder. This opinion would be the same if the Court concluded that Mr Martin laid in wait for the intruders and deliberately shot them."

As Badger said, "What a load of cobblers." One of the Artnik team, an Old Etonian, also ridiculed the notion that such low-grade abuse could have such traumatic consequences: "If he'd been to Eton and been properly sodomised, I guess he'd have herded up all the local gypsies and marched them into his own private gas oven." But as paedophilia has become the contemporary benchmark of evil, psychiatrists view it as an irresistible trigger for adult mental pathology. Indeed, this is probably why Tony banged on about it to them. He reads the papers. In fact, he also did this in his third interview with Peters and Newton, going on at length about how being burgled was like being molested and that anyone who has been molested is especially sensitive to any violation. This section was ruled inadmissible at trial. But the significant point is he has only paraded this kind of connection with people whom he needed to win over to escape conviction.

Both Joseph and Craissati's qualifications allow them to put a lot of letters after their names. Climbing up the ivory tower must be good for your salary and image but it can put you out of touch with what is happening on the ground. Most of us approaching a convicted murderer coming up for appeal would have it in the forefront of our mind that he is likely to lie. Especially as the jury had believed the prosecution's persistent accusation that he had lied and lied in court. This doesn't seem to have occurred to either Joseph or Craissati. It does not figure in their reports at all. They take Tony at face value. Woolf commented: "It is apparent that Dr Joseph accepted that Mr Martin was a truthful witness." You wonder what it takes for them to build into their interpretative framework or paradigm the likelihood that their subject is deliberately lying his head off. After all, it doesn't prevent that person having personality disorders or suffering from some mental illness.

Indeed, Joseph actually read Tony's evidence before interviewing him and that alone should be enough to convince anyone that this is someone transparently lying through his teeth. However, as he does not concede that Martin is lying, Joseph cannot address that. This is why he is at his most threadbare when he tries to psychologise away another of Tony's whoppers – that he cannot remember leaving the stairs during the shooting. Joseph concludes that this was caused by amnesia: "I believe he may therefore have suffered a genuine period of amnesia, when he was standing on the stairs and he may have walked further down the stairs without being aware of doing so." Yet, apart from uncertainty about how many shots he fired, Tony remembers everything else and he suffered no loss of memory when he visited the Leets immediately after the shooting.

Tony lies. Even his staunchest supporters such as Helen Lilley concede that. As Badger stated: "He's a lying bastard. Anyone who knows him, including my two girls and he's known them since they were 15, know'd he'd kill a gypsy. He's had it in his mind that long. Twenty-five years minimum. That wasn't a sudden thing that happened that bloody night. It was meant.

"You know where he got it: his 'ero, his uncle Fountaine. He was married to one of Hilary's sisters, Rosemary, who don't like Tony one little bit. All three live in that house – it's like a bloody witches coven, I tell you. I met him (Fountaine) once. He looked just like Adolf Hitler: the little 'tache, the hair in a fringe." Badger put two fingers under his nose, then moved his forefinger midway across his forehead. "Bloody strange family...

"Sometimes Tony would go home a different way at night, so anyone watching the back wouldn't see him go in the back. Look at the Helen's CCTV recording of him walking across the car park after he'd shot 'em. She's kept it. He's walking like he was John Wayne. If he was so frightened then, why isn't he frightened now. Come on. With no protection. Everyone knows where he drinks and has lunch in Wisbech."

Again the experts just don't see what everyone who knows Tony says about him: he is not a frightened man, more a cocksure, over-confident one. Tony himself told us when asked if was frightened that evening, "I was never frightened, but having been robbed and threatened on a number of occasions, I felt I had to do what was necessary to protect myself."

Moreover, if Joseph had factored in Tony's expressed hatred of gypsies and his intention to shoot one the first chance he got – as was given in evidence at trial – he could never have concluded that Tony's paranoia meant that he was more likely than an ordinary person to believe his life was in danger and that this diminished his responsibility even if he "laid in wait for the intruders and deliberately shot them". Clearly Joseph could not have read Ballinger's instructions to Maden that contained the detail that Tony was currently "reading *Mein Kampf* not because he was a Nazi but because Hitler's methods for dealing with thieving gypsies (shoot the bastards) was far more effective than the methods used by the Norfolk Police..."

Even if we concede that Tony is paranoid that does not alter the fact that he was not a frightened man on the night of the shooting and nor is he now. As Horwood-Smart put it to the jury, he was an angry, revengeful man, who took it upon himself to cull, as he had promised, some light-fingered pikies. "And he did," as Paul Leet put it. On the other hand, that does not alter the fact that most people – including the Artnik team who worked on this book – identify with what he did, no matter what the law says. Sympathy with his action, though, is obviously no reason for hiding from the truth of what he did.

Badger was the first of Tony's friends to visit him after he was arrested. "They would not let me see him at the police station, although they let me buy him a steak. Which I did. But a few days later I visited him in Norwich nick, he was in the hospital. I said to him why didn't you ring me and I'd have come over and we could have phoned an ambulance and the police. He just said he went to see if he could find them. He said it was fearful what he did. It was his favourite word. He said when he went to let the first one off, it didn't fire. There wasn't one up the spout. He definitely fired four because he emptied the mag. He's proud of what he did, you know. He also asked me how far would a cartridge fly when you pumped it. I said it depends how hard you pump it… So he was working out where he's put the empties and whether he's made mistakes."

Badger who is a big, rangy, 63 year old, paused and added enigmatically, "He had a camp bed in the garage. You didn't know that, did you? I know 'cos I've seen it. Ask Roger (Cotteril). It was known on occasions that he slept in the garage. I'll say no more. He wasn't in that house at all. He slept in that bedroom until it got full of rubbish. And I mean full… I wouldn't have thought he'd slept in that bloody bedroom for a couple of years. It was knee-deep in newspapers, empty wine bottles, Kentucky Fried Chicken boxes with the bloody bones still in 'em. Right? I mean knee-deep. The rubbish was level with the bed...He knew I knew what he was up to. He followed them in...that makes it premeditated bloody murder to me. Because he let 'em walk past, then followed them in.

"It weren't disturbing burglars. It was laying in wait for them. When you start to look at it, it don't take a lot of working out. If you were frightened of your bloody house being burgled, what do you do? Alarms. The fact of the bloody matter is if you care about your property put some security in it. But he always had a gun around the house. You know they found a sawn-off shotgun." He grinned. "I gave him that." It was found, all rusty, hidden in the garage.

"I'll tell you another thing. I used to shoot. If someone shoots you like that with a 12-bore you gotta be out (for the count), you gotta be. Get up, climb out of a window, then crawl...no way. Impossible. It has always been my opinion and Roger's."

It is difficult to know if Badger is reporting what Tony has told him or inferring or working it out himself. One of his favourite phrases is "I'll say no more" accompanied with a conspiratorial look that is the equivalent of tapping the side of your nose.

If Barras was hit by the first shot at point-blank range with English Shot No 6 – from the angle of the wound it was assumed he was bending down putting the silver jugs in the holder – he would have been thrown across the room onto his face. With the kind of wound he sustained it would have been almost impossible for him to get up, make his way to the window in a rubble-strewn, darkened room, then climb out and crawl to where he died. Almost impossible but sometimes, though fatally wounded, soldiers in their death throes do perform incredible feats.

What is impossible, however, was for Barras to have been hit in the manner described, to have spoken quite audibly and coherently, then to have clambered up and been on Fearon's shoulder before climbing out of the window immediately after him. Fearon lies almost for the sake of it but his account of seeing the flash, hearing the bang and Barras' cry, then feeling and hearing the lad behind him has been his story all along. What he described Barras as saying points to the lad being hit, as Fearon was, in the leg, leaving him in agonising pain but still able to walk and talk. If he'd taken the first shot in the back, quite apart from the way he could not have kept up with Fearon, his speech would have been almost an inarticulate groan. The first shot didn't hit him in the back. That is impossible.

Badger is correct.

They both took shots in the upper thigh inside the breakfast room. Fearon pulled out the window frame, then went first and as Barras clambered out Tony got him with the last shot as he was silhouetted against the moonlight. He fired the first few shots down but as he saw the last burglar making his escape he couldn't resist it. He shot Barras in the back. This is why he knew he was going to be arrested and why he always lies about not seeing the moonlight coming in through the empty window frame.

"The lies he has got away with," Badger marvelled. "You don't expect him to tell the truth in court…When he got off on appeal, got reduced to manslaughter on appeal. What a result. What a result….but at one stage he was on about I'm gonna clear my name! Clear my name!!" Badger's astonishment was accentuated by his voice rising an octave. "What's he mean by that? Clear his name? Shot in the bloody back. That's an execution. And all these shite stories in the media. Bloody cobblers."

At the Ritz Hotel with Artnik, Martin recounted stories from his days down under. He recalled how on one occasion, in Queensland, sitting round a small fire late at night with some white Australians he was asked where he had come from.

"Cambridge, England" he replied.

"There's no such place, Limey," the sheep shearer replied. Martin recalled with some bitterness that he was continually teased about being English. "I used to make them irate, that happened a lot. I can piss people off if I put my mind to it". Martin hates being the butt of the joke. "I mean, what did they expect me to say? I have always been proud of sounding Australian, but it annoyed people down under... Sometimes I'd show off about being English...and that went down even worse."

He was asked what he was doing in Queensland.

"Shearing sheep...driving around." And for fun?

"I engaged in a basic breeding programme...we are no different from monkeys really... There are things that you can do there, when you're on your own that you can't do with anyone else." Why were you living in Australia? he was asked. "Australia, I was there because I shot someone," he replied with a grin. As mouths flapped open and brows furrowed, he started off again.

"I loved the wide open spaces, the wilderness that place gave you, The Gibson desert... I used to just drive into the wilderness, I was...what is the word I'm looking for – deranged, that's it. I experienced hallucinations...no, visions. I dreamt of plunging into a tub full of ice-cream..."

We were back where we started – cobblers.

Badger likes his beer every bit as much as he likes repeating his favourite words and phrases. He was asked – not for the first time – about Tony's killing someone in Australia and having to bolt back to Wisbech. Badger looked wary, "He told me, yeah. He's told my two girls. Bloody proud of that as well. But if it can be corroborated, I am looking at a lotta...but no, a *lotta* money. Alternatively if the police are informed properly he'll be arrested. If it is still laying on file right, he'll get arrested. What I can tell 'em is so serious...but I don't want to hang him. And the Australian police might say, 'That is a load of bollocks'. That'd be the end of it. I tell you what – it would alter the bloody title of your book. But unless he leaves the country I will not stitch him up. No way. No way. No way."

When he was told that probably Australia had a statute of limitations on crimes over 30 years old, he shot back, "Still make a good story, won't it."

Even though Martin boasts openly about the Australian shooting, Badger would not been drawn on it, but clearly Tony has boasted to him in detail about committing some serious crime there. Perhaps it was the beer talking, but he added, "It's amazing that they haven't looked in that cesspit of his. Cos some local people think he's probably done it before." One harbours the hope that even Tony, for all his dislike of the Norfolk Constabulary, would not wish this task of searching his cesspit upon them.

Why did Tony come up with such a stupid story? A child could do better. Badger thought about the question, "If it'd be me, being prosecuted…I'd say I shouted warning after warning and they still come at me. Isn't that what you do? Not Tony, he can't be bothered. Tony doesn't think things out… Like everything else he bothered to do. He started then give up. If Tony can get out of doing any work he will. But he'll make out he is a very busy man. Never worked hard in his life…

"If he's got anything, he's got Asperger's that's what he's got. My grandson has got a touch of Asperger's. So I know what Asperger's Syndrome is. Words. He get 'em all jumbled up. And he can only concentrate on one thing at a time. He will look at that door and hold a conversation with you without even looking at you. Weird. They admire themselves in reflections a lot. All Tony, all Tony. This is why he gets on so well with Roger's (Cotteril) children…they are autistic. But he probably didn't think much beyond the gun. He'd know he'd go down on that..."

Indeed, Tony himself once said to Artnik, "I'm not a very original person. I'm autistic."

Badger rambled on but even without any letters after his name still shed more light on the peculiarities of Tony than all the shrinks put together. Joseph says somewhere in his report that the extraordinary state of Tony's farmhouse has to reflect the mental disorder of its owner. It's the most perceptive observation he made but he doesn't pursue it or develop it. Like a lot of his kind, he knee jerks on childhood psycho-sexuality.

Yet, an even better way than Bleak House of getting a working handle on Tony is the way he talks. It's characteristically odd and all the shrinks pick up on it but, just as Joseph doesn't develop his observations about the farmhouse, neither do they.

Although Craissati, to give her credit, does note in her summary that one of the features of a "paranoid personality disorder, with avoidant and schizotypal traits...[is] Vague, circumstantial metaphorical, over-elaborate, or stereotyped thinking, manifested by odd speech or in other ways, without gross incoherence".

Tony Martin grew up if not with a silver spoon in his mouth at least with a silver-plated one. His father was a wealthy fruit-grower and landowner. He went to public school and while he had slight learning difficulties he was never backward or retarded. At school, he was always an outsider and not, as it were, one of the boys. But while he was not a joiner, he was not bullied, as he was combative and had a fierce temper. Clearly he was groomed by Richard Turney and it seems possible that Tony was involved in some kind of homosexual relationship that he later became acutely ashamed of and repressed. Richard Portham, who gave evidence at his trial and campaigned on his behalf, commented perceptively on this, "I think Tony is homosexual but he won't let himself be that way. And he hates himself for it."

The only person in his extended family who made a mark on the public stage was the National Front founder, Andrew Fountaine; Tony admired, identified with and learnt from him. He actually does believe that the white race is superior and that other races are inferior, and his views on gypsies are exactly what he gleaned from Fountaine. "Hitler had the right idea...coons...wogs." Another word that Tony now incorporates into his rantings is *nonce*, which is prison slang for a person convicted of sexual offences. Gypsies are also nonces to Martin.

He left school at 17 without any qualifications but was supported by his parents. He developed a wanderlust and worked as steward on the cruise-liners. However, he jumped ship in New Zealand and was arrested as an illegal immigrant. He served time before being deported back to the UK. He had a spell on the Scottish oil rigs, then he returned to the antipodes, spending three years bumming around Australia. At one time, he worked in a circus, looking after elephants. However, he left Australia under a cloud, which he has told people was the result of a violent act.

Back in the UK, he set up a pig farm, using inherited money, on some land owned by his father. Apart from a tendency to talk rather than listen and to dogmatically assert his views, people found him quite normal. He boasted about his womanising days of this period, which is now the late '60s: "I used to go over to Wisbech because the women were easier. I'd always drive over, because women are impressed by a sports car, and they like a man who dresses well. They couldn't resist a blazer with chrome buttons."

He then fell hook, line and sinker for Anne Masters and, when she rejected him, he was heartbroken and, after he'd recovered from his nervous breakdown, the decline gradually set in. Rejected and exposed to his own sexual inadequacies, he gradually rejected and withdrew from the social world. Not being able to care about people, he cared about teddies, dogs, trees. After the Anne Masters episode his characteristic speech patterns and peculiar grandiosity became more noticeable.

He inherited Bleak House in 1979, which then boasted a tennis court, central heating, period furniture and a beautiful Aga-style kitchen. Gradually he wrecked it, with his botching, bodging and tinkering. He likes to rationalise it with one of his bon mots that he repeats ad nauseum, "I'm a perfectionist. Perfectionists don't get things finished." Yet, just as Anne Masters had exposed him to his own sexual inadequacy, so the mess he made of Bleak House exposed him to his own personal incompetence. He projected his society onto society generally: the country was going to the dogs, what with immigrants and "Gestapo Socialism". As he retreated into his own personalised laager, the criminal elements among the local gypsies came to personify the forces of evil that were ruining the country and making his life unbearable. It follows that a mind in thrall to such cognitive distortions is going to lose its grip on everyday reality but this can hardly be classified as the development of a mental disorder that absolves the person from being held responsible for any criminal actions.

In terms of criminal liability, whether Tony is actually autistic or paranoid is neither here nor there. His condition is within the experience of laypeople. They don't need psychiatric jargon to understand Tony. Woolf quoted from definitive authority on this very issue: "an expert's opinion is admissible to furnish the Court with scientific information which is likely to be outside the experience and knowledge of a judge and jury. If in the proven facts a judge or jury can form their own conclusion without help, then the opinion of an expert is unnecessary." The jury heard Tony's interviews and his evidence in the witness box, it visited Bleak House. It already knew enough about him to form a judgement. Evidence from the psychiatric experts would not have changed their verdict.

Tony meets people from a disengaged stance, never interested in what others are doing but only in his own world, his business and his perception of the world around him. In any social grouping, he has to be centre stage or he won't play. He talks at people not to people. In argument he will not be checked or challenged, preferring diversion and decoy to meeting any call to account. His innate sense of superiority not underpinned by high intelligence or education has led to him being cavalier with the truth. In turn, his disengagement and withdrawal from social life has led to him being cavalier with his lies, too. His mother has kindly dubbed him his own man; but also a man only his mother could love.

During his police interviews and in court, during arguably the most important conversations he was ever to have, Martin lied on a grand scale. But he had habitually being lying badly for so long, even when his freedom was at stake he could not lie well. He is certainly intelligent enough to have constructed a plausible account that would have met the fairly tolerant expectations of a sympathetic audience, but he was thirty years out of practice.

For thirty years, he has been his own man and, with sufficient money and no familial claims, been able to walk away from the world when it wouldn't pander to his version of reality. This time he could not walk away as he was in a forum that is socially constructed and empowered to hold people to account. He tried talking Martinese to waffle his way out of trouble but the police and jury were not cronies versed in the rules of his style of social interaction: Rule 1, never ask Tony Martin a direct question; Rule 2, never expect a straight answer.

He went down…and he went down characteristically, too – he didn't really care.

CHAPTER 9

BANGED UP
WITH THE ENEMY

The journey from Bishopsgate, by Norwich Cathedral to the prison on Knox Road is not a long one, but for Tony it seemed to take an eternity. He looked longingly out of the small, wire-grilled window in the side of the 'meat wagon' at what he realised might be his last glimpse of the outside world for a long, long time. As he would later tell *The Mirror* "I remember feeling disorientated…On the journey I saw a side turning for Narford Hall where my uncle had lived. It was quite a strange feeling."

Meat Wagon. He thought of the pigs he'd sent to slaughter… Maybe they looked out not dissimilarly to him as they were dispatched to be processed into supermarket bacon. Was that what he was reduced to now – an animal condemned by the enemy to live out his days in the equivalent of a human farm? What would happen to *his* farm, *his* apple trees? Who would look after Bleak House? What about his dogs…his mother.

Tony's mind, always prone to surreal free-association, conjured up his childhood reading of Bleak House. There seemed something uncanny about the fact that his farm shared its name with the home of that character, what was his name? Jaundice? Jarndyce? Yes, Jarndyce. Tony saw himself much as the put upon Jarndyce and he remembered an observation Dickens had made with reference to his novel: "The one great principle of English law is to make business for itself." Tony wondered to himself how much those two-legged rats, lefty Scrivener, fee-hungry Ballinger and, cravatted Makin... how much had they made for themselves out of putting him in prison for life? He tried to get from cravatted to garotted but it proved difficult and he gave up.

Bloody lawyers and their disbursements. They will never call a spade a spade. Fee is what a disbursement is. A fee. But that's what lawyers do – they try to make things out to be what they're not. He remembered some quote from Shakespeare that he'd come across... "First kill all the lawyers." Fancy letting someone who wears a cravat to do the job. He should have defended himself. He would have made a much better job of it. As he began blaming everyone but himself, he began to feel better.

At HMP Norwich, Tony was taken through induction at reception. He saw the prison medic who asked him how he felt about being convicted and sent down for life. Tony replied, "Well, I've done nothing wrong, but I'm not really terribly shocked. The guilty are let out of prison and the innocent are put in prison. That's what this country is coming to. I thought about killing myself but not yet as I still have things to do. So I am detained at Her Majesty's pleasure, ehh? What pleasure can she get out of locking me up? You run these places in her name but I bet she has never seen what they are like..." He wittered on.

He was designated a category 'B' prisoner – meaning that he was considered a 'substantial' risk to the public and must be kept in closed prison. With his history of thrombosis, it was decided to house him in the prison hospital. He was put on suicide watch for the night but this was rescinded the next day.

The other inmates watched his progress with some curiosity, but not much. One cleaner in reception spoke to him, a fat shambling caricature of something out of 'Porridge'. "I know 'oo yous are. You's that farmer wot killed that kid. You gonna get wots cummin' to you in 'ere."

Tony stiffened his backbone and, in his best public school accent, replied, "If I were to get what was coming to me Gunga Din, I wouldn't be here talking to you." The cleaner looked confused, then sloped off with his broom.

At lock-up, the warder, a kindly man with a moustache and an engaging smile, whispered conspiratorially, "You farmer what shot gypsy?"

Tony, unsure what was coming, nodded with resignation.

"Well, I think you're hero, and there are plenty others of us here who think same."

After two uneventful days, Tony was transferred to Bullingdon Prison in Oxfordshire. Bullingdon is an angry boil on the picture-postcard landscape of the Cotswold town of Bicester. Built in 1992 in what was described as a 'New Gallery' design – some wag said that meant it had pictures of all its rogues on the wall – the prison locked up just under one thousand. But it had an endemic problem of bullying and a deputy governor, Terence McLaren, who was arrested in 2002 in Operation Ore's crackdown on paedophiles who download child pornography from the internet.

Tony hated his time there. He was subjected to systematic abuse from the other prisoners, including death threats. He was put on suicide watch, which meant his cell was checked every 15 minutes. Tony protested at the way his cell light was continually being switched on and off to check he hadn't cut his wrists or something. When this wasn't enough, he threatened to go on hunger strike. To make matters worse, soon after he arrived Makin and Ballinger descended on him with Malcolm Starr and Paul Cumby, one of the Trustees for the Tony Martin Support Fund deed.

There were a number of issues on the agenda: the grounds for his appeal, the usual disbursements problems and also the advice of all those present that he give Malcolm Starr and Paul Cumby power of attorney to handle the farm and his affairs. Malcolm Starr, a people-pleasing smoothie in his mid-50s proved to be a good friend to Tony but Cumby, an 'oil prospector' in Saudi Arabia, had expressed an interest in acquiring Bleak House.

To formalise proceedings, another solicitor, Angela Porter from the local firm of Herbert Mallam Gowers was kept informed of the proposed delegation. Porter took a sympathetic interest in the farmer's predicament and quickly allied herself with him against what she perceived as a potentially dangerous arrangement. The proposed deed read: 'I, Anthony Edward Martin appoint Paul Cumby and Malcolm Starr jointly to be my attorneys for the purpose of the Enduring Powers of Attorneys Act 1985 with general authority to act on my behalf in relation to all my property and affairs.'

Porter swiftly insisted on the insertion of an extra clause: 'subject to the restriction and condition that none of my property including my house may be sold without my express permission.' It was later discovered that the address Cumby had given when he signed the deed was false.

They all made an effort to raise Tony's hopes that the appeal would be successful. He was more cynical, "Why should my appeal be anymore successful than the trial?" They assured him that they would look for new evidence, that the judge had misdirected the jury and so on. Makin cited the example of Justice Owen comparing him to Stalin and Hitler. Tony replied laconically "That's not the way I heard it. And anyway what's me being kind to children got to do with anything..." Among Tony's more endearing traits is the pleasure he takes from being contrary.

He returned to his cell thinking that to cheer him up they were all clutching at straws. What did raise his spirits was the mountains of mail that he continued to receive from well-wishers across the country. One in particular made him proud to be part of the true-breed Englishman that as far as he was concerned was fast becoming an endangered species.

The elderly Brigadier, who had read of Tony's plight with outrage, had pledged to donate a percentage of his pension each month to the Tony Martin Defence Fund. This had continued until the Brigadier's wife had to be committed to a home, and in the letter the Brigadier apologised for no longer being able to send his monthly donation as the money was needed to pay for his wife's care. Instead, the loyal supporter enclosed his war medals and hoped that their sale could be of some assistance to the cause. This and other well-meaning offerings were filling up the coffers of the Defence Fund.

However, Bullingdon was living up to the name Tony dubbed it...Bullydom. Some pikies had marshalled the enemy – the prison vermin, perverts and two-legged rats – to move against him. There were a lot of gypsies in Bullydom and they taunted him about the reward that was on his head.

On one occasion he was attacked in the prison showers but he gave as good as he got and didn't back down. Then during the Euro 2000 football championships, England lost 2-3 to Romania and all the gypsies on a nearby wing began chanting, "Hang the farmer. Hang the farmer." That kind of hatred shook him up but didn't make him eat any humble pie for shooting Barras.

One highlight of this period was a letter from Martin Bashir, asking for Tony's co-operation in doing an ITV Special to clarify the issues on his case 'prior to the Appeal'.

Bashir wrote, 'I believe that such a programme could have a powerful effect in judicial and political terms.' Tony preened – he was being interviewed by the same person whom Princess Diana trusted. The only dark spot, which Tony pointed out to Sainsbury in his characteristic indelicate manner, "Shame he's a bit of a wog."

The final straw of his time at Bullingdon came on a Saturday afternoon, when Tony was taking advantage of his hour's period of exercise in the prison's yard. A group of pikey-looking prisoners approached him purposefully. Tony quickened his pace to avoid any confrontation but they boxed him in.

'Do him!' cried their leader. The others quickly piled in, wrestling Tony to the ground. Then, as one member of the pack shoved a filthy rag into Tony's mouth, another produced a box of matches and, bizarrely, attempted to set Tony alight.

This time the chant was, "Burn the farmer! Burn the farmer!" But Tony's prison tracksuit proved matchproof. Before long the staff *heavy mob* broke up the melee and dragged the bullyboys down the punishment wing. Tony was shaken but, luckily enough, not hurt, merely roughed up. The incident, however, alerted the prison authorities to the pressure Tony was under and it was arranged that he would be transferred to HMP Gartree in Leicestershire. He arrived there on July 6th 2000.

At Gartree, Tony was happier as well as being more comfortable. He had his own seven foot by eight foot cell with a stainless steel lavatory and basin and he set about the task of decorating his cell and covered one wall with pictures of castles cut from magazines. The other walls were decorated with pictures of the animals, trees and flowers that he was once again able to gaze over from his bedroom window at Bleak House.

His relations with the other inmates were much better than at Bullingdon. One of the cons even lent him a radio and another offered his ration of Tony's favourite cereal, Alpen.

By this stage the newspapers, fanned by Max Clifford, Malcolm Starr and the POW Trust, featured Tony almost daily, either with some descriptions of some new indignity to which he had been subjected in prison or with news of his irrefutable grounds of appeal.

Peter Sainsbury said of the campaign, "We wanted maximum publicity to force the High Court to act. And Malcolm was brilliant, absolutely brilliant, the way he controlled things. Everything went through him. You know how lazy the press are – we drip-fed them new stories, new angles, new developments all the time. And Malcolm controlled access to Tony. That was the key: only let them get at Tony once we'd hammered how the story would go."

Tony had played up his thrombosis and was excused from prison work, so he was virtually a man of leisure. He read every news story about him, but was outraged that someone who featured daily in the press could not have the papers delivered to his cell.

His day revolved around the newspapers, his letter-writing and monitoring what was happening with the appeal. The bullying a thing of the past, the status of 'hero' accorded him by the press had revived the old arrogance that had been less visible in Bullingdon. Tony settled into the now familiar routine of playing the martyr.

Tony was keen that he have a television installed in his cell and wrote to Peter Sainsbury, asking him to organise it for him, "If I am to be locked away in here it is only right from a dignity point of view that I am allowed to watch television. I like to watch nature documentaries, and I would rather watch the behaviour of animals on my television screen than have to watch the behaviour of the animals in this prison. I also think that it is only right that I have newspapers delivered daily to my cell."

The indefatiguable Sainsbury duly wrote to the corpulent Governor of Gartree, Jill Lacy, listing Tony's demands. She patiently wrote back explaining, as had been explained to Tony a hundred times, that Gartree's policy on television dictated that all new prisoners must undertake a three month assessment prior to qualifying for a television. The issue of newspapers, she insisted, had also been explained to Tony. "They had to be purchased by the prisoner through internal purchasing procedures via our prison library."

Tony retorted to Sainsbury, "I know this place is a pig sty but that's one very good reason for not putting a fat sow in charge of it."

In turn Sainsbury got one of POW's trustees – Teresa "cut off their ghoulies" Gorman – on the case. She wrote to Paul Boateng, who was then at the Home Office: "What are you doing to get this man out of prison?... his privilege of having a TV in his cell has been denied him... Can you imagine the horror that Mr Martin is going through just for protecting himself and his property in the dark from burglars and accidentally killing one of them..."

Teresa was a Tory MP at the time and notorious for being an enthusiastic proponent of castration for sex offenders.

Tony spent the next few months driving Gartree warders spare with his now perfected rhetoric about how to put the Great before Britain again. Some were card-carrying members of the National Front but even to them Martin was like some Grand Wizard of the Klu Klux Klan. Then, in December, Tony received a letter that left him speechless for so long he wondered if it had infected him with lockjaw. It was from Fearon who was still in HMP Stocken serving his 3 years and was addressed to 'Dear Tony'.

Fearon had been following the Martin stuff in the press... The typewritten letter, purportedly composed by him said:

'I must stress that your influential sincerity to the papers was overwhelming. I feel you will gain your sense of truth in time...I was there that night... We were not there to take your belongings merely to escape your dogs...I have since been visited by the victim support group in relation to my feelings about you gaining parole in the future… My feelings are with you. I hope you feel remorse as it's the only way forward.'

Although it was a very spiritual letter, it did not contain any exhortations to find salvation in Jesus. After he'd recovered the power of speech, Tony found that all he could do was foam at the mouth.

"He can't even read and write… Victim support – pervert support, that's what these counsellors are…" The wing's assistant governor was informed. Referral to the counselling services for an anger management course was considered but in the end it was agreed that it was best to leave howling dogs to the moon…

As his first Christmas approached Tony smothered nearly one wall of the cell with Christmas cards. Mohammed Al Fayed sent him one of Harrods' largest teddy bears as a Christmas present. 'Happy Fugging Christmas' the greeting read. Tony was very upset when Princess Diana died and blamed the crash on Dodi – "a good-for-nothing who'd only ever sponged off his father's fortune". But he was flattered by Fayed's gift and he told Sainsbury, "He may be a wog, but you have to hand to him, he is a gentleman."

Early in the following year, with his Appeal looming Tony was caught up briefing Joseph and Crassaiti on how being molested was responsible for him being a Victim of Circumstance. Meanwhile the press continued to trumpet the injustice of his conviction. Then, in October 2001, he was transferred to HMP Pentonville in London for the hearing of his appeal at the High Court.

Tony didn't like the fact that he was doubled up with another prisoner in a cell that was built nearly two hundred years for a single prisoner, but otherwise he liked the Ville. By now he had learnt the ropes on buying phone cards from other prisoners and with lots of indigent short-termers at the Ville it meant he could use the wing phone at will. He spent hours ringing Starr, Sainsbury, Badger, Helen Lilley...

There was also a new set of warders to harangue: he had already incorporated into his litany of why the country was going to the dogs the assertion that prison was so cushy most prisoners found it a relief from the strain of going out everyday to thieve their daily bread.

Tony reated his own prison routine by involving himself in answering the mountains of mail he received, listening to R4, Classic FM and reading the papers. He read the *Daily Mail* and *The Telegraph* every day, but ever in character he told a *Daily Mail* journalist that he read the *Daily Mirror*.

He also occupied himself with what he grandly referred to in front of other prisoners as his 'fanmail'. Many of his letters were from women, and he realised with some amusement that he had become a bit of a pinup to hundreds of middle-aged ladies from all over the country.

After Tony got a result on the appeal, he was moved to his fifth and final prison, HMP Highpoint near Newmarket. His great mate there was 68-year-old, ex-engineer Jack Tully who was serving a 6-year sentence for the attempted murder of his wife whom, while he failed to kill her, he had put in a wheelchair for life. With no one to push her wheelchair she forgave him. Like Tony's absolution for murder from Middle England, Tully assumed his wife's forgiveness exonerated him from guilt.

The pair of them were full of folk dogma about how the country was falling apart, which included the injustice of their being in prison. Tully told Artnik, "We had a lot in common Tony and me. We believed in the same things. Decency, hard work, the traditional people of England... Things have gone wrong. It's not our country anymore, we both had the same ideas about where the country was going."

A gross, thick-set man, Tully has thick hands and sausage-like fingers that he drummed on the side of his chair as he spoke. "The first I heard from Martin was when he came out of his cell and shouted out, 'Some nonce has stolen my teddy bear.' One of the pilferers had stolen it...he never got it back.

"But we became friends and we spent hours just talking in his cell. He never undressed, and slept on top of the bed. He would stay up late reading and writing. Then he would wake up at about 11:30, go and get lunch.

"He was a bit of an oddball, a bit of a personality, and the staff pretty much left him to do what he wanted. He'd go off to educational classes in the afternoon. He liked to read his fan mail aloud, I remember one letter where some bird wrote that she liked the look of Tony. At the end of the letter it said, 'P.S. if you don't fancy me then perhaps you'll like my daughter.'

"Was he heterosexual? He never tired of telling us what a good-looking young man he once was. He claimed to be heterosexual but...err...there was something wrong there. Let me put it this way I would not be surprised, if he wasn't.

"He used to get magazines and catalogues about teddy bears... he had photos of his dogs up on the wall. He would buy phone cards like there was no tomorrow and was on the phone all the time. I liked him. We live about 11 miles from each other, so we were kind of neighbours...

"Basically Tony is a self-centred, very devious man...he evades questions, you'll never get to the bottom of him.

"At one time, a cousin of Fred Barras threatened to kill him. Tony just laughed. He didn't take it seriously. The man said, 'You may laugh but one day you'll wake up and find a man with a mask on and with a gun up your nose.' I thought he meant it but Tony took in his stride.

"He told me things I'd never repeat, never repeat." About Australia? "He has told me bits and pieces about Australia. He did a bit of farming and droving."

He did a bit more than that. "Yeah, I know."

Did he mention it? "Some things."

But he left under a cloud. "I think that's about right. Ask him. If he doesn't want to tell you, I'm not going to."

Murder? "Well some things you do take with a pinch of salt. But you're looking for a scandal. Whatever you put in his book could affect the way the rest of his life pans out. At the moment he has the sympathy of all the over-50s…in England at least.

"Let's have a hypothesis here, you're saying he killed someone else. If you chuck in another murder that happened before in the book, he will lose that sympathy for a start."

Tully was released in 2003. He pushes his wife's wheelchair, keeps his tongue on what Tony coughed to about Australia but is prepared to finger him as a closet homosexual.

Around the time he was mates with Tully, Tony was considered for parole. The trouble was the two Probation Officers doing the assessing were appalled by the fact that Tony didn't view himself as a criminal and, consequently, had not attended any rehabilitation courses. As social workers, they assumed that as he hadn't addressed his offending behaviour, then he was likely to repeat it.

Probation Officer Chris Dewsnap was a shaven-headed, single-parent who sported a ring in his left ear. Dewsnap used to be a 'product replenishment manager' – or shelf stacker – in Sainsbury's, but had taken a part-time Open University degree to gain his social worker qualifications. He read *the Guardian*.

Dewsnap's report found Tony "egotistical...and demonstrates an attitude of discrimination toward sections of the community". Even worse, Tony "demonstrates no remorse for his behaviour or victim empathy and refused to undertake any offence focused work". Mention was made of the "Think First Accredited Groupwork Programme".

Tony just regarded "Dewsnipe" as another lickspittle socialist parasite who was in league with the enemy. Dewsnap refused to recommend Tony for parole concluding that his "entrenched views make him a high risk of behaving similarly in future".

As this was around the time that a paroled Fearon, funded by legal aid, sued Martin for damages for unlawfully causing his injuries! The tabloids went ballistic. "**Final Insult**...**Plain Crazy**... **Outrageous**..." Tony was back as Middle England's front page folk hero. Meanwhile, Dewsnipe was probably promoted to Head Probation Officer and was designing a new generation of 'Think First Accredited Groupwork Programmes'.

Tony returned to championing Middle England in his letters...
"People like Fearon were making it difficult to run my business as I was becoming more and more housebound. Surely I have rights as well. There is people murdered every day in this country because of theft or easy picking.

"They would not know their arse from their front. Dewsnap is the one who is prejudicial and what I said to him was forthright and the public agree...remember I am Daniel in the Lions Den.

"The cat soon will be out of the bag and the genie free.

"As they say at Pentonville this is all *Bollocks*. Those people in power simply want the end of their noses banged real hard, then they would understand the folly of their remarks. Jesus wept. When will the blatant stupidity stop. Kenneth Williams is the one I want he has much substantiation to do he can't just hide behind 'no comment'.

"Why are there so many cretins? There is so much of the case to get out, the public know it but officialdom does not want to know. I suppose that I have read that so many other people have had it so much worse, though that doesn't alter my situation. The criminal world and the police are on a par with the ill treatment that I have received. We are supposed to live in a civilised society. It's not the way I have been treated. People are not aware of what it's like in the countryside. Criminals prevail. It can't be right.

"We must stand firm against the indecency of our country or what is left of my country. This is a dark day for our country to support the thugs for attacking the old. No decent man should ever be allowed to be put in my position where he can't protect himself: A man's house should be sacrosanct and it is only his right to say how he should defend himself because he knows his position better than anyone else.

"Everyone is talking about me and supporting me. People say I am a hero. No, I am not a hero. But what has happened has liberated fearful people. If we can't protect our property and ourselves to live decent lives what is the point of life. Shall we all become uncivilised and be free to spoil each others lives standing up for what is right?

"The time is coming regardless of Blair's problems with the war to write to him and I'll get a reply. It makes no odds really, they will have to answer at the end of the day in the public interest. Not the political interest, but the people's interest. That is what true democracy is all about is it not? Not a secret society."

PS to Peter Sainsbury:

"You may know the politically correct brigade may replace

Nelson in Trafalgar Sqare with Ken Livingstone who obviously thinks that he is doing a good job, so we all have to make allowances. The whole thing is preposterous.

"Do I meet you when I am released? Not only will people be watching me, but they will be watching you.

Best wishes,

Tony Martin   Norfolk Farmer"

Tony Martin was refused not only parole but also home leave, which given that it is granted to virtually all long-term prisoners shows how spiteful Highpoint Prison's social work brigade had become over his rejection of their services.

Tony's EDR (Earliest Date of Release) was Monday, July 28th 2003, but because of the intense press interest and the reward still on his head it was decided by the Prison Department to whisk him away to a secret location and release him from there. Accordingly, on the Friday before his EDR, he was picked up from Highpoint by the police and taken under armed escort by a Victim Protection Unit to a safe house in Southend-on-Sea. He was held there over the weekend, still as a serving prisoner but released into the arms of the *Daily Mirror* on July 28th 2003.

This is how he described it to Artnik: "I was released on July 28th they are evens the 2 and the 8. I like even numbers. Double 28 because you've got two even numbers and its 56. Go back to the imperial – that's a 56 pound weight– and, if you double that, you have two even numbers again – it comes to a hundred weight. Now 20 hundredweight makes a ton.

"My release was a ton of bricks on the enemy.

"That's how I think."

A RIGHT TO KILL?

CHAPTER 10

FROM PORRIDGE TO NORWICH

The *Daily Mirror* took more precautions collecting Tony from the safe house than White House security took when G.W. Bush went to Baghdad for Christmas turkey with the troops. The Mirror's Deputy Editor, Eugene *Hush-Hush* Duffy, commanded the Mirror Corps. The pick-up was planned and run like a military operation. Mobile phones were banned. According to Hush-Hush, they could be tracked by newspaper rivals. A fleet of cars were used: some as decoys, others to block any possible pursuers.

After they took custody at 8 am of their Exclusive, the cavalcade then careered off in the direction of Somerset where the hand-picked staff in a safe house in the country were awaiting their arrival. They changed vehicles on the way. Tony rather liked all the cloak and dagger stuff. It upped the ante on all the attention he was getting.

The Sun, having been pipped at the post at the end of the bidding war, was on the case and desperate to do a spoiler. The early negotiations had been conducted by Tom Hendry of IMS News whose company is based in Reading. *The Mirror* had bid £125,000, which comfortably saw off those from the *Daily Mail* and *The Sun* both of whom had been more supportive of Tony's case than *The Mirror.* Tony went with the money.

Given that *The Sun* had raised over a £100,000 from its

readers for Tony to fight the damages claim brought by Fearon, a few eyebrows were raised at what looked like a deal straight out of the school of chequebook journalism. Yet, as late as January 2004 the cheque is still at *The Mirror* awaiting Tony's collection. Malcolm Starr explained why he leaves it there, "If anyone asks, Tony can in all honesty say that he has never taken a penny from the newspapers for telling – not selling – his story."

Piers Morgan, *The Mirror*'s editor, bid high for the Martin story because he had decided to try to drag the his paper out of the tabloid mire of footie, kiss 'n' tell, and celebrity-itis. He thought the Martin story would be a springboard for a more responsible coverage of issues that really matter. The Mirror ran it big. It was front page for four days but the first splash was "World Exclusive" with just a picture of Tony Martin in a corn field with the headline "I'm Free". His story virtually filled the paper: "Tony Martin in his own words, see pages 2,3,4,5,6 & 7."

The Mirror team worked their socks off trying to get something exclusive from Tony but, as he told Artnik, "I told them nothing." And he didn't. Although the story ran and ran, most of it was trivia. The by-line was by Jenny Johnston. *The Mirror* journalists quickly found out two things about Martin: first, he was more forthcoming with females and, second, that he has a personal hygiene problem. Six women were drafted in to work with him in two hours shifts as the smell was a trifle overpowering. They were also subjected to the trials of constantly having to listen to Martinese. What proved especially irritating was Tony's habit of using the phrase "at the end of the day". To shut him up, whoever was in the room would chorus straight back at him, "At the end of the day…you go to bed." He didn't like being sent up but nevertheless it encouraged him to kick the habit.

Although the hackettes could only get trivia, *The Mirror* was not fooled by Tony's act. There are parts of the Exclusive story that go right to the heart of Tony Martin. Jenny Johnston wrote, for example, "We had a lengthy discussion about his beloved dog – his only surviving pet. Otto's two siblings died during his custody, and he was moved almost to tears talking about Bruno's death in January. 'I cannot wait to see my Otto,' he said. 'It was very upsetting to hear about Bruno, but someone did tell me his coat was in a lovely condition when he died, which is comforting.

"'In a way, it was easier for me to deal with because I was inside. I didn't have to steel myself for any of the practicalities. It would have been worse to have found him dead myself. My best friend, like that.'"

It was Bruno that 'shook his mouth' at Fearon and Barras. Tony loved Bruno as a best friend and when he died he took comfort from his coat being in a lovely condition. Here is a man who truly is Living among Strangers, even canine ones.

Johnston noted, "During the three-hour journey, however, he did not ask after a single human being. When I asked about how his mother had coped with his prison sentence, he said simply, 'I've had varying reports.'"

Two months after he was released, Artnik asked him how many times he'd seen his mother in the intervening period, he replied, "Once."

Another part of *The Mirror* story read: "In the car in which they picked him up, he did apologise for not washing for two days… the car stopped and we emerged into brilliant sunshine to take some photographs. He waded into the middle of a cornfield, and whooped with delight. He scooped up the grain and threw it over his head. 'Surreal,' he shouted, as it cascaded down his courtroom suit. 'What did I tell you. The only word is surreal.'"

Johnston opined, "Martin had only recently learnt the word surreal and when he learns a new word, he likes to use it." In fact, in his first police interview he'd described his position as surreal. Nevertheless, a defining trait of Tony's character how he picks up on erudite words, which he then obsessively deploys in conversation. Still, by such clever linkage of what he said, the articles fleshed out how Tony is.

Johnston was exposed to the usual claims, "He reminds me several times that he used to be 'quite a hit' with the ladies... 'I don't know an awful lot about guns. I'm certainly no expert. In the house that night was the only time I had ever used that gun... I was not familiar with it. To me it was like the difference between an RSJ and a longbow.'"

And asked whether he felt any sympathy for the Barras family, Martin answered, "I feel nothing for them. Nothing good, nothing bad, just nothing. I don't feel anything about anyone or anything." He also replied to the comment that he nearly cracked in prison, "They kept saying, 'You're losing it, you're losing it.' But I wasn't. *I was just acting.*" (Artnik's emphasis)

Yet, although these articles are brilliant in the truth they shed on Tony they are abysmal in the way they funk what the paper set out to do: answer the questions about "what he did and why". Instead it merely gives Tony a platform to trot out all the twaddle that his jury at trial and the Appeal Court rejected out of hand. Like so many of us, *The Mirror* team had lost touch with what the Crown presented to the jury at Martin's trial, which was upheld by the verdict and later confirmed by the Appeal Court. Realistically, Tony's case should be given no more credence than a flat-earther's.

Of course, there is a kind of journalism that is only interested in telling its readership what they want to hear. But *The Mirror* is not in that camp. Their Martin team, like many of us, had probably just been conditioned by the never-ending propaganda that Clifford and Starr had drip-fed the press ever since Tony was arrested.

Tony liked it with the *Mirror* team. Although after 6 days they had milked him of anything newsworthy. Certainly the paper's Martin Exclusive spiked sales in the first couple of days, but they were not sustained. So telling their readers what they wanted to hear – not that Martin gave them anything else – did not increase circulation. However, *The Mirror* still felt that holding him for another week would kill the story as far as other newspapers were concerned. Tony liked the attention and agreed to stay.

While he was at Somerset, Starr struck a £25,000 deal with the *Tonight with Trevor McDonald* show to do a special on Tony. When that was finished, *Hush-Hush* Duffy decided that for security reasons they should move to another safe house. This one was in Ludlow. After two weeks, the media were still baying for more, so *The Mirror* had one more dip before leaving him to the rest of the pack.

They drove him up to Lincolnshire where Otto was still in kennels. They then took Tony and Otto back to Bleak House for a photo shoot, before going to a hotel in King's Lynn where Malcolm Starr joined them. He was and is a Patron of POW, so he tried to get Tony to fulfill his promise to ring Peter Sainsbury. Tony declined, despite his promise to ring the POW Secretary as soon as he was released.

After a night's revelry on *The Mirror*'s expense account, Tony shacked up in an empty caravan on Richard Portham's land. He was there around six weeks but Richard expelled him after Otto pinned Portham's child – who has Down's syndrome – against a wall. Richard Portham supported Tony through thick and thin – he was a witness at his trial – but even he has become disillusioned with Tony post-release antics. "I have heard him on the radio and it makes me cringe to hear the things he says," he told Artnik. Portham is also more open than perhaps he would have been in the past about Tony. He admitted, for example, that the reason Tony left Australia was because it "…was murder, wasn't it…he has skirted round it but he has also told me other things…"

Portham also tells of an incident in a supermarket in September when Tony approached a mutual friend of theirs, Linda, and asked how she was. She said that she was alright. "And Tony tweaked her tits and said, 'You look perky.' She was shocked. She had recently had part of lip removed for cancer. But I told Helen (Lilley) about it and she said that she had seen him do it before."

Artnik asked Portham if he thought this was Tony trying to show publicly that he is not homosexual? Portman answered, "I think you've hit the nail on the head there. I think Tony is that way but he won't allow himself. He hates himself for it." Starr made a more diluted but similar point to Artnik concerning how there have been no Martin romances since his release, "He visits a lot of females who wrote to him in prison but he hasn't got time to do any courting. He is probably one of those men who enjoys female company but doesn't like to take it any further. I'm sure you probably got that impression."

After his eviction from the caravan, Tony shacked up in a derelict hotel on the edge of Wisbech that Malcolm Starr and Mike Coleman were seeking planning permission to turn into a school. They gave him the use of a flat and, in return, he doubled as a kind of caretaker. Meanwhile, the speaking invitations were coming in thick and fast and Tony decided that he would now become a figurehead in the campaign to legally strengthen the rights of householders when faced with intruders. He was whizzing back between Wisbech and London. In mid-October he popped into *The Sun* to "open up his heart to" their readers and thank them for raising a £100,000 legal war chest to fight the Fearon claim for damages.

He sang to the paper from the same old song sheet: "When they broke into my house I was terrified and I had no option...There doesn't seem to be any decency at the moment..." In early October the Tory party conference gave him three rousing cheers. He had another standing ovation a few days later at the UK Independence Party conference. He spoke to them despite admitting he knew "nothing about the Independence Party's policy".

It didn't matter: "I'm against Europe, I mean we've been here since 1066. Going into Europe will cost us a bloody fortune. It's what young men died for in two World Wars. I don't belong to a political party but if any party has got anything to do with decency, I'm all for that..."

He forgot motherhood and apple pie.

Back in Wisbech he developed the habit, while holding his gin and tonic, of pontificating on any topic that anyone liked to mention or which popped up in his head. He and Otto also had the run of Starr's office where he'd put his feet up on the boss's desk while Otto hassled his girlie staff for titbits. Tony would read his mail and take calls from whomever wanted his words of 'wisdom' on everything from the iniquity of the Norfolk police to the spinelessness of Parliament. He also developed the habit of dropping into Malcolm's home just when his wife was serving supper. She "resented" him and laid into her husband about there being three in their marriage; she also reproached Malcolm for always being at Martin's beck and call. Martin occasionally saw Roger Cotteril, who was managing the Bleak House farm, but he did no farming himself.

On 20th October Tony was invited by a group of crusties to give a speech at Oxford University – they had heard that he was worth a sniff. Tony thought it would be a walk-over. He had prepared a few jokes and one-liners to warm up the crowd before he went into his "horrendous" experience.

Following his formal introduction to the assembled students and a light ripple of applause Tony launched into his big ice-breaker. "Let me say as a bachelor I prefer other men's wives because it's easier. Now, a man climbs through the window of his married lover and starts making love to her on the bed. No sooner has he got into her than the man hears his lover's husband coming in through the front door.' 'Quick! Where's your back door?' he whispers. 'I haven't got a back door,' she replies.

"And the man says, 'Then where d'ya want it?'"

This was the punch line of the joke!

It was so feeble that it would not have raised a titter with a Bernard Manning audience and even students with their anti-PC credentials on parade found it in poor taste. They stared in disbelief at the stout, pompous middle-aged farmer, though there was one lone raucous laugh, presumably out of courtesy or personal experience at boarding school. Without further ado Tony launched into his half hour ramble. On this occasion the police were high on his hit list:

"Regardless of the treachery of Norfolk Police I am a victim of circumstances. Nothing more. Nothing less. All they did was they went down the road to denigrate me. All they were doing was covering up a gross dereliction of duty. The police don't like you to go out speeding. They don't like you to go drinking and driving... I am a Fen man. We have been there since 1870 and I ain't budging because of reprobates..." Reprobate was one of Tony latest words.

"I have been called many things – famous, hero and whatever ... I would like to think I'm a champion of decency."

It was incoherent stuff but he got some laughs and, as it was that bad, plenty of over-the-top cheers from the new-wave fans of ironic cringe. Tony took it all in his stride. Now he'd proved a hit at Oxford, he decided that the university circuit was his stamping ground. On the 4th November Tony Martin slipped on his old school tie and strode confidently into the debating chamber to be greeted by a full house at the Cambridge University Union Society. The media were excluded to give the cubs on the student rag a chance. He reeled out the same old 'back door' joke, then did his victim of circumstance routine. He spoke confidently and, as he said later, "it was the first time that I felt that I was back amongst my equals since school". But he was less crass than at Oxford.

After his address, he took questions, many of them on the theme of remorse. His response was always the same: "I personally don't think I have done any wrong at all…The people who burgled my house? No…Well, if they come in my house it's their tough luck."

When Artnik took Tony out for dinner after another night on the university stump, he clearly assumed that he was still giving students the benefit of his erudition. Under the influence of all the attention and applause, the Martinese had acquired a Churchillian grandeur as he took to the boards as the self-appointed spokesman of all right-thinking Fenfolk.

"When you listen to what I have to say you have to think about infinity. We can't understand infinity. You are hearing this, in a particular room in a particular town in this world, which is in a galaxy, which is in the universe…it goes on forever and that is something that we can't understand. This is why people believe in God because they want immortality but they are not going to get it.

"As far as I am concerned I want to have a nice time whilst I'm here and enjoy it before I'm gone. People who believe in God say that when they leave this planet, they go to a better place. I don't think that it's unreasonable to say to them 'then cut your throats and go'. To me there are just those who believe in God. It doesn't matter what religion they keep – Catholic, Presbyterian, whatever. It is if they genuinely believe in a better place after death. And once again – why don't they go there?"

It was toe-curling stuff, especially to Artnik's on-the-job listeners who were only there to put to him that he'd lied about never using the pump-action shotgun before he shot Fearon and Barras. But he proved impossible to interrupt.

"There is a thing called revenge, restitution, vengeance. Whether you believe in God or not, and it is so true, when it comes to vengeance, it says in the bible: 'Vengeance is mine alone sayeth the Lord' and whoever or whatever the Lord is nobody can complain with that.

"What I'm saying is, is that we all think we are clever, but we are not. The young generation today has technology that has made them confident, they have things that I didn't have when even I was a child." Tony paused in full flow, as if struggling to recall something. He took a swig of water from his glass, changed tack and began again:

"I told the Cambridge lot this, and it bears repeating," he stated solemnly. "You can look at a young mouse when it is first born and it looks like the human foetal stage, with no hair. You can sometimes find a nest in the grain shed late in the year because that is where they nest, given the chance. Now, as a farmer, I have to get rid of them. I could look after them I suppose, but that would be quite complex as you have to keep them warm. So I break the nest and I tread on them. I don't like doing that, but I'm doing myself a favour, not that it's going make that much difference because there are so many of them. But when you look at that tiny little pink thing – it's not made by a machine – it is just made by a sperm and an egg. It is amazing and it's so complex and you think, where did it all come from?"

There were forays into film and literature, before Tony fell back on his own childhood experiences to illustrate his personal creed: "At school I boarded because, well, if you are a bad boy you have to be sent away. Oh yes! Sent away to be beaten by the matron. But I've never been beaten – the world knows that". Puffed up by his oratory, he stood up from the restaurant table, declaiming not just to his company, "I did get the cane though. Six of the best. Of course, today we don't have the cane, children just stab each other in the playground, which is deplorable. At the school I went to there wouldn't have been any knifing, they would have nipped that in the bud." The restaurant had stopped eating, some with forkfuls of food frozen in mid-air, as they listened to Tony in full flight.

"I mean people are just like cattle. You get different types of cattle, different moods, different types of dogs. We are all wild animals, not everyone has to be civilised but some of us have to be. People have their places and those who don't understand that get into trouble. For example when you go to somebody's house you can get in real bother…"

At last one of Artnik's team did manage to ask, "Now about that pump-action Tony?"

He sat down and lowered his voice, "I have to go down the road: I am a Victim of Circumstance. I mean I could turn around and say, 'Well, actually I'm a very clever, devious person. I'm actually an attention seeker and I said to Fearon, 'Break into the house: you get the stuff, I'll get the insurance.' So I'll let him break into the house and tell him 'We'll make a bit of money out of it'. But the twist in the story is when I let him break in the house – he didn't know I was going to shoot him."

After hours of recording Tony in London, Wisbech and at Bleak House – not even we can claim to have interviewed him – this was a good example as any of the only way he tells the truth: as a joke, a

Freudian slip, an inversion, a metaphor…never forthrightly. But he knows the truth just as surely as the jurors at his trial knew he'd lied to them. Nonetheless, while Tony is not as clever as he thinks he is, he is still cleverer than many people think he is.

Tony led Peter Sainsbury a merry dance. Sometimes, when Tony came to London, Sainsbury would trail after him in the hope that their erstwhile client would, after Fearon threw in the towel on his claim, funnel some of the money collected by *The Sun* to the POW Trust. Sainsbury has an artificial hip and the field-striding Tony liked to make him suffer a bit. Once, while with Artnik, Sainsbury fell behind in Hamley's – Tony was on a teddy bear hunt – and the researcher said to him, "Don't you think we ought to wait for Peter?"

Tony replied with a sneer, "Don't worry, he won't lose us. He'll be waiting downstairs." He was. When Tony saw him, he said quietly to the researcher, "Told you."

Eventually, Sainsbury decided that, if only for his own pride, he had to confront Tony on the way he done nothing for the charity that was largely responsible for him being free. They met in Starr's office at Wisbech in December 2003. The confrontation quickly degenerated into a slanging match with Tony calling Sainsbury "a parasite, in the same bag as Fearon". Sainsbury, unfortunately, did not know why Tony was on the warpath. Some of those contacted by Artnik in Wisbech had been taking Tony down a peg or two by taunting him about what the book would reveal.

Sainsbury lost his temper, too, and called Tony" an ungrateful bastard". After the meeting broke up, Sainsbury wrote Tony a vituperative letter and they have never communicated since, except through the national press.

An irate Tony summoned one of his tame journos, *Daily Telegraph*'s Daniel Foggo who then wrote an article just before

Christmas. Tony briefed Foggo in Starr's office. The article gave Tony a platform for lashing out at Sainsbury – he and POW were "a bunch of shysters" – and also Martin's own book, *A Right to Kill?* It's editor John McVicar was tagged "convict turned author" condemned as "a reprobate" and "His book is malicious and the things he is going to put in it are untrue". Foggo did not tell his readers that he himself had started a book on Martin but gave up after his two written chapters failed to find a publisher. Nonetheless, he quoted Martin on Artnik's book: "Whatever the rights and wrongs of my case, the title of the book is beyond belief. It is crass, deplorable and insensitive. Nobody has the right to kill."

As December 2003 drew to a close, listeners to R4's *Today* were voting on what law they would like an MP to present as a private members bill in Parliament. *Today* had leftie MP Stephen Pound, lined up to nominate Listener's Law. Pound had his own do-gooding proposal. However, the Bill that was the runaway winner was: "If you discover that someone has broken into your property during the night, you should have the right to assume the worst (i.e., that you are in mortal danger, and not that it's just a 'harmless' burglary) and act accordingly." Listeners' Law became Tony Martin's Law. When the result was announced by the embarrassed *Today* presenters, Deputy Prime John Prescott laughed like a drain, "That blew up in your face, didn't it."

Pound just muttered, "The listeners have spoken, the bastards."

The hacks were quickly onto Tony asking if he would kill again in the same circumstances. He replied, "In the same circumstances, yes, if I am terrorised. People are highly jeopardised in this country. I personally think we are looking bloody stupid in the world." The next day's *Daily Express* front page headline read: **I'd Kill Again**.

A week or so later Foggo, now riding shotgun for Martin, got back on the case and discovered that Sainsbury had past convictions and had served 3 years for fraud. He doubtless did a press clipping search as it all came out five years ago in the *Daily Mail*. Still, with Martin in the news, it made for a front page column: "Tony Martin charity is led by fraudster"(January 4th 2004), complete with more quotes from Martin: "If I'd known then what I know now I wouldn't have touched the charity with a bargepole!"

POW was to retort: "Had it not been for us, he would be making his soppy pronouncements from inside, not outside prison, where he would be languishing for another 15 years or so."

No one, though, was exempt from Tony's Christmas blues. Poor Hilary, his mother, got it in the neck. too. For some years she has let him farm 7 acres of orchard land near the March bypass, which is near Wisbech. Tony, alarmed at his 90-year-old mother's emphysema, asked her to put the land in his name in case she popped off over Yuletide and it went to his older brother, Robin. She refused.

Tony stormed out, shouting that she'd never see him again. She didn't see him over Christmas nor did she receive a card. If she had, it would probably have been signed:

Tony Martin: "Victim of Circumstance."

"DROP-KICK ME, JESUS, THROUGH THE GOALPOSTS OF LIFE"

In December 2003, Tony Martin responded to a *Daily Mail* invitation for its readers to name the quirkiest song that had made an impact on them. He wrote in his published letter: "The most memorable song title I have heard was that of a record played frequently on RTE 2 in the Republic of Ireland in the mid-Eighties. The song was by Jesse And The James Boys and was entitled 'Drop-kick Me, Jesus, Through The Goalposts Of Life'. I still chuckle when I think about it."

The song has the verse:
"Make me, oh make me, Lord, more than I am
Make me a part of your master plan
Freed of the earthy temptations below
I've got the will, Lord, if you've got the toe."

One thing that Tony Martin does a lot is chuckle. Indeed, the acknowledgement to this book reads: "...The publisher further wishes to compliment Mr Tony Martin for being most gracious to her, and for his unique sense of humour, which brightened up her trips to Norfolk considerably." Martin's humour is an acquired taste as it is invariably at the expense of other people's foibles and weaknesses. Nonetheless, despite the grind of doing this book in such a short time, the one thing that has consistently lifted the spirits of the office has been examples of his Martinese. Countless times one of us has spotted some choice remark he's said or written and rushed to bring it to everyone else's attention. In some ways, Martin is a hoot.

But he never spoke a truer word in jest than: "I can assure you: Most people who have had an association with me are never quite the same again." It certainly applies to all of us at Artnik but the person who most springs to mind when I read that is Fred Barras. He can't even **be**. According to the law, Martin murdered Barras and some might say got away with it. The same people might also feel that the black humour that laces this book, the story of the shooting, is in bad taste. Murder is never funny and the story of how a murderer circumvents justice is even less so.

As editor, I set the tone of *A Right to Kill?*, so I take responsibility for that and, just as Martin does not feel any remorse for the murder, I don't for highlighting Martin's funny side. There is something about the whole saga of Barras's murder and Martin's conviction, reduced to manslaughter, leaving him to serve only three years and four months, that is straight out of an Ealing Comedy. That this could occur in a mature democracy with such checks and balances in place as the independence of the judiciary and the freedom of the press is farcical. It is farcical that *Today*'s listeners would, in the wake of the misreporting of the Martin case, vote overwhelmingly for a new law that would give householders the right to kill intruders in the hours of darkness.

Everyone already has the right to defend themselves and that includes the right to kill if they believe that their life is at risk or they are under threat of serious harm. The objective test of that is whether a jury decides that the violence used to defend oneself is proportionate or reasonable. This is a perfectly *reasonable* way of regulating vigilantism in a civilized state. There is also the further democratic safeguard in a country that uses the jury system, which is the safety net of the 'grassroots verdict'.

It is not lawyers that decide whether the force used in self-defence is unreasonable but twelve ordinary people picked at random. In a micro-model of democracy, they listen to the evidence, retire, then argue among themselves in the language of reason – not prejudice – to arrive at a consensus. Moreover, for the accused to be found guilty, the consensus must be at least 10-2, as it was in the Martin trial. On the other hand they can, when in all conscience they think the violence was disproportionate, decide to give the accused the benefit of the doubt. The accused enjoys the presumption of innocence and a jury can, and often does in these cases, take the view that despite the force used being disproportionate the accused was, in the circumstance, justified or his use of such force was excusable.

Jonathon Cooper, a leading criminal barrister, said about the Listeners' Law proposal: "The law as it stands at the moment, despite its critics, is functioning... We do not live in the wild west. This legislation that is proposed effectively may well turn us into that." Cooper is correct: the law is functioning. Do we want capital punishment for burglars – many of whom are a lot younger than Fred Barras – being brought in by the back door? If such a law was passed, as soon as some irate householder mowed down a couple of 13-year-old burglars, there would be uproar and it would be revoked. What Tony Martin and the proponents of Listeners' Law want is farcical, unworkable and uncivilized. It is also undemocratic.

Democracy has little to do with what the majority want. That is the route of mob rule. People propose laws – like the woman behind the winning Listeners' Law, Amanda Lindsay – but in a democracy they have to argue their case and meet the objections to their proposals in the language of reason. And if they fail to meet the opposing argument, they are under an obligation to change their viewpoint. I personally would like to bludgeon to a pulp the scumbags who keep nicking my car radio. But if I proposed that to *Today*'s listeners I presume that many of them would say the culprits are likely to be deprived young teenagers and suggest that what I propose is barbaric. Once I was faced with this argument, and if I could not gainsay it, I would change my mind. This is how democracy works and it is not a million miles away from how it is in the jury room. Democracy is never just about people voting.

Leftie politician Stephen Pound who turned out to be the patsy – he only wanted a do-gooding Bill – in the Listeners' Law vote said of the result: "My enthusiasm for direct democracy is slightly dampened. This is a difficult result." Politicians like Pound are only happy with "direct democracy", i.e. mob rule, when it fits their own Nanny State agenda. And here we do touch on the reality of the Tony Martin phenomenon.

Why did his case touch such a nerve among so many people? Why did the popular media grotesquely misreport the case? And let's remember how grotesque it was. Anyone who attended the trial or read the transcripts could discover that Martin did not act in self-defence, he ambushed Barras and Fearon. You don't have to be some hotshot investigative journalist to discover this. Paul Leet said mischievously in front of his wife to Artnik:

"He just said that he'd come from his Mum's and found these blokes in his house. That's the bit that I can't understand, you see if he come home from his Mum's how was he upstairs in the house, then come downstairs (Jacqui Leet: Yes, how was he upstairs in his house, yeah?) How was he upstairs in his house, then come down, that's the little bit I can't make out. (Jacqui Leet: Yes, he told you he come back from his Mum's and found them, yet then the next minute it was in the papers that he was upstairs asleep.) That's the only bit I can't fathom out… I can't make out how he was upstairs.

It don't make sense. I believe the gun was already in his car. I believe he sees the light as he was going in his house. He comes home from his Mum's, saw a light, his gun was in his car... I believe he went in and saw them and shot them."

The prosecution case was that Martin ambushed the burglars, it was what the jury believed and nothing in the Judgment by the Appeal Court altered that. Why do so many people believe otherwise, and why did and does the media support this misrepresentation?

The Tony Martin case is a contemporary touchstone of political correctness. It polarises opinion and taps into the rage and frustration that more traditional, patriotic groups feel about the "New Establishment", a term that Richard Littlejohn favours and one that Peter Hitchen used in his book, "The Abolition of Britain".

The Old Left did not die with the death of Socialism. They regrouped and with the same dogmatic virtue drew up a new agenda for controlling other peoples' lives. They relinquished trying to do it through public ownership of the economy, instead – still in the name of the good society – they worked at doing it culturally.

They applied the only lesson they learnt from the failure of Marxism, which was that you need capitalism, business and private enterprise to generate tax revenues. So promote the market, but use the taxes it generates to revolutionise people's private and cultural lives along socialist principles.

For over ten years, the New Left has mounted an assault on the commanding heights of the taxpayers' money. Their mission after infiltrating the media, local government and the State: to protect people from making mistakes, rather than to leave people to learn from their mistakes. The New Establishment is the nanny state and the place they want us is in the nursery.

In 2003, a certain John Ashton articulated the New Establishment's mission statement: "Individuals cannot protect themselves from bio-terrorism, epidemics of SARS, the concerted efforts of the junk food industry, drug dealers and promoters of tobacco and alcohol... A civilised society will provide a legislative framework to protect people, and in particular the most vulnerable. Criticism of the nanny state is almost always misplaced and is frequently nonsensical. The State is the guardian of the weak and underprivileged... it has a duty to ensure that those less well-off in society have safe, warm, low-cost housing, convenient transport links to shops and amenities, and the protection of police on the streets." Ashton is an apparatchik of the Nanny State: a champion of the vulnerable, the underprivileged, the excluded.

He is Regional Director of Public Health in the North-East, and his "partner", who is director of Public Health in Preston, recently co-operated in the conception and birth of a child. They named him Fabian Che Jeb in honour of their muses: The Fabian society, Che Guevara and the prophet Jebediah. It is this type of man and his New Left policies that turn not just the Tony Martins but lots of us into self-justifying, rabid, ranting homicidal maniacs.

The Martins of Britain hate the Ashtons of the New Establishment who stop them hunting foxes, using firearms, discriminating against minorities, ridiculing homosexuals, driving back from the pub drunk...they loathe them because they fund the race relations industry, make homosexuality a lifestyle choice, promote gender politics, let criminals out of prison on parole as soon as they have been "rehabilitated", wage war on the motor car, promote a "multi-cultural" Britain, redistribute income from the rich to the poor and raise taxes to fund all the bureaucrats and quangos necessary to pursue these policies.

This is the political context in which Tony Martin mounted his ambush and it is the same context that made him the champion of Middle England and much else besides. It is the Tony "I'm a pretty straight sort of guy" Blair Government that has changed, often by the undemocratic manipulation of public opinion, the political climate so much that many people feel like Tony Martin, albeit they don't act like him.

It is Blairite policies that let the Fearons and Barrases out on the street no matter how many crimes they commit. The same policies license all the do-gooding busybodies that are employed to implement the agenda of what Tessa Jowell (Secretary of State for culture, media and sport) calls our "empowering, co-operating state". They also license social workers and Probation Officers like Highpoint Prison's Dewsnap to recommend parole for a Brendon Fearon and not for a Tony Martin. They pay for victim support counsellors to write the kind of letter that Fearon sent to Martin hoping "you feel remorse as it's the only way forward".

The story of the Norfolk Farmer standing up to the protected black sheep of the Nanny State was just too good for the press to miss. With a few notable exceptions they went with it and eventually, the Martin rural myth became too big to correct.

Instead of mounting an utterly implausible defence, perhaps if Tony Martin had argued that he was provoked by the Nanny State beyond what any normal person could put up with, his jury might have been more sympathetic. The media's reaction might then have helped drop-kick our Nanny State into touch a bit earlier than it will now take the electorate to do so.

John McVicar

Artnik's compilation of its best Martinese:

I can really drive people mad if I put my mind to it.

I have suffered many injustices in my life.

(Dec 2003) I would say at the moment I am an icon.

I don't actually know who I am, really…

(On comparing his sojourn in prison to lunching at the Ritz)
I can assure you, I live a very simple life…it's better here than at
Highpoint.

I am not afraid of anyone.

I am a perfectionist…and perfectionists can never finish anything.

I hate trainers, real men should wear real shoes.

I can assure you: Most people who have had an association with
me are never quite the same again.

I don't buy furniture – people who want furniture come to me.

(To Artnik in Hamley's toyshop) Put these under your hat. I am
Tony Martin – I don't have to pay.

I showed someone a photo of me as a young man. They said:
'What happened, Tony?'

I don't go looking for trouble, it finds me.

(On the Cubana restaurant) I have never heard such a racket in all
my life… I wouldn't be so rude as to say anything at the time, but
give me a bloody shotgun and I'd soon quieten that place down.

(On the Knightsbridge eatery San Lorenzo) I didn't like the lamb – they had no mint sauce with it.

What pleasure did Her Majesty get out of locking me up?

But on this occasion everybody else is to blame for this. I am a totally innocent person. The blame lays with the police and the criminals. They are in cahoots.

(On prison) I wasn't a cleaner, I'm no Jonathan Aitken or Jeffrey Archer.

I wanted to write to Jeffrey Archer. He should title his prison diaries Comedy of Errors.

MPs are like Christmas decorations. They do nothing about the ordinary man in the street. They have no backbone.

I'll make sure they do change the law.

(On not helping the charity that was responsible for his release) I am very indebted to the POW, but I can only look after number one.

The POW Trust helps criminals.

(On discovering that the Secretary of POW, Peter Sainsbury has a 1990 conviction for fraud) If I'd known then what I know now, I woudn't have touched the charity with a bargepole.

(On his Rottweiler) Otto is a person – an actual person. *Of course he barks*, he is a dog.

They are so poor in Romania, women are standing on the roads with no clothes on.

Women are a dish to be savoured. Women are a bit like peas. If you are a farmer who plants peas, you are either a fool or a very rich man.

I always buy women fine chocolates, knowing their vanity.

A woman is a complicated man.

(On avoiding marriage) Because I must admit that women, well, it's like Jason and the Argonauts. I mean he knew what to do. He strapped himself to a rock because of the terrific pull.

The English language seems to be latent in me.

I'm a bit of a sadist, or is that a masochist? Well, to be honest, it doesn't really matter what you do in life as long as you don't do anybody any harm. Life is just purely esoteric. You get a number.

I only shoot two-legged rats, but I'm not allowed to anymore.

Rats and I have something in common.

There is no such thing as a gypsies. People go around calling themselves things, but it doesn't mean anything, giving people names. Basically they are all just conmen. They are simply itinerants.

People used to say that I talked a lot of rubbish, but personally, I just think that they didn't understand me.

Portham, Richard – 154, 206, 231, 232
Pound, Stephen MP – 238
POW Trust – 174, 175, 216, 237, 238
Prisons:
　HMP Bullingdon – 168, 213, 215, 216
　　HMP Gartree – 216, 217, 218
　　HMP Highpoint – 220, 225
　　HMP Norwich – 81, 98, 162, 212
　　HMP Pentonville – 219
　　HMP Stocken – 123, 218
Pritchett, John – 82
Renshaw, Graham – 183
Sands, Derek – 43
Sainsbury, Peter – 174, 175, 177, 216 - 219, 224, 237, 238, 239
Safe Houses:
　Market Harborough – 90, 98
　Swadlincote – 98, 99, 107, 109
　Norwich – 109
Saunders, James – 175, 176, 177, 190
Scrivener, Anthony – 101, 111, 113, 121, 124, 125, 129, 133, 134-138, 157, 171, 174, 178
Shepard, Gillian MP – 92
Shetty, Giresh – 187
Spalter, John – 42
Spalton William – 119
Starr, Malcolm – 91, 107, 165, 213, 214, 216, 217, 219, 228, 230, 231, 232, 233
Stobard, John – 111
Taylor, John – 65
Thacker, Steve Superintendent – 90, 91, 92

Tiernan, Dermott Gerard – 63, 126, 127
Tomlinson, Justice – 171
Tully, Jack – 220, 222
Turney, Rodney – 191, 192, 206
Uncle Arthur – 24, 77
Waterhouse, Keith – 98
Webster, Christopher – 14, 15, 18, 19, 93
Welham, Jim – 120, 121
Widdecombe "Widders", Anne MP – 84, 85, 167
Williams, Kenneth – 167
Williams, Martyn – 84
Wilson Alastair – 30
Wolkind, Michael – 176, 177, 181
Woolf, Lord Chief Justice – 177, 178, 179, 182, 183, 184, 199, 208
Wright, Justice – 177
Wright, Martin – 50, 61